THE DECLINE OF URBAN POLITICS

D1521690

Volume 162 Sage Library of Social Research

RECENT VOLUMES IN . . .
SAGE LIBRARY OF SOCIAL RESEARCH

THE DECLINE OF URBAN POLITICS

Political Theory and the Crisis of the Local State

M. Gottdiener

Volume 162
SAGE LIBRARY OF
SOCIAL RESEARCH

SAGE PUBLICATIONS
Newbury Park Beverly Hills London New Delhi

For information address:

SAGE Publications, Inc.
2111 West Hillcrest Drive
Newbury Park, California 91320

SAGE Publications Inc. SAGE Publications Ltd.
275 South Beverly Drive 28 Banner Street
Beverly Hills London EC1Y 8QE
California 90212 England

SAGE PUBLICATIONS India Pvt. Ltd.
M-32 Market
Greater Kailash I
New Delhi 110 048 India

Printed in the United States of America

Library of Congress Cataloging-in-Publication Data

Gottdiener, Mark.
    The decline of urban politics.

    (Sage library of social research ; v. 162)
    1. Metropolitan government—United States.
2. Municipal government—United States. I. Title.
II. Series.
JS323.G58   1986   320.8'0973   86-14020
ISBN 0-8039-2713-4
ISBN 0-8039-2714-2 (pbk.)

CONTENTS

To my sons
Felix and Zev

CHAPTER 1

INTRODUCTION:
THE DECLINE OF POLITICAL CULTURE

Over the past several decades profound changes have occurred in the organization of urban environments. Not too long ago most people lived in residential communities agglomerating around a single city or town center containing important functions such as commerce, industry, and retail services. At that time, for most Americans before 1940, there was a comparatively close fit between the political jurisdiction of local government and the control of key resources necessary to community well-being. If economic development was still uncoordinated in the laissez-faire world of early capitalism, local governments, nevertheless, possessed a comparatively strong ability to respond to community needs by tapping available resources when required.

This early concordance between agglomerations of economic resources and their respective political jurisdictions worked so well for the benefit of local government that it was most often a regime led by a party boss with considerable political power. To be sure, this period prior to the Great Depression was not a halcyon time of unrivaled public welfare; quite the contrary, as cities were the sites of social pathology created by the unregulated growing pains of industrial capitalism. Yet, in comparison with the present, there was a functional correspondence between the jurisdictional control of local government and the sources of economic well-being affecting the local region.

One of the earliest tasks of urban sociology was to document the progressive disintegration of this concordance. In the 1950s it was observed that the resource and economic infrastructure of the United States had begun to deconcentrate away from the central city and company towns, and, instead, had been cut loose in a massive shift of jobs and people toward the urban periphery (Gottdiener, 1985a). Corporations evolved from tightly knit organizations that layered administrative, management, and production functions all within the same location, to national and even global systems of production and distribution. Currently, corporations possess hierarchical forms of organization, bureaucratic modes of decision making, and a complex, functional division of labor, all of which are deployed differentially across space so that separate functions are located in separate places (Chandler, 1977). At present, most people live within an expanding milieu of large-scale public institutions, places of employment and commerce, industrial and financial centers, and networks of family and friends, the linkages of which often involve travel over distances of many miles, and which involve spaces no longer confined within the boundaries of single political jurisdictions (Muller, 1981; Fischer, 1983).

At present our great cities have become specialized economically, turning more toward harboring service centers and headquarters sites for financial and industrial conglomerates, while the suburbs prosper as the home of progressively more industry and commerce. These changes are the consequence of nearly five decades of manufacturing decentralization away from city centers and toward the peripheral areas of the metropolitan hinterland, or to other countries across the globe. Of greatest importance among all the recent trends since the 1950s, however, is that fewer and fewer Americans each year have called the central city their home. By the 1980 census, approximately 65% of the nonfarm population was living within urban regions outside central cities (Long, 1981). At one time such areas were considered specialized suburban bedroom communities, but today we recognize that the immense regional spaces adjacent to our large central cities have long since matured to multifunctional uses very much like the urban agglomerations of the past, except for their deconcentrated form. Currently, they possess a full complement of economic, political, and social functions that cater to a wide variety of needs (Gottdiener, 1985a). In some cases, such as Los Angeles, San Francisco, Boston, Minneapolis, and Detroit, the areas comprising the adjacent region outside city jurisdictions have eclipsed the cities themselves in economic and political importance.

The 1980 census has also revealed that our largest cities, those with three million or more inhabitants, are languishing with slow population growth; a dramatic reversal of the urban implosion characteristic of industrial societies for at least the past 150 years. More surprisingly, cities such as New York, Chicago, Boston, Baltimore, Philadelphia, Detroit, Cleveland, and St. Louis have even experienced an *absolute* population decline. At the same time smaller central places in the United States have accelerated their growth in the 10 years since 1970 (Long, 1981). In short, present-day patterns of development have restructured urban areas from concentrated agglomerations into massive metropolitan regions possessed of a differential deployment of functions and with a residential and industrial center of gravity lying outside the historic city. Everyday life for most Americans currently transpires in the more amorphous deconcentrated areas of the metropolitan hinterland where governments are small and economic resources are spread out over an expanding space that cuts across local political jurisdictions. The sum total of these fundamental transformations affecting local areas can be called "sociospatial" restructuring because its patterns represent deep-level changes in social organization that are simultaneously linked to new forms of urban space. Together these sociospatial forces of change have produced the contemporary landscape of regional metropolitan growth.

Over the years these profound changes in metropolitan development have affected local government in a number of striking ways. In the 1800s a French aristocrat, Alexis de Tocqueville, visited this country and made a series of remarkable observations about it. At times prescient in his ability to grasp fundamental factors behind the development of American society, Tocqueville was particularly impressed with the nature of this country's form of democracy. He observed that Americans were highly involved in government, especially local government. They were organized into a pluralist society with a wide variety of formal associations. Local political forums were used as a debating platform for separate interests and ideas. A high level of participation meant a high level of exposure to contrasting and even contentious values or judgments regarding what society needed and how best to provide it. Above all, Tocqueville marvelled at the manner by which public decisions could be made based upon this pluralist democratic process without the need for an enlightened elite or select group of representatives to lead the way. Today we would say that local government at that time exhibited the properties of "self-management" because needs and proposals to meet them were articulated, diagnosed, and acted upon without interference from mass media, party elites, or government representatives from outside the area.

Many things have changed since Tocqueville walked these shores and clearly a nostalgic yearning for simpler days cannot divert us from serious analysis of the present. To begin with, the United States is now a fully urbanized nation. While most Americans continue to prefer towns of limited size, this figure is relative. Since Tocqueville's time the quaint villages that he visited have given way to the massive metropolitan regions discussed above. By the middle of the nineteenth century the very scale of living and working arrangements had been fundamentally transformed. So too had the scale of governance, which evolved into a complex matrix of interlocking laws and regulations comprised of several distinct levels of political jurisdictions under federalist arrangements.

Yet, for about 150 years, between 1800 and 1950, pluralist democracy remained roughly intact as a form of political organization. To be sure, the town-hall meeting had been replaced in most areas by back rooms of party offices and egalitarian interaction had disappeared before the onslaught of bosses and aggressive political leaders. These changes, however, affected the form of democracy more than its content. Participation, for example, remained high and voter turnout was not its only measure. Local political life was characterized by strong daily involvement in parties, precincts, and wards. Political leaders did not cater solely to powerful interests. Rather, within the constraints of incrementalism they performed a pluralist juggling act catering to business demands, infrastructure requirements, and partisan local interests (McDonald and Ward, 1984). As the revisionist literature on political machines suggests, if many of these boss-led governments were corrupt, they were also responsible for a blossoming of democratic involvement in the new cities of America.

Beyond the age of bossism and right on through the Progressivist era, local urban governments performed admirably despite changes in form by helping to fuel industrial expansion. If depression-era changes slowed this growth to a standstill, local governments remained a principal administrative means of adjusting to the grip of crisis. During the Great Depression cities became veritable structural vessels for a wide variety of plans, administrative transformations, and policies aimed at the restructuring of the U.S. economy. Once again the fundamentally pluralist nature of American democracy shone through during this crisis as the needs of capitalists were tempered and altered by the State to fit the larger social need of recovery. Although not every interest had its demands addressed, the State framework consisting of the federal, state, and local levels, worked autonomously from specific special interests to effect a restructuring of the economy for the benefit of a general interest that may be called crisis management (see Habermas, 1975).

Around the 1950s this picture of pluralist participation and interlevel administrative harmony began to change. Fundamental social forces started to affect American life in basic and irreversible ways. First, a new affluence appeared in the postwar expansionist years. Many families could afford to break up into generational units and the nuclear household took over from more extended kinship forms. Husbands found work in locations outside their own local area and housing in general became available on a mass basis in the suburbs. The suburban dislocation had begun. Finally, minority groups were discovered in large numbers by white society. For the most part this segment of the population, growing all the time relative to whites within the central cities, was segregated into expanding ghettos and their own political and economic rights were socially constrained.

A vast and accelerating growth explosion of local governments, special-service districts, and extralocal administrative jurisdictions came to characterize local government in the 1950s (Wood, 1961). By the 1960s, cities no longer dominated metropolitan politics and state legislatures could act favorably on interests centered in suburbia and rural areas with little effective challenge by urban regimes. Indeed, the population itself split up between an increasing number of regional alignments, city-suburb conflicts, urban-rural contrasts, and intense competition among the separate municipalities for revenue producing resources. It's not that territorially based political rivalries were new to America, clearly they had existed before; in the years after World War II, local politics was fractured by a growing number of locationally distinct power bases. By the 1960s, for example, the Chicago metropolitan area comprised more than 1,000 separate political jurisdictions (Zimmerman, 1975).

Although it was commonly felt that the contemporary period had brought lasting and deep-seated changes to local political life, these were not always clearly or universally understood. Early analysts like Stein (1960) or Nisbet (1968) cast the transformation in terms of a loss of community. Nisbet was especially concerned with the disappearance of the type of pluralist democracy admired by Tocqueville and its progressive replacement by proto-totalitarian forms of mass politics. He, like Stein, however, viewed local politics as linked strongly to the well-being of the traditional American community, rather than as involving a separate, political path of change. According to this theory, the passing of the localized community represented ominous portents for the future of democracy.

More recently, the health of community life has become less of a concern among social scientists and the earlier work on its demise seems in retrospect somewhat premature. In fact, there is a new school of thought that finds the decentralized networks of friends characteristic of the modern metropolis to be as profoundly sheltering as were earlier conceptions of the centralized community (Fischer, 1983; Wellman and Leighton, 1979). The same cannot be said for local politics. Beginning with the 1970s, a burgeoning literature continues to document what can best be described as the death of local politics in America. People still vote, representatives continue to be elected year after year in locally run contests, parties still seek out funds and run slates, even patronage positions and charges of bossism can still be heard across the American landscape. But, the very heart and soul of local politics has surely died. A form without content remains. The present shell of politics surrounds a progressively empty center. The democratic life of the polis sucks out through a vacuum at the very core of the city.

If people need incentives for them to want to participate in politics, if the fruits of involvement are the rewards of pleasant change, if having a public life rather than focusing on callous self-interest depends on the good civic works that it can bring, then old reasons for the existence of a local political culture have ceased to prevail. Local politics has long since passed over into the hands of professional managers, giant multinational corporations, local capital caught in a predatory jungle of fierce small-business competition, provincial politicians making do on dwindling party resources, and, certainly not least, federal interventions promulgated by the long series of crises befalling the country since the 1960s.

The irresistible force of federal initiatives has, almost single-handedly, changed forever the nature of urban life striking up strong commonalities between patterns of development in the United States and those of communist countries such as Hungary or Poland. State intervention in urban growth is little recognized as significant by most mainstream urbanists, yet its role is pivotal. Massive metropolitan deconcentration, for example, would not have occurred were it not for the convergence of a strategic assortment of federal schemes and regulations, such as those supporting the construction of interstate highways, tax relief for homeowners, GI-bill subsidies for home buyers, and suburban defense employment. Beginning with the 1960s, however, a series of social and economic crises affecting cities accelerated the federal presence in local affairs. Ghetto riots were the most spectacular of these events. Those that took place in the mid-1960s, principally in 1964, ushered in a new age of concern about the deprived conditions of urban minorities. Political and academic commissions studying the aftermath of ghetto insurrections pointed to the long history of discrimination and disadvantages afflicting urban minorities, especially blacks. Under the Johnson Administration a monumental war on poverty was put in motion that would eventually channel billions of dollars in funds to local areas over the years.

Just as the federal programs of the past 20 years collected and ultimately assembled an immense reservoir of disadvantaged clients, they also enabled social service bureaucracies to expand their personnel and scope. Under the Nixon administration, when program targeting was replaced by general-revenue sharing, a significant source of funds was made available to municipalities for the further expansion of their local administrations, whether more government activities and employees were needed or not. Brick by brick each federal dollar built a massive bureaucratic edifice interpenetrating but also overshadowing the political and public business of local government (Fossett, 1983).

By the 1970s a second serious crisis afflicted local areas, namely, the specter of default. The fiscal crisis felt first in the cities of the frostbelt and most spectacularly played out by New York, changed the very basis of local public finance (Bahl, 1981). An expansionary balloon of local government involvement in urban affairs burst, exposing city residents to the chilling austerity of budgetary cutbacks. During the period of fiscal restructuring that followed this crisis, control of city finances passed over into the hands of state, federal, and private financial interests and out of the grasp of local residents and their elected city officials. The last vestiges of local control of municipal resources were snatched from the voters by changed arrangements for city solvency (Newfield and DeBrul, 1981).

Finally, a third crisis, one of long duration and beginning in the 1950s, has also afflicted urban areas, namely, the profound collapse of manufacturing as the industrial base of the city. During the decade following World War II, large numbers of new plants providing employment opportunities bypassed cities and popped up in suburban areas. Then, in the 1960s, demographers charted the absolute decline of all blue-collar work across the country and the shift to white-collar and service industries as the consequence of fundamental changes in the U.S. economy. Cities were hit especially hard by the erosion of the manufacturing infrastructure. By the 1970s, the revenue base of most cities had quite simply fallen to a level at which municipalities could not be run without outside aid.

More strikingly, cities, towns, and villages across the country became the sites of disruptive plant closings as their industrial bases dried up. We know now that what appeared first as a recognizable stage in the boom-and-bust cycle of capitalist development and thereby called on the unemployed to garner their patience in anticipation of better times, was in reality the beginning of a *new* phase of capitalist development in the United States not previously experienced here. At present, many analysts now believe that America has been emptied of its industrial strength and that the economy will function in the future as a more limited, second-rate manufacturing power. Such a prognosis takes into account the effects of the global transfer of industrial jobs elsewhere by giant multinationals and the growing obsolescence of this country's production infrastructure (Bluestone and Harrison, 1981; Melman, 1983). A process begun in the 1930s, the progressive redundancy of labor, has now accelerated in a new stage in which many people will be perennially without regular work.

In sum, three decades of change have transformed the city from a formidable engine of growth to a federal and state client dependent on a form of municipal welfare. Once painted in glowing terms signifying progress, political scientists now speak of the city according to its limits (Peterson, 1981; Wirt, 1983). Local politics is hemmed in presently by the power of corporations, programs at higher levels of government, and a failure to generate enough revenue without the need for finance capital's administration of public budgets. In between the crush of federal and state programs, banker demands, and corporate manipulations, the autonomous local political forum and its pluralist mechanisms of countervailing power have all but disappeared. If, in the 1960s, we could still speak of the threatened extinction of local community life, we can now talk more perceptively about the eclipse of the polity itself.

Not all political analysts would see the present in this light. There are several ideological modes of interpretation that argue against the view presented here. A formidable tradition,

for example, conceives of social development as an organic
process of evolution. According to the ideology of organicism,
present-day political arrangements may not be ideal, but they
do represent the best of all *possible* worlds. This is so because
the present has evolved through systemic processes of adapta-
tion and adjustment. Such ecological change accommodates
social needs through an inherent wisdom that more contrived
plans would upset. Where critics of the status quo see the pulver-
ization of local political life and its anomic, alienated forms of
involvement, mainstreamers perceive the inevitable products
of complex social change that bring greater levels of system
decentralization and personal autonomy.

For example, the fragmentation of the metropolitan region
is viewed in terms of opposites by defenders and critics of the
status quo. On the one hand, "public-choice" advocates believe
that such fragmentation functions well in supplying in a
decentralized manner necessary social services to a heterogeneous metropolitan population in an efficient way. The end
result of this process means a variety of communities will exist,
each offering a different bundle of public services. In this way
people can choose what is best for them. On the other hand,
critics of metropolitan fragmentation point to the stratification
and uneven development of urban areas. They see dispersal as
extracting a formidable cost from less advantaged populations
in the form of fewer services, poorer quality services, environ-
mentally hazardous living, absurdly high costs in time and
money for commutation, glaring inequities in the distribution
of life's essentials such as medical care, and an increasing
inability to orchestrate metropolitan planning. At present, the
defenders of the organic view seem to hold sway in academia
and the discussion below will examine this debate more closely
in order to arrive at some truth about the perceived need,
among radicals, for reconstruction.

A second ideology supporting present development comes
from those urbanists who assert that the pursuit of economic
growth is the policy of local government, which achieves the

greatest success. Progrowth policies, it is therefore believed, should be the principal business of local government (Peterson, 1981). The opposition "pro-" versus "no-" growth is a fundamental one in this society (Gottdiener, 1985a). Briefly, those that are boosters find little wrong with the functioning of local politics save that it provides residents who challenge new development with the opportunity to prevent or stall ambitious construction schemes. "No-growthers," in contrast, often view municipal governments with much distrust and as something of a real-estate development business (Feagin, 1983). For them the political process has already been usurped by powerful capitalist interests so that it is necessary, in order to block growth, to step outside normal political channels and protest by such measures as initiative referenda, picketing, law suits, boycotts, and the like. No-growthers rarely perceive that local political processes work for them, and they are most often right.

Despite the many costs of growth (Kapp, 1963; Mishan, 1967) the ideology of development possesses great appeal as the universal panacea for the ailments of society and is most often pursued with only minor concessions to those asked to pay for its social burdens. A narrow fix on pursuing growth chains local government to the unquestioned acquisition of development projects, often of a spectacular nature, such as football stadiums or world fairs, with limited real payoffs to local areas. Mounting evidence now shows that, because most of the subsidies that towns bestow upon business to promote development take place without public knowledge, government boosting of growth circumvents the democratic process (Judd and Smith, 1983; Sbragia, 1983).

Transposed against Pollyannaish ideologies preaching contentment are certain concrete facts about the American electoral system. Taken together they paint a dismal picture of democracy. Voter turnout, for example, is abysmal. The legitimacy of representative government is questioned by the presence of an electoral majority of nonvoters; parties have lost the ability to mobilize the masses. The people most in need of democracy, namely, minorities and the poor, seem to be reached least by the present system and fail to have their voice heard in elections. Finally, among all voters the feelings of alienation about politics and politicians soars above other attitudes, such as the positive ones once associated with the promise of politics and public visions of the future. All of these trends have been documented by a vast and growing literature (Abramson and Aldrich, 1982; Almond and Verba, 1973; Auletta, 1982; Burnham, 1982; Cavanagh, 1981; Crotty and Jacobson, 1980).

This book is about the decline of local political culture. It argues that what was once distinctive and beneficial about city or town government has progressively disappeared. This change has been incremental and largely unmonitored. It has come to assume a kind of naturalness, as if the present limited government and public powerlessness had always been so. This perception is reinforced by a set of attitudes deriving from organicism and a conservative opposition to social engineering arguing that incremental adjustment is, in fact, the superior method of public planning. Hefty arguments try to convince us that depressed central cities deserve our benign neglect rather than transformative social programs (Banfield, 1974), that low levels of political participation are, in fact, a sign of democracy's health and vitality (Lipset, 1963), and that social-welfare programs produce more pathology rather than alleviate it (Murray, 1984). These arguments are all false because they only deal with appearances. They fail to help us understand why society has developed in the way that it has. They are descriptive without explaining fundamental causes. In short, they do not help us to learn about the nature of local government and its relation to society.

In order to face squarely the problems posed by the attenuation of local political culture, it is necessary to chart out a trajectory of change that can provide the present with a historical referent. I shall address this issue in the next chapter. However, I shall not dwell on a long historical description of decline; given the evidence that we already possess, I take this for granted. The concerns of this discussion, instead, focus on its implications for the present, rather than the need to detail the history of change in local governance. For the purposes of the present discussion, the decline of political culture can be described today by the following three broadly conceived characteristics. Each will be developed in more detail in subsequent chapters. First, levels of voter participation are so low as to question seriously the validity of representative elections; second, there has been a progressive uncoupling of decision making from public forums and a growth of quasi-democratic modes of State management; and, third, there is a failure of local government to perform redistributive tasks of social justice required by democratic society and, consequently, a relative disappearance of societal issues not pertinent to economic and political administration from local public discourse. It is the latter feature that indicates the progressive decline of political contents, in a qualitative sense, from the affairs of the local State.

This discussion will proceed in stages. First, before we can decide what local government should do, it is necessary to inquire after the tasks that it has been asked to perform by residents of the metropolis. This identification of the *contents* of local politics becomes a way of documenting the death of political culture by attention to the present purpose of government.

Through analysis it is discovered that, regardless of their personal political philosophies, people look toward the local State to manage the quality of community life. In place of a concern with a vision of societal development and a publicly felt need to engage in decisions regarding the future through dialogues in political forums, local government has become preoccupied by the balance sheets of growth and the management of uncoordinated development. Political effects are produced today by the uneven nature of social change. In the face of threats to the quality of community life, residents seek from their local governments the administration and management of regional change and its burdens.

This new political discourse takes place within extreme limits on the ability of the local State to do anything about regional circumstances. Capital flight, industrial restructuring, fiscal crises, the powers of higher levels of government, and the autonomy of bureaucrats all combine to hem in options for political adjustments. The local State is ascribed a role by citizen interests that it cannot perform.

Chapters 3 and 4 concern themselves with contemporary approaches to local politics in the shadow of this dilemma. Following the assessment of contents, these chapters explore the ways of understanding that contemporary analysts of metropolitan politics have offered us. I make the useful and now routine distinction between "society-centered" and "State-centered" approaches here. Chapter 3 devotes itself to the former and includes assessments of Public-Choice theory, the "new" political economy, and neo-Marxism. Chapter 4, in turn, concerns the latter approach and examines neo-Weberianism and State-managerialism perspectives that assign to the State a certain autonomy from society-centered influences. One purpose of the discussions in these two chapters is to demonstrate the limits of all one-sided approaches to local politics and the need for a more synthetic view.

I assert that too often, out of the needs of positivist social science, analysts call upon us to choose between equally reductionist versions of political causality. Consequently, the concluding section of Capter 4 reexamines the issue of public-policy determination and argues for an approach that synthesizes State- and society-centered perspectives. Two recent phenomena that have been the subject of considerable empirical work are used to demonstrate the limits of extant perspectives, namely, the fiscal crisis of the city and the issue of equity in the supply of social services. I conclude that, because current approaches to local politics fail to develop a deep-level understanding of the State, they are doomed to reproduce conceptual errors of analysis.

Subsequent chapters reach for this greater understanding of the State. A special effort is devoted in this book to the local State because it is a greatly neglected subject and one that bears directly on the question of local politics itself. My discussion of the theory of the State takes cognizance of the almost overbearing volume of recent work carried out on this subject. Care is taken to minimize discussions of well-worn positions and to ferret out new ideas. Chapter 5 devotes itself to a theory of the State itself. After a brief critique of extant perspectives including pluralism, power elitism, instrumentalism, structuralism, and the more recent approaches emphasizing the dynamics of power, I develop a typological means of locating alternate versions of State theories.

My purpose here is to avoid the kind of pigeonholing found in surveys of the literature that typecast approaches according to their alleged analytical focus (for example, see Carnoy, 1984). The problem with such a method of classification is that it limits the breadth of different approaches merely to contrasts constructed at the level of explanation. This is in keeping with the positivist perspective endemic to contemporary social science and its passion for causality. In contrast, I will survey theories of the State below according to their epistemological premises. This emphasis on ways of knowing is a better means of grasping the issues that all State theories must address and for which their explanatory paradigms should be held accountable.

Chapter 6 switches to an assessment of the local State and theories meant to understand this level as distinct from the State in general. Surprisingly, the literature has little to offer on the subject and work here is so limited that much of what has been said on a theoretical level about the local State is, quite simply, wrong. My purpose in this chapter is to extract, from a broad range of perspectives, what is unique about the local State. That is, do there exist manifestations of political relations that are somehow unique to the local level and if so, how can we specify these qualities theoretically? After an assessment, I arrive at the conclusion that the most singular attributes of the local State, when compared with the State in general, concern its intimate relation with social control, for the case of the United States. This is a conclusion that differs somewhat from the extant literature, which views the local state, first and foremost, as a mechanism of societal reproduction. From my perspective the local State is animated most consistently, in the United States, by the field of power relations and, as Foucault (1979) suggests, by the political technology of the body techniques that are continually being perfected in the surveillance and regulation of human beings. Among other things, this approach to the local State exposes the issues of equity and social justice as ideological smoke-screens that cloud the consciousness of analysts, thereby preventing a true assessment of the role of State power in everyday life.

The understanding of power alone, however, cannot explain the local political process. The State performs other functions as well as those of social control. These can be analyzed by paying particular attention, not to State power, but to its institutional apparatus. Chapter 6 details the complex nature of the institutional qualities that house the political process and the sources of determinacy that modulate and shape what otherwise would be a free play of political interests. In this way I explain the political process in terms of the dialectical relation between structure and agency.

While Chapters 5 and 6 pay particular attention to the structural aspects of the State, or what I demonstrate is a two-tiered structure, Chapter 7 focuses on agency and the clash of interests constituting local politics. This chapter addresses a formidable dilemma and tries to explain it. If the political process is underdetermined by economic interests, as I contend, and if the dialectical relation between power and apparatus, or structure and agency, is contingent and open to significant degrees of freedom, then why is it that the most powerful interests in society seem to dominate the political process? As will be seen, there is no glib or easy answer to this question, despite the many views of power elitists and Marxists on this subject. My explanation seeks to deal with this dilemma by understanding power in a manner that goes deeper than previous approaches. By paying attention to the Janus-faced quality of power, and its deep-level relation to political processes, greater understanding of the limits to democracy is achieved.

In the end, this discussion calls for political change. But it does so by seeking to avoid reformism and the ideologial issue of social justice. If political culture has died, there can be no substitute for its resurrection before schemes of social reform can be entertained. As a first step in this revival, let us address the nature of the local State.

Before proceeding, please note: In the following pages it has been necessary to distinguish between the state level of government in federalist arrangements, that is, the town, county, state, and federal levels, from the system of governance and decision making known as "the State." As indicated, the former always appears in the lower case, while the latter is always capitalized.

CHAPTER 2

THE NATURE OF LOCAL GOVERNMENT

In the modern societies of Europe the apparatus of the State is heirarchically differentiated into separate levels of government, and its mechanisms of coordination for social development are a part of this integrated structure. The United States possesses no such comparable framework. Indeed, the ideology of "separation of powers" fragmented the political authority of even the nation-State itself into three branches of the federal government. In this country the dimensions of political control were worked out under federated arrangements that helped resolve a contentious relation between state governments and the federal level. Such a compromise was codified in the many laws that distinguish between the authority delegated between these two principal levels of government. In America the State is not only decentralized administratively, its powers are separated and reside in different institutions.

While the presence of a local government existing below the state level is taken for granted by most citizens, it is surprising to learn that no provisions were originally made in federalist arrangements for it. Recently, Windsor and James (1975) reminded us of this critical fact and its implications for urban political analysis:

> There is strictly speaking no fully developed theory of local government in the American federal system. Constitutionally, under what is commonly called Dillon's rule, local government does not exist. The constitution of the United States is a

compact between sovereign states and the federal government
that defines and divides their respective powers, rights and
responsibilities. There is no mention of local government in
Article Ten of the constitution. All local governments are
legally agents of the states, to be created or dismissed in the
state constitution or in statutes at the will of the legislature or
the people [1975: 87].

The fact that we can pause, look around, and become aware
of local government today cannot detract from the structural
handicap imposed upon it by federalist arrangements. What
we take for granted in the way of community politics does not
derive from any special mandate or vision as is the case with the
ideas behind "state's rights," for example. Because of its
peculiar, ersatz status, local government in the United States is
an empty shell of decision making surrounding a power
vacuum that has been created by the courts and opportunistic
state legislators. Having no distinct charge nor philosophy of
governance it has been open to control by the most powerful
interests intent upon seizing it, however subtly accomplished.

This does not mean that some governing directorship of
capitalists sits comfortably behind the reigns of State. Local
government is an open forum for the play of social forces and
the interests they generate. In any arena we can find the *vox
populi*, representatives of capital and even organized unions.
What matters in this apparently pluralist array is the manner
by which such separate and often contentious interests force
public decisions according to specific biases. What matters
then is how public policy formulated on the basis of these
decisions is implemented through government action. Over the
years the rudderless nature of this framework has resulted in a
drift across centuries consisting of several distinct periods.
These are neither more progressive nor enlightened than those
of the past and they may even overlap. They merely represent
particular historical stages within which the contentious forces
fighting over local control consolidate or condense around a

specific *modus vivendi* which is then observed to reproduce itself in a distinctive political style for some time. Through the play of forces in the vacuum of State administration, each successive period defines for itself the meaning of local government. To consider the local State means to acknowledge the fluidity of political forces, the relative irrelevance of social vision or important political ideas, and the mission of governance as the prey of concerted group action.

Continuity and Change in Local Government

From the earliest days of colonization, the local community embodied a version of political relations more attached to medieval principles than in the present. According to this view a centralized State is to be feared as much as trusted. Political relations did not pervade interaction within the community, rather the State was merely one association among several that also possessed compelling claims to power, such as the family and the church (MacIver, 1969: 165). In short, many early settlers lived in communities reminiscent of medieval towns that had a political culture founded on associational rights and limited attachments to government outside the local area.

This form of politics differs markedly from both the Greek city-State and from the Roman notion of citizenship. Prior to the Middle Ages individuals as subjects of the great ancient empires were linked to the central State as much as to their extended families. What mattered increasingly in this ancient world was the individual's social status and his or her relation to the State itself. Within the political community of totalitarian empires the associational rights of people were weak, if they existed at all.

The Middle Ages changed all that because in its towns political authority became only one type of social authority. Max Weber (1962) studied this phenomenon in exhaustive detail. He found that the classic medieval town possessed a

robust assortment of separate, pluralistically powerful associations. Residents were not only citizens of the town itself
but active members of the medieval associations located within
it. Weber paid particular attention to the "conjutorio," those
self-help, mutual-aid groups that through tightly knit interaction enabled town residents to survive and raise families in
an otherwise hostile world. Some analysts have argued that
Weber viewed cosmopolitanism as the unique contribution of
urban culture (Sennet, 1968). Nowhere in Weber's writing on
the city can this argument be found. Instead, for Max Weber,
the richness of local public life produced by the decentralized
nature of medieval associations became the cornerstone of
urban culture and its most distinctive attribute when compared
with social and political forms of the past.

As Nisbet (1968) has shown, the power of decentralized
mutual-aid associations, craft guilds, and the like were all
swept away with the breakdown of medieval social relations
and the rise of the nation-State. The many seats of authority
were progressively replaced by an all powerful State. To a great
extent the trajectory of this development continues to the
present as the power of centralized State institutions persist
hegemonically in both the West and the East. According to
public-choice advocates the decentralization of government
administration tempers the power of the central bureaucracy.
As Althusser (1971) has observed, however, State functions
operate with uniformly maintained political and management
practices through the linked systems of separate regional
authorities, police stations, tax offices, planning boards, and
so on. The facade of functional differentiation cannot hide the
systemic unity of the State apparatus operating through its
nationally coordinated political and administrative practices.
Virtually absent from the present framework of power are the
types of countervailing forces once prevalent in pluralistically
democratic societies. Within the present social context, what
then has become of the rights of citizens?

Political thought in the United States is dominated by a tradition that became codified during the time of Rome. According to this view the relation between the individual and the State requires no mediation. Liberty is protected by the concept of natural law, which asserts that, regardless of the form of government, there are basic rights of individuals that no State can legitimately take away. If the natural rights of people are acknowledged by the system of power, then individual freedom is assured. Thus, the courts and *not* countervailing associations with their own power are the last refuge of persecuted individuals. This formal doctrine of natural law became the cornerstone of both the French and American revolutions. As the United States developed, this tradition produced a structural bias in favor of managing individual liberties at the expense of nurturing legal concepts based on the importance of associational freedoms.

Over time, towns and cities in America that were once free associations were altered to accommodate the hegemonic role of individual rights within the political community. The judiciary became highly developed because of its central role in the mediation of disputes and a close relation was cemented into place between lawyers and government leadership. In the end the concept of the associational town was replaced by the individual rights of the town through the formal category of the "municipal corporation." At the same time, by expropriating the opposition between associational authority and government authority as a distinction between public and private rights located internally within the domain of State jurisdiction itself, the power of government grew with every dispute about individual freedom and liberty. Regardless of how the outcomes of such disputes resolved these issues, the domination of the State was never threatened by the development of some other associational power. Their only effect was an explosion in laws and litigation. This apotheosis of individualism found its most responsive chord in the early development of capitalism and its ideology of free enterprise unrestrained by organized groups of capital and labor. In sum, the shift in the power of the State against associational rights stood in concordance with the ideology of capitalism forging a potent regime of accumulation in the early phases of U.S. growth.

This development, which is essential to an understanding of the eclipse of the polity, was mirrored in the evolution of the municipal corporation. The purpose of the corporation is to promote the value of urban land through the use of public authority defined as a separate and sometimes constraining entity relative to the natural rights of individuals. It is often supposed that local government emerged as an incorporated presence through processes manifesting themselves in the earliest days of this country's history. As Frug (1980) indicates amply, however, while some early proprietory towns were corporations, such as Philadelphia, most were unincorporated associations with no institutionalized rights within their borders other than those guaranteed under the constitution to individuals. The corporate status of cities in the United States, which conferred a formal apparatus of State power upon the local level, was an historical creation of the courts in the 1800s. Incorporation as it was practiced by state legislatures and the courts deemphasized the basic associational rights guaranteed to individual residents of urban agglomerations in favor of institutionalizing legal defenses of private property (see Frug, 1980). This period might be considered the second stage of municipal development following the earliest era marked by the vigorous exercise of associational rights and a weak central State.

By the 1800s city incorporation became a vehicle for propertied interests defending themselves through the government against the class struggle, on the one hand, and state legislatures, which were the scenes of the complex interplay among various mobilized interests in early American history, on the other, including several antagonistic fractions of capital. Furthermore, during this period the State apparatus, through the particular concept of the "municipal corporation," was able to move against associational forms of local autonomy, such as the New England town councils. Most Marxists view the process by which cities were incorporated as the political expression of the consolidated efforts of a group of local capitalists (Markusen,1978; Hoch, 1984). This is correct as a general observation. More specifically, however, select groups pushing for incorporation were not necessarily the most important elements of the capitalist class, but were comprised of opportunists who understood that the concept of the public corporation provided those in control of local government with a *separate* source of wealth and power. This was so because the evolved form of the concept of the "corporation" consolidated in one mechanism the fundamental sanctity of property rights as the basis of political associations over against all other associational rights. In effect, through the concept of the municipal corporation, the city became a legal individual. Thus the municipal corporation not only protected the private-property rights of individuals living within the city, especially the early capitalist industrialists, it also sanctified the concept of *public* property and established the notion of the government's right to property. This incentive was so strong that it hardly mattered to those in the 1800s that basic associational rights were ignored in the political creation of cities. As Frug (1980: 1108) suggests,

It is for this reason that the classification of American cities as corporations mattered; it can be understood as helping to repress the notion that associational rights were being affected in defining the laws governing city rights. No rights of association needed to be articulated when discussing the rights of "private" corporations, since property rights were sufficient to protect them against state power, and there was nothing that

required rights of association to be imagined in discussing the
subordination of "public corporations."

Thus while control over economic resources was central to
capitalist development and became a source of power in
nineteenth-century America, control of the municipal corporation became a second route to wealth and power safe-
guarded by the laws of incorporation passed during meetings
of the state legislature.

The codification of Dillons Rule (1872) consolidated the
political formation of incorporated places and institutionalized an autonomous formal separation between the
public corporation, or local government, and the activities of
society. This "particularization" of the local State is specific to
the case of the United States and it resulted in the formal
separation of two distinct domains of interest in society. Such a
development represents the third stage in city formation.
During the period corresponding roughly to the time between
1880 and 1920 city government became a vehicle for the
realization of wealth through the benefits obtained from
control over *public* property. As the defender of *all* property
rights the local State advanced its own interests at the very
same time that it helped private capital consolidate its control
over an often militant urban proletariat. I shall return to this
critical activity of local government in Chapter 6 when I will
discuss its relevance for the theory of the State.

As observed, the granting of municipal corporate status was
a power of the state level of government. Consequently, state
legislatures in the late 1800s became the scene of battles among
rival fractions of capital along with their proletarian and
political cronies for the right to incorporate publicly but
largely for personal gain (Wickman,1970). Antagonism developed, therefore, among fractions of capital from outside areas
wishing to move in and local bases of power. The state level of
government was easier to penetrate from the outside than was

the municipal corporation causing considerable friction between separate fractions seeking to maneuver for control of development. Eventually a movement arose to return some autonomous political powers back to the local area. As Greer has observed (1962: 47), this drive for "home rule" was a legacy of the egalitarian reformism of the Jacksonian era. Wherever successful, "home rule" preserved for local places a measure of freedom from administrations at the higher levels of government. However, during the reformist days of Jacksonian democracy the fundamental premises of the evolved concept of incorporation were never challenged. For this reason the separation of the State from society, in the case of the United States, remained centered upon property and *not* associational rights.

The main thrust of home-rule reforms centered on consolidating the political power of the municipal corporation, especially its bureaucracy. At first cities were run by the famous form of the boss-led machine. This represents a fourth stage of local-government development. By "political machine" is meant any political party headed by a single leader with or without possession of public office, that dominates elections and the public administrative apparatus through the use of illegitimate as well as legitimate means (Scott, 1972; Mushkat, 1971; Mandelbaum, 1965). The boss-led machine of the nineteenth century was comprised of precinct or ward subdivisions conforming to the demographic districts of the city. Usually, the political arrangement of the machine party apparatus was in direct correspondence with the named areas of the city constituted as ethnic or racial enclaves. In such an arrangement, the legally defined political jurisdictions of the city, such as wards or precincts, were led by party "captains" who then administered to the needs of the local population in return for political support during elections. In short, the party was *the* political association and no others were necessary because of its skill in establishing this exchange relation.

The characteristic basis of the machine was its administrative and *not* its partisan nature. It was a true "machine" with no values of its own save the need for personal and party advancement. As a citywide mode of political control it represented broadly all the diverse interests making up the polity (Shefter, 1977). In exchange for votes and party work residents of the city could look to it for help; consequently it rivaled other protoforms of mutual aid and even became a structure that sheltered workers from the vagaries of capitalist accumulation through the form of patronage, thereby competing with unions themselves. As Lineberry and Sharkansky (1978: 119) note,

> There is but one common denominator of the organization that we call the political machine: It is a non-ideological electoral organization, depending heavily on lower-class votes. Machines are almost never ideological. They are rather broad umbrellas that are large enough to cover every shade of opinion and interest.

It is important not to romanticize the place of the political machine in American politics and several studies have helped to document the essentially corrupt nature of many of its practices (Scott,1972; Huntington,1968). More important, today there is a virtual absence of machine politics from the American scene, even in places like Chicago where it once flourished, so that the entire phenomenon has limited instructional value for an understanding of contemporary politics (Lowi, 1967). Yet there are two aspects of the machine that are worth highlighting. First, it represented a source of continuity in the development of the municipal corporation, which circumvented and in fact discouraged the free growth of private associations and mutual-aid frameworks outside the form of government. Second, it enlarged greatly the city bureaucracy under home-rule arrangements and solidified its control over the political resources created by Dillons Rule. Because the city of the nineteenth century also contained most of the economic wealth of the region, it represented a concordance of political and economic power within the same sociospatial environment. The political machine aggregated local citizen needs with business and civic booster demands within a framework whose jurisdiction coincided with control over much of the economic activities that were important for regional material well-being.

Since the turn of the century the above aspect of local urban administration has swiftly eroded under a variety of influences. Perhaps the principal political changes that occurred were those affecting city administration brought about by the progressivist movement. As the twentieth century arrived, progressivist reforms struck at the very heart of the machine's sociospatial framework. This period represents a fifth stage in the open-ended evolution of local government. For example, the locationally sensitive features of the machine were destroyed by the drive for a city manager or nonpartisan form of government that held elections at large and that eliminated ward and precinct districts. Progressivist reforms also dismantled the structural mechanisms of political aggregation characteristic of the machine. They cut the city off from political involvement by exercising the principle of home rule and by procedural measures such as staggered elections. In short, where before the machine had been an effective means of channeling the demands of heterogeneous urban enclaves, progressivist reforms substituted a nonpartisan mode of governance that no longer required a vote-for-favor exchange relation. The informal and day-to-day link between city hall and the polity was broken.

If progressivist reforms broke up the concordance between political representation and localized interests, it did preserve the first feature of the machine, namely, its assault against associational rights. In fact, progressivists did the machine one

better. They enlarged greatly the city bureaucracy. Even more
significant, they appropriated many of the associational activities of private citizens and made them concerns of the State
under the banner of social engineering and reforms. Thus they
established the massive nonelective service bureaucracies for
health, education, recreation, and the like, which were run by
the classic bureaucrats of the civil service. As a result,
progressivism, while perhaps overrated as a period of structural
reforms in the democratic process, effected fundamental
advances in the appropriation of associational rights by the
State bureaucracy.

The cities of today are far removed from the coincidence of
economic and political power characteristic of machine-led
urban areas. As we have seen, the local political apparatus now
has little control over important economic interests organized
as national and international activities. More important, there
is an absence of a framework that might canalize local
neighborhood needs and integrate these in some aggregated
fashion so that the political leadership of the city can respond
to special interests and social development in a coordinated
way. Not all of the blame for the lack of an integrated structure
of governance can be placed upon predepression progressive
reforms. In fact, the further erosion of an integrated political
framework for the city occurred ironically as a consequence of
post-World War II programs aimed at addressing the deteriorating conditions of the nation's cities. In particular, massive
spending from the liberal agenda of the 1960s expanded greatly
the numbers and powers of city bureaucrats even if it failed in
promoting the type of social change that it was meant to
produce (Murray, 1984). This mode of intervention cut new
inroads into the associational needs of society making entire
city populations wards of the State.

In addition, federal intervention on a monumental scale in
urban revitalization changed the face of the city forever. On the
whole, analysts of every political persuasion agree that these

efforts failed to rescue central city communities and their deteriorating housing (Anderson, 1964; Mollenkopf, 1983). While local neighborhoods suffered from renewal, the value of central-city real estate was preserved making the programs of revitalization an important means by which powerful interests in the city were able to subsidize their own needs (Gottdiener, 1985a). This period, which takes us up to the present, represents the sixth stage of political development for local government.

In short, while the cities of today possess a political apparatus, its ability to channel, integrate, and actively coordinate the needs of the population in order to sustain effectively community well-being for all its residents remains a social problem. This inadequacy of political structure is not felt by everyone alike. Clearly, certain segments of the polity, especially the more affluent, are better served by the present system than others. As I shall indicate below, however, the need for structural change does not rest on questions of equity, or the differential ability of people to pursue their own interests through local government. Rather, despite differential opinions regarding personal satisfaction with the status quo, there are qualitative judgments that can still be made about the nature of democracy. The present discussion addresses this problematic and not the reformist one of social justice because only solutions to the former can supply a basis for solutions to the latter.

Unguided by mandate and restricted to the corporate form of municipality, development of local government in the United States has come to focus on the narrow fix of promoting growth, while the everyday needs of resident populations not related directly to this aim are often ignored. This emphasis has occurred not through any directed process or plan but because of the relative ability of city administrations to operate within an increasingly constrained environment. The pursuit of growth is the function that the city seems best able to perform (Peterson, 1981). Are we, however, to be content with this status quo? There are many reasons stemming from the concept of equity and social justice why we should not. I shall get to them momentarily. But if we are concerned about rescuing local government and returning to it a role in the constellation of powers and delegated authorities prevailing presently, then we must know more about its place in the larger system of social organization.

In this context I am less interested in what governments can or cannot do regarding their identifiable limits, than in understanding what they have been asked to do, what functions they have been called upon to perform, by the local political process, and, most important, why. In the case of the United States it is essential that an approach to the local State begin with just such an examination of the *contents* of local politics precisely because, in this country, the role of urban government has revealed itself over time. Therefore, we must try to identify the needs that citizens have asked local government to address over the past several years, whether or not it has been found capable of meeting them. If we can tease out of the historical record a pattern to local demands, then we shall be in a better position to argue for an overarching mandate aimed at supporting what local government should be doing and not just what it seems best able to accomplish because of present limits on its effectiveness.

It will be asserted in the next few chapters that the contents of local politics is described best as a concern for the quality of community life. Essentially, this concern embodies a paradox. On the one hand, local residents wish to limit and manage the growth of the State. Some even object to its progressive regulation of social activities, which in previous times were left to the private sector. On the other hand, residents continue to look to the State to solve many of the problems of social life. While people wish that government's powers were less, they expect it to do more. Lloyd Free and Hadley Cantril (1967) were the first to discover this behavioral set of American values and they call it the "bipolar" alignment of voter attitudes. According to Burnham (1982),

> American voters are arrayed not on one attitudinal dimension, but two: ideological and operational. Ideologically they are predominantly conservative, regularly producing large majorities against "big government." Operationally they are liberals, just as regularly "voting" for specific programs that require government spending—particularly those from which they expect to benefit personally. However messy this may be from a logical point of view, such an opinion structure is admirably suited to support a nonsocialist but interventionist State that deals in the currency of particularized benefits [1982: 254].

The ascribed function of the local State as the protector of community quality has revealed itself over time. That is, this concern is an emergent, historical property of local politics. It is not an intrinsic feature of local governance, nor is it some concrete mandate charged to local areas by the division of administrative functions in the hierarchy of governmental jurisdictions. Rather, it is a characteristic that has surfaced following three decades of post-Depression metropolitan regional development and economic restructuring. If each age defines for itself the special mission of local government, as I have argued, because it lacks a basic political mandate, then only a content definition of local politics can provide us with a clue to what the current conjuncture is like.

At present political effects are the consequence of un-coordinated economic and spatial restructuring that has been taking place in American society since the Depression. The uneven nature of metropolitan development patterns and the lack of overarching social planning coupled with the plethora of fragmented programs at every State level have contributed to the production of these political effects. Consequently, concerns over the quality of life have surfaced to dominate the local political agenda. Conflicting ideologies professing to have grasped the basic factors responsible for improving community quality clash in the city and town public arenas of the nation. It will be my task to examine these political theories as they relate to the quality of life and to explain at a deeper level why the relation between the State and the society, in the United States, manifests itself in this precise manner today in conformity with such a political content.

The Quality of Community Life

What is meant by this much used concept, "the quality of life," and how is it related to local politics? There are two dimensions with which this concept can be gauged. Furthermore, they have both been modulated by recent historical changes in social development. The first involves the quality of local community resources, while the second concerns their availability to all local residents. In the first case, the notion that the quality of individual well-being is linked with that of community well-being is called the transcendental approach to the quality of life (Gerson,1976), and has been a central tenet of political philosophy at least since Plato. In order to study the relationship between the local State and community well-being it is necessary to assume the existence of this prior linkage between private existence and local social circumstances. Such a link is most explicitly espoused by welfare liberalism. It implies that regardless of attributes associated with personal background, such as class or race, which quite directly affect life chances in a stratified society such as ours, there are also community institutions that mediate background resources and help achieve individual well-being or that can even provide individuals with resources that can overcome the social deficiencies of birth. Thus, one aspect of the quality of life focuses on the role of local community institutions in providing individuals with certain life chances that they cannot acquire privately because of their personal circumstances, and it is precisely for this reason that sustaining the quality of community life is a central, socially perceived and ascribed role for the local State.

The quality of life is also dependent on material resources. The availability of jobs, the nature and extent of this work—whether it is physically or mentally demanding, cyclical or steady, and so on—are also critical factors in determining community relations, even though many labor related needs are confined to group action at the place of work. The separation between home, producing the individual as a citizen, and work, producing the individual as a worker, is an artificial one created by capitalist relations of production. Community well-being depends on the health and management of the local economy. Aggregate assessments, such as the overall success of a region or nation cannot be allowed to confuse the differential impact of business on community quality. Thus failed companies and unemployment in laggard sectors can affect local political needs despite the well-being of other enterprises and workers in a city.

In sum, the quality of community life is dependent on both public and private resources. Each has its own role to play. In addition, however, the well-being of these two spheres is interrelated. Because the local State depends for much of its revenue on the private sector, it is in the interest of government, in order to fulfill its public function, to promote and sustain the well-being of the local economy. Precisely due to this link, urban analysis has called forth an approach called "political economy" that attempts to study the relation between the two spheres. Its major contribution has been to document the intimate links between the local State and the needs of the private sector (see Chapter 3), that is, the *social* nature of economic development, on the one hand, and the collective foundations of State services, on the other. Finally, just as local political culture has died as its associational basis and the decision-making role of public forums have disappeared, labor at the place of work has also become more isolated and less able to help in the management of community resources for the greater good. Consequently, one important implication of the focus on the problematic of the quality of community life is that forms of self-management and participation in the neighborhood must also be connected to such forms at the workplace as well.

Mainstream work on assessing the quality of community life is quite limited. It ignores the social constitution of resources that depends on collective modes of interaction and social responsibility (Schneider, 1975). Instead, the dominant approach among social scientists involves quantifying aggregate indicators of well-being (Bauer, 1966; Liu, 1976). Some of these indicators are linked to services provided by social institutions such as health care, welfare, parks and recreation, mass transportation, and education. Others are products supplied primarily by the private sector, such as housing, entertainment and cultural activities, and the level of economic activity. Still others are privately produced but socially managed, such as levels of pollution or environmental quality, and crime.

This quantitative approach to community well-being is useful only as an aggregate indicator of factors that can be quantified easily. In addition to neglecting collective aspects, as we have seen, it also ignores spatial problems of access that affect community quality even if resources themselves are adequate. Thus, while the provision of health care, for example, may be rated high on the basis of the number of hospitals, the concentration of medical specialties, and so on, a majority of residents may not possess access to such resources. In a second example, the presence of public space as an indicator of well-being must be, but rarely is, evaluated by assessing the ability of residents to enjoy such spaces, especially when they are no longer safe places to be in. Finally, despite the availability of high-quality services, rapid development may block the ability of residents to gain access due to over-crowding or other growth-related problems, such as the disappearance of open space. Consequently, there is a socio-spatial aspect to the quality of life that is a function of social as opposed to individual characteristics and resources that is not measured by the quantitative approach using social indicators. Such considerations also play a central role in local politics.

In sum, I suggest that at the same time the local State has become more involved in the provision of public services, it has also been called upon to ameliorate their access problems. This is exemplified best in the case of suburban efforts at growth-management policy, but it is also illustrated by massive projects combining public with private auspices, such as urban renewal within central cities. It is precisely for this reason that quality-of-life concerns possess two aspects that must be discussed together. Access and quality are related.

Recently, social changes have affected the ways in which quality-of-life concerns have been viewed. This transformation is the subject matter of this book as it has led to the eclipse of the polity. Since at least the 1930s sustaining community quality has become increasingly more problematical for the institutions of society. The family, churches, and business enterprises, in particular, have all faced crises that have been difficult to resolve in a private way. Consequently, over the past 50 years the State has been called upon progressively to play the role of manager for a host of problems that society cannot resolve. At present the State has become the veritable regulator of everyday life. The issue raised by this intervention is whether or not it represents a democratic mechanism of social management. Does the local State regulate in the interests of all? Can each social group find redress of grievances as development proceeds? Finally, are all interests represented by the actions of State? Precisely these questions will be addressed in the next few chapters.

The historical movement of government toward increasing regulation of everyday life has meant that progressively fewer concerns are articulated in open public arenas. Pluralist democracy has been wiped out and replaced by three-way battles between interests in favor of growth, local citizens burdened with its social costs including elements of capital as well as labor, and professional city bureaucrats with an iron hand on State controls. Because the final outcome of policy is decided by representatives of government, rather than some equitable form of public self-management, democratic processes have been changed fundamentally in this country. Political differences about policy become converted into modes of management by local bureaucrats. The practice of government administration hides the often contentious battles that policy outcomes represent and makes it more difficult for such decisions to be renegotiated by the public or even examined at a later time. Over the years and as a direct result of successive local crises, the State has increasingly intervened in more areas of private life, while political mechanisms have atrophied that once left the solution to social problems open to vigorous debate without the auspices of government bureaucracies. Regulatory activities once set in motion, such as the capacity of the State for surveillance, are rarely monitored by the public and take on a life of their own. Over the years incremental advances in the capacity of State regulation aggregate and become a force in human affairs (see Foucault, 1979, esp. chap. 5).

In sum, the thesis of this discussion is that concerns over the quality of community life form the core of local metropolitan politics and provide a content definition for its issues and conflicts. These manifest themselves in different ways. Yet, they are unified by the social impulse that links the local State in increasingly greater intimacy with concerns about sustaining or improving the resources of the community. Finally, this content of local politics is produced by the changed relation between the State and society, particularly the dual role of the

State and the eradication of countervailing powers.

The relationship between community well-being and the interventionist State is a contradictory one. Contradictions exist on many levels, such as those internal to the State itself in the performance of political administration, as well as the contradictory nature of the relation between the State and society. For example, the quality of life rests heavily on the level of material well-being, as already mentioned. This is in large part an economic quality or rather a function of the level of economic performance. On the one hand, in the United States, the more robust is this economic activity, the higher will be the standard of living. On the other hand, vigorous growth produces social costs detrimental to the quality of community life. These include environmental pollution, rapid redevelopment and growth within communities, overcrowding, and crime.

On balance, then, there is no implicit correlation between growth and well-being (Mishan, 1967; Judd and Smith, 1983), a fact that strikes down the importance of studies such as Peterson's (1981) that equate in an ideological manner these two aspects. Consequently, both the nature and level of development must be matched to the nature and level of community well-being in a strategic or planned way. No private-sector mechanism exists that operates through the activities of social organization carrying out such a guiding strategy. Only some form of political control can accomplish this task. Lacking such a mechanism, any match made for the moment between economic success and public well-being is by nature an historical coincidence of a temporary kind. Thus, the activities of the private sector are both the source of social well-being and also of our social problems. It is this contradiction that makes the need for an interventionist State necessary. Furthermore, as localized areas have been forced progressively over the years to accommodate themselves to massive regional development and restructuring, this failure of governance has become more apparent. Small wonder that it is manifested in the growing concerns of local residents and in the expectations ascribed to the local State by the polity regardless of self-professed political persuasions.

Despite the growing need to manage the quality of life, the local State is not adequate to this task. In fact, State intervention in society contains its own contradictory tendencies, and these shall be examined in the next few chapters. According to the view developed below, it is a mistake to impute a functional role to the State at any level, as many contemporary analysts are fond of doing. State interventions can exacerbate contentious issues in society as well as manage them. In fact, there are several aspects of the present system of governance in metropolitan areas that can be considered structural limitations that are unproductive and that do not advance the level of local well-being. As I shall indicate in Chapter 5, the study of the State according to its functions is a form of idealism (see also Badie and Birnbaum, 1983).

By way of concluding this chapter, let us examine some of the ways in which current political arrangements fail to meet the needs of an effective polity. The purpose of this discussion is to isolate the important structural reasons why local government is weak and which bear directly on other factors already assessed that have contributed to the decline of political culture. I shall show that in evaluating the structural inadequacies of local governing frameworks, a variety of contemporary perspectives have taken issue with common assessments about the significance of such weaknesses. It will, therefore, be the task of the next two chapters to assess, in turn, these *new* approaches to local urban politics before we can entertain more theoretical questions regarding the relation between the State and the society.

Limitations of Local Government

In general there are three fundamental limitations of local government that apply to all areas of the metropolitan region.

First, political participation at the local level is very weak. For example, municipal elections draw one-third or less of those adults eligible to vote (Alford and Lee, 1968; Abramson and Aldrich, 1982). In fact, voter turnout has declined to less than one-half of those eligible in all political contests (Crotty and Jacobson, 1980; Hadley, 1978; Gans, 1978). Involvement in local politics, once the hallmark of community life, has declined over the years (Verba et al., 1978; Burnham, 1982). So, too, has involvement in local political parties, which have weakened considerably in the course of time (Fishel, 1978; Crotty and Jacobson, 1980). Many voters, for example, can be counted on today to switch party preference during elections or even declare themselves as independents. Consequently, local political parties have considerable difficulty supporting themselves. Finally, analysts suggest that diminishing faith in the efficacy of local government has also increased over time so that the polity has become progressively more alienated from the local political process (Crotty, 1977; Abramson and Aldrich,1982).

A second feature of local politics is that the metropolitan region is excessively fragmented into overlapping jurisdictions and proliferating municipal boundaries. Urbanized areas are so balkanized among separate and often contending municipalities as to question seriously whether any form of co-ordinated governance exists for the region as a whole. Some analysts, however, argue that such an overarching structure is not even necessary. I shall discuss the origins of this political fragmentation and the debate over its relative efficacy more fully below. Finally, throughout the metropolis there is a spatial separation between the rich and the poor, black and white, and between white-collar and blue-collar workers (Neiman, 1975). In addition, locational inequality or segregation is merely the spatial representation of functional and systemic inequality characteristic of a society stratified by class and race. Thus the growth process of regional expansion and development can be described best as uneven and inequitable (Browett, 1984; Gottdiener, 1985a). The sociospatial nature of this process plays a fundamental role in local political concerns.

All three of these features act in concert to make the structural framework of local government weak and ineffective. Several analytical questions are raised by the presence of these attributes. What are the reasons for these characteristic features? In what way(s) are they related? Are there underlying processes of development that contribute to or even produce the defining aspects of local politics? And finally, what significance do these features have for the assessment of conflicting theories about the nature of local urban politics? Let us examine our three features in more detail in order to gain a better appreciation for the distinctive way in which an integrated approach to metropolitan politics focusing on the State's role in managing the quality of community life can answer these and other questions

The Weakness of the Polity

William Burnham, perhaps more than others, has devoted several decades to research on this topic and has concluded that the American polity is now so weak that democracy requires reconstruction. He spotlights specifically the decline in voter participation in politics as the principal factor in this social problem. Talking mainly about the national level of politics (1982: 197), he suggests,

> The choice appears to be between a continuing, gradual euthanasia of the American electorate, or the revitalization of democratic forces in this country. As in the past, the size, shape, and composition of the "party of nonvoters" will quite sensitively reflect which path is being taken.

The main argument advocating needless concern over the lack of participation in politics comes from Lipset (1963) who suggested that low participation means satisfaction with democracy. The prestige ascribed to Lipset's study merely points out the ideological stranglehold that his generation of sociologists has exercised in academic life in choking off the growth of critical social theory. Over the two decades since this Pollyannaish interpretation of statistics on voter decline has appeared, this argument has been exposed as false and misleading (Burnham, 1982). Instead, it is now understood that the growth of nonvoting has reached crisis proportions that question the very legitimacy of our elections (Gans, 1978; Tarrance, 1978). Furthermore, as Crotty and Jacobson (1980) have shown, if people do not vote, they are not likely to be engaged in any other kinds of political activity. Thus, two-thirds of all nonvoters do not become involved in any other form of politics, even avoiding to influence the votes of acquaintances (1980: 11), while only one-half of all those who do vote become involved in other forms of politics (1980: 13). As Crotty and Jacobson (1980) summarize,

> The number of voters participating in elections continues to decline to levels low enough for us to begin to question the relevance, and should the trend continue, the stability of American political institutions. The picture is bleak. The electorate has become polarized between the higher socio-economic status adults who remain in the 30 to 50 percent of the eligible population that continues to participate in elections and the lower socio-economic status groups who have dropped out. How representative is a governing system that does not include in its decision making in any meaningful way those most in need of effective political representation? [1980: 248].

As we have seen, the decline of political culture in the United States is reflected directly in low-participation rates and possesses at least three separate dimensions. These are: the growth of the population of nonvoters, a drop in party support, and the increase in political alienation. This discovery does not mean that municipal government has ceased to function, nor that political contests have no importance. What it does suggest is that due to its weaknesses, political culture no longer provides enough inputs for democratic processes to function. This observation is based on the argument of pluralists regarding the importance of electoral competition who suggest that without a substantial *level* of involvement by the electorate to feed the quest for votes, there is little else of consequence to pluralist mechanisms of democracy (Verba and Nie, 1972). It is also based on arguments, such as Pateman's (1970) that substantiate the benefits of participation itself in direct opposition to views, such as Lipset's, that fear the mobilization of the "masses" in the political process. According to Pateman (1970),

> The existence of representative institutions at the national level is not sufficient for democracy; for maximum participation by all the people at that level of socialization, or "social training", for democracy must take place in other spheres in order that the necessary individual attitudes and psychological qualities can be developed. This development takes place through the process of participation itself. The major function of partici- pation in the theory of participatory democracy is, therefore, an educative one, educative in the very widest sense, including both the psychological aspect and the gaining of practice in democratic skills and procedures [1970: 42].

Participation means socialization and experience in political life. When this is denied to the vast majority of citizens through social trends fostering nonparticipation, political culture sim- ply dies.

There is some evidence to suggest that the decline of political culture is correlated to the increasingly limited social role of the local community and localized attachments to place. As neighborhood involvements have lost out in favor of com- muting and social networks of dispersed friends, political participation also suffers (see the study by Wellman and Leighton, 1979). According to Orbell and Uno (1972), for example, greater mobility is itself a cause of decline. Many people solve the problem of their personal involvement in community disputes by exercising what Hirschman (1970) calls their "exit" option, that is, by moving elsewhere rather than by staying and carrying out a political struggle within their community. In many cases, however, it is no longer possible to move because either housing or commuting costs or both have presently become prohibitive. Those factors such as the influence of the housing market, which once supported the exit option, now contribute to increased resident militancy (Cox, 1982). For these reasons it is important to understand the link between changes in societal processes shaping community involvement and historical changes in the relative strength of local political culture. As indicated in Chapter 1, it is simply incorrect to equate automatically the decline of community with the eclipse of local politics, because the forces shaping their relative strengths and weaknesses vary in their effects.

In many cities structural changes have been put in place to try to revive the participation in politics of those groups historically least active, namely, the poor and the minorities. Urban administrations have responded with the creation of new mechanisms for channeling political interaction including decentralized planning boards, neighborhood governments, and even "little city halls." The main effect of this change, according to Katznelson (1976), is that the structure itself of local government largely determines the relative ability of groups to exercise political influence. Katznelson (1976: 21) calls this approach to understanding political involvement the assessment of "class capacities" because "political arrangements themselves may act as dependent constraints on the capacity of a class to realize its interests." This concept was originally meant only to refer to a capacity of a class to realize its own interests (see Poulantzas, 1973), but it has now taken on a new meaning through usage to refer as well to the ability of classes to use the public decision-making structures of the State. In effect, classes carve out domains of power for themselves through influence at the local level.

The study of local politics today charts out the relative success of different group capacities to affect public policy. This is one way of evaluating the performance of the local State. Analysts differ among themselves over whether local government is more responsive to some groups than others. Some public choicers (see Chapter 3) suggest that over the years the demands of the relatively less affluent have defined public spending priorities even to the point where a fiscal crisis has occurred. In contrast, neo-Marxists (also discussed in Chapter 3) marshall evidence to suggest that it is the demands of business that have the greatest political capacities to influence government activities. Finally, systemic stratificationists (see Chapter 6), and neo-Weberians (see Chapter 3) find progressively more evidence that government structures and State managers are themselves implicated in the limited ability of the less powerful to affect public policy. In the next and subsequent chapters it will be necessary to assess these separate theories.

Metropolitan Fragmentation

Since at least the 1960s there has been a lively debate among political scientists, sociologists, and planners over the specific effects of metropolitan fragmentation. Despite significant areas of disagreement, the fact remains that almost all local metropolitan regions are chopped up into a large number of separate municipalities and that public service provision is atomized into a patchwork quilt of overlapping districts complicating further the ability of residents to center themselves within any single public jurisdiction. Perhaps this decentralized local government structure is the most distinguishing feature of the American political system since, as Dahl (1972) has pointed out, only France among Western societies is more fragmented.

There are two separate issues in the metropolitan fragmentation debate. The first concerns its origins and the second its effects. With regard to the former, according to Neiman (1975), cities in most areas of the country were restricted in their ability to annex fringe-area development. In contrast, state legislatures consistently enacted laws that made it relatively easy for areas outside cities to incorporate themselves. Consequently, "it was more feasible and rational to move and defend the new locational strategy through municipal incorporation" (p. 21). Such observations have been supported by fiscally based arguments that see the growth of fragmentation as a way in which populations have been able to capture the benefits of the local tax base through the selective inclusion and exclusion of activities in specific locations (see Hoch, 1984). As Downs (1970) has observed, this need is almost exclusively the consequence of reliance upon property taxes as the major revenue generating mechanism of local government. This in turn often leads to a form of fiscal conflict between municipalities within the metropolitan region with begger-thy-neighbor consequences for local tax bases (Hill, 1974; Logan and Schneider,1981).

By far the most debated explanation advanced for metropolitan fragmentation is the "lifestyles-value" model first proposed by Tiebout (1956) and subsequently supported by Warren (1964) and Williams (1968). According to this perspective, social stratification deploys itself in space as the demographic differentiation of lifestyle values. Individuals have sought out local communities with the same values as their own and have consequently defended themselves against potentially discordant influences by barricading the local area behind municipal boundaries. Thus, according to this argument, the local polity is viewed in its associational context alone and the municipal infrastructure is merely a means to pursue specific private values associated with styles of consumption. Due to the differences in lifestyles and the fiscal requirements necessary to support particular bundles of services, large numbers of local jurisdictions have proliferated across metropolitan regions. This thesis was tested in 1969 by Oates and again in 1975 by Shephard and little evidence was found to support it as an explanation for metropolitan fragmentation. According to Shephard (1975), for example,

> One must search for other explanations of political fragmentation. Speculations are that local political control may be sought by many metropolitan residents not with any clear goal in mind but as an end in itself. Local political control is not sought initially to promote lifestyles or attain a particular bundle of goods and services. Rather control is valued alone as an attractive political symbol, as an assurance of quite possibly never exercised access as a mechanism for allaying the anxiety created by uncertainty in political life.

Without question the origin of political fragmentation is multifactorial as it seems a variety of influences have converged to produce the distinctive pattern of metropolitan decentralization. What is at issue in the metropolitan fragmentation debate is not so much why separate jurisdictions have proliferated, as whether such a structure of metropolitan governance is good or bad. Critics of fragmentation such as Wood (1959), Neiman (1975), and Newton (1976), point to the impossibility of coordinating governance, the difficulty of planning and of pursuing regional public interests, the fostering of racial and class segregation, and finally, the discouragement of political involvement as consequences of metropolitan decentralization. Supporters of fragmentation, in contrast, such as Ostrom (1983), Kotler (1969), and Bish (1971), indicate that there is no empirical evidence to support the contention that fragmentation implies a lack of governance or the inability of local jurisdictions to aggregate their individual political efforts into some substantive pursuit of the public interest.

Ostrom et al. (1961) have quite rightly asserted that whether a polycentric political system is any less efficient at governance than one that is more centralized remains an empirical question and critics of fragmentation have yet to substantiate their claims. Bish and Ostrom (1973: 93) in particular have studied the relative increase in efficiency brought about by metropolitan consolidation and have concluded that "sufficient evidence does exist to doubt that centralization is the answer."

Despite these well-placed observations, there are several empirically substantiated *negative* features of metropolitan life that are nevertheless associated with political fragmentation, even if the question of efficient governance itself has yet to be answered. In particular, we do know that regional class and racial segregation have accompanied decentralization over the years. Even if one is not the cause of the other, the present structure of governance has done nothing to alleviate the problems of segregation or, as Lineberry (1970: 675) has observed, the "non-congruence of policy-making units and problem units."

Second, I have already observed that local political involvement is extremely weak. Newton in particular has pointed out in a series of papers that there is a direct relationship between fragmentation and the "death" of political participation (1976; 1978). According to Newton (1978: 84), fragmentation has reduced political conflict and competition because social groups of varying means cannot confront each other in spatially segregated political arenas. As he observes,

> The politics of a large number of political units is unlikely to be much more than the sum of its parts, simply because carefully maintained boundaries make it difficult to put anything larger together. The result is a series of parish-pump and parochial politics in which small issues rule the day for want of a political structure which could handle anything larger [1978: 86].

In a case study of a suburban township adjacent to New York City, research verified empirically these observations of Newton (Gottdiener, 1977).

Furthermore, according to Newton (1979: 89), the inability of local governments to aggregate response makes it difficult to solve regionwide problems. This discourages citizen involvement in local politics and encourages them to leave when environmental concerns become serious enough to affect the quality of life. According to the argument of Newton, then, metropolitan fragmentation produces voter alienation, a result empirically verified elsewhere (Abramson and Aldrich, 1982), and this, in turn, also contributes to the weakness of local politics. Finally, and most important, Newton (1976: 38) observes that while the structure of regional government is fragmented, the control of power is not, and is concentrated in a few hands. Thus, metropolitan governance may *appear* to be functioning efficiently and regional populations may *appear* to be content with decentralized administration, yet the interests reflected by this structure may only be that of the ruling class.

Public choicers try to refute Newton's argument, but focus more on the alleged effects of inefficiency rather than equity in their dispute (Ostrom, 1983; see Chapter 3 for a detailed discussion). Yet, there is more recent evidence substantiating the claim that political fragmentation is responsible for the weakening of local governance and the limited power of municipal decision making (Sbragia, 1983). There is also considerable new evidence that demonstrates the formidable power of the capitalist class in determining policy that circumvents, and in many cases remains hidden from, the public eye (Judd and Smith, 1983). This material will also be examined further in the next chapter.

Until this moment I have commented on the weaknesses of metropolitan fragmentation in general and the city in particular. Yet our urbanized regions also involve suburban municipalities in its structure of governance. What do we know about the efficacy of suburban governments? A common conception, following the "lifestyle" or "public-choice" theorists is that political fragmentation has been functional and beneficial for suburban residents because it has broken down the formidable distance between citizen and public administrator characteristic of large city bureaucracies (see Fischer, 1976). Consequently, it is believed that suburban residents are comparatively more engaged in local political activities than their central-city counterparts. According to several studies exploring this question, such an assertion is a myth. In particular, suburban governments reproduce the weaknesses of the local form of governance granted to city municipalities within a suburban setting (see Gottdiener, 1977). For example, as Murphy and Rehfus (1976: 3) indicate,

> The suburbs of most metropolitan areas, however, usually are governed by a large number of small units that lack the economic, political or home rule powers essential to deal with local issues.

This structural weakness is compounded by the wide political diversity exhibited by different suburban communities even within the same region (Greer,1960; Dobriner, 1963; Wirt, 1974; Gilbert, 1967). Consequently, suburban political structure is not only weak but suburban areas have made relatively little impact on national politics despite possessing a plurality of registered voters in the country (Murphy and Rehfus, 1976: 28). Available empirical evidence suggests that the primary source of interest aggregation, if one exists at all, in suburban regions is the national political party. Consequently, the only recognizable impact of suburban politics seems to be the occasional ability to return large pluralities in voting during presidential elections, especially for Republican candidates, when all voter turnout is traditionally the largest (Eulau et al., 1966; Mains and Stine, 1959).

The relative weakness of suburban politics has been documented by a study revealing that suburbs have the lowest

participation in elections from among six categories of settlement spaces including large cities and small towns (Verba and
Nie, 1972: 229-248). Of those few residents who are involved in
politics, most reflect status and homeownership-related interests and, unlike central-city areas, do *not* express either
ethnic, religious, or community attachments (Alford and
Scoble, 1968).

Suburban governments are most often thought of as being
more responsive to resident needs than city regimes. For the
most part, however, the suburban political agenda is too
parochial to serve as an effective decentralized forum for
regional governance. Suburban political issues are most often
narrowly defined. Specific questions usually deal with environmental or public-service delivery adjustments to growth
(Murphy and Rehfus, 1976: 52; Gottdiener, 1977: chap. 4).
According to Downes (1971), conflict in the suburbs does not
follow class or cultural lines and is most often over the best
public strategy that should be adopted for dealing with specific
practical concerns. The narrow scope of issues, limited participation of citizens and public administration concerned with
problem solving support the contention of Stephens and Olson
(see Greer, 1962) that suburbs are serviced by "Toy Governments."

These limitations of suburban government are compounded
by the presence of extralocal, regional, and nonelective
authorities with broad powers, such as the Federal Department
of Housing and Urban Development, or the New York-New
Jersey Port of New York Authority, and elected governments
at the state or county level that supply local services, such as
police protection or education. These diminish further the
prestige and patronage power of suburban governments.
Without extralocal influence suburbs have little control over
the administration of regionwide policies and programs. Aside
from party politics, there appears to be no structural means of
channeling interests or aggregating political involvement for

regional programmatic initiatives (Wood, 1961).

In sum, suburban politics exhibits a second version of structural weakness alongside that of the central city. The metropolitan regions' governing framework is fragmented, as we have seen. In addition, however, there appears to be no overarching mechanisms for coordinating development in such a manner as to modify the impacts of growth. Metropolitan politics is a hodgepodge of balkanized party activity, actions by nonelective superagencies involved in regional public good provision, and of government programs funneled down from the higher circles in a bewildering variety of fiscal and sociopolitical contexts. At its core, this fragmented and multileveled structure rests upon an extremely weak base of low voter turnout and political apathy. Government acts, public policy intervenes, yet the local State fails to coordinate development in the interests of some overarching goal or toward greater social justice.

UNEVEN SOCIOSPATIAL DEVELOPMENT

Whether we consider centralized or decentralized structures of governance, the fact remains that in every metropolitan region there is a "geography of well being" (Smith, 1973). For quite some time ecological studies of American central cities have noted the segregated nature of residential settlement patterns. The comprehensive picture drawn by the early "Chicago School" sociologists showed clearly the class and ethnic boundary lines within the predepression city (Burgess, 1925). Subsequent research produced exhaustive analyses that added race to the list of segregation factors (Taeuber and Taeuber, 1965). By the 1960s American social scientists had constructed a clear picture of the dimensions of locational divisions among populations within cities. One implication of these findings bore directly on private-sector employment problems, especially the mismatch between job opportunities and the location of poor or minority populations in the city (Kain, 1968; Gold, 1972; Bederman and Adams, 1974).

A second area of concern had direct implications for the functioning of local government, namely the discovery that spatial segregation was matched by an inequitable distribution of public services. Thus, the important realization emerged not only that cities were segregated, but that local government was implicated in the inequitable provision of public services on the basis of that spatial segregation. Studies documenting this fact have been conducted for education, which is the central way inequitable patterns of stratification are *reproduced* (Sexton, 1961; Coleman, 1976; Oakes, 1985); police protection (Bloch, 1974; Mlandenka and Hill, 1978; Weicher, 1971); street repair (Antunes and Plumbe, 1977; Boots et al., 1972); and for other social services (Levy et al., 1974).

These findings make the issue of inequality a serious social problem. While social stratification is often defended as the inevitable price to be paid for a system that brings out the best in people through competition and rewards people differentially on the basis of that performance, no such defense can be made for the role of local government in reinforcing and amplifying the uneven effects of capitalist competition. For this reason, the discovery of inequitable patterns of public service deployment has become a legal issue that has eventually made its way to the courts at all levels of the judiciary (Megret, 1981). As we shall see in Chapter 4, current perspectives on local government vary in their assessment of both the manifestations and of the implications of social service inequities. Mainstreamers have discovered that no conspiracy is behind the distribution of public resources because its inequities are "unpatterned"(Lineberry, 1977). Neo-Marxists, however, take issue with the way such an approach has been framed. They consider it fallacious to study the delivery of social services by themselves and outside the links between them and their role in reproducing aspects of the larger social system (Katznelson,

1981). As the assessment in Chapter 4 will show, this inquiry addressing the issue of public-service provision has become the central focus of urban political science.

It was not until the metropolitan fragmentation debate went into full gear during the early 1970s that analysts recognized the regional scope of inequitable disparities in the public-service provision pattern. One study of a suburban area, for example, documented the inequitable supply of educational, medical-care, fire-protection and recreational services to residents based primarily upon the patterns of demographic spatial segregation by class and family income (Gottdiener, 1977). Elsewhere the metropolitan fragmentation debate uncovered the fact that across the region local communities varied in their ability to sustain community quality in the face of massive metropolitan development. As Neiman (1975) observed,

> In effect, the latent function of the metropolis, as an aggregate macro level entity, is to maintain and increase, through structure and policy the unequal access of individuals to "the good life"—through impediments to movement for one set of individuals and various subsidies for the pursuit of locational strategy for other individuals. The function is latent since it is implicit and unarticulated in contemporary institutions. This raises serious equity questions, once it is recognized that metropolitan institutions and their historical context may have an important relation to the distribution of locationally situated advantages and disadvantages.

In short, we now know that spatial segregation is regionwide and that the political structure of the entire metropolitan area acts as an institutional mechanism spatially deployed, which *reproduces* the class and racially segregated nature of society (see Browett, 1984). Furthermore, the major significance of the discovery that social-service provision and the quality of life varies in the suburbs as well as the central city is that in the former area blame is almost wholly a function of government land-use policies. Thus suburban inequities in housing and public service provision constitute a more distinctly *spatial* way in which stratification is produced and reproduced than is often considered in central-city analysis. The origin of sub-urban locational inequality has been studied most especially within the context of growth-control practices commonly referred to as "exclusionary zoning" (Gaffney, 1973; Daniel-son,1976; Babcock and Bosselman, 1973). Other studies (Windsor, 1979) suggest that it is rather the market, that is, private-sector mechanisms, that are the main culprits behind segregation (see Ostrom, 1983). In Chapter 4 I shall discuss whether it is possible to separate so glibly the public and private spheres in the determination of public policy and its patterns of uneven development.

The regional extent of uneven development and the limited ability of local government to do much about it are a third, debilitating weakness of metropolitan governance (Peterson, 1981). This is so because everyday activities play themselves out against the backdrop of a stratified society that limits the life chances of individuals according to class and race. The public arena is one battlefield, in addition to the workplace, where those who are less well-off can organize to renegotiate the distribution of social wealth. Furthermore, over the years local government has been called upon with progressively greater frequency by all segments of society to sustain or improve that quality because of the contradictory way in which private-sector activities produce public problems for everyone living within the same community. In a final irony, the contradictory manner of local State intervention through the aggregate effect of its actions results in a pattern that re-produces social inequality rather than leveling it. This only serves to intensify further the need among the less well-off for more State involvement to ameliorate the costs of growth.

In sum, the common basis of local politics is the articulation of the local State apparatus, on the one hand, with publicly manifested concerns about the quality of community life, from all segments of society (business as well as the working class), on the other. The source of this political agenda is the contradictory and inequitable nature of the capitalist-development process and the institutional split that promotes attempts at overcoming private-sector problems in a public way through State intervention at all levels of government. Because government intervention itself promotes rather than resolves the stratified nature of the social order, the need for intervention reproduces itself just as it also reproduces the class and racial divisions of society. The dual and contradictory role of the State as the promoter of capitalist development and the manager of its effects defines the relation between society and local government. Concerns about community quality manifest themselves in one of two ways: either as sociospatial conflict associated with urban and suburban development, government regulation, and the management of growth, or, as conflict over public-service provision. Recently, a variety of approaches to local politics have appeared that attempt to understand the new realities and limitations of local governance. Let us turn our attention to these in the next two chapters.

CHAPTER 3

NEW THEORIES OF
URBAN POLITICS—PART I

Perspectives on local government do not address themselves directly to the decline of politics. Yet, surprisingly, most analysts, working from a variety of political persuasions, find inadequacies in the *structural* features of governance. Interposed between basic assumptions on the meaning and purpose of political life and the voluminous empirical material generated by academic research, are certain findings implicating the mechanisms of public decision making in many of the social issues of current concern. Conservatives, for example, lament the largeness of government. They view democracy as disappearing behind the faceless facades of municipal bureaucracies and overstaffed administrative agencies. The political process cannot solve social problems. It can only bring more and more interests into the local arena and create ever more issues for public debate. A conservative perspective that has recently drawn attention is public-choice theory. Its basic assumptions are that politics only works democratically if it is pluralist and only governments of limited size can function efficiently. Consequently, public choicers defend the decentralization of metropolitan government and consider inequities of segregation to be products of exopolitical processes, such as the housing market. This serves to displace concerns away from politics and toward economic policy, thereby separating the two domains.

At the other end of the conceptual scale are located the neo-Marxists who view government of *any* size as functional for the needs of capital. Neo-Marxists cannot conceive of separating politics from economics. The State in contemporary capitalist society performs two fundamental roles: the promotion of capital accumulation and social control or legitimation of the status quo. In studying the first function a new school of thought has arisen that includes many non-Marxists as well and that can be called the "new political economy." These analysts study the intimate relation between State activities in the promotion of growth and the needs of capital according to its business cycles. This link is historical. Even conservatives acknowledge the important role that the State plays in fostering economic well-being (Novack, 1982: 9). The "new" political economists, however, question whether local government subsidization of capital ever brings about the effects that the ideology of growth suggests will occur. While not addressing the decline of political life as such, they see government as a cover for supplying the needs of capital at the taxpayers' expense.

A third perspective on local government, also neo-Marxist, pays more attention as a theory to problems associated with the supply of social services in the city. It considers local government as an arm of the welfare State. From a Marxian perspective, its main function is the reproduction of social relations for capital, hence the importance of both social control and the supply of public goods and services to the urban population in sustaining the quality of life. A particular branch of this approach, called collective-consumption theory, has addressed itself to the supply of use values by the State for the labor force. It suggests that this function is the preeminent way in which to define the uniqueness of urban government, as the conflicts surrounding the provision of social services constitute the basic contents of local urban politics.

All the above perspectives share a fundamental assumption

regarding local politics, namely, that activities are driven by needs residing outside the sphere of government itself. On occasion, such as in approaches similar to public-choice theory, which rely on pluralism, these perspectives commit the fallacy of assuming that the State operates solely by being responsive to the demands articulated by the public. The myth of the responsive State and the functionalist view of local government are all characterized as "society-centered" approaches. There is another perspective, however, that balances this against a "State-centered" view. In England it is called neo-Weberianism, while in the United States it is more often called State managerialism. The basic thesis of State managerialism is that government has needs of its own in addition to being responsive to those expressed by the public. At every opportunity, but especially in times of crisis, the State tries to expand its power over society. Neo-Weberians have a slightly different emphasis and are more concerned about the way in which aspects of the State affect the outcomes of political processes independent of other determinants.

According to neo-Weberians, State managers are an intervening variable in political outcomes. The more the State is given to do by society, the greater are the opportunities for the interests of State managers to intervene in the process of public administration. For this reason, neo-Weberians are also interested in the collective-consumption problematic and the nature of the welfare State. As administrators involved in the supply of public goods and services, State managers can produce political effects that cannot be explained by the actions of groups lying outside government, such as differentials in the supply of social services and the differential effects on economic activities produced by State regulation.

Yet, acknowledging the presence of "State-centeredness" or an active and autonomous State interest, does not amount to suggesting that local government possesses a political vision for society's future. The autonomy of the State is a decision-making property that, although aiding it in legitimating and expanding its hold over society, is used to make social organization run more smoothly on the course provided for it by powerful forces. Consequently, ordinary citizens cannot find any asylum in the autonomy of the State from the vagaries of capitalist development. State-centered theorists, while not concerning themselves directly with the death of political culture, are not necessarily any more sanguine about the functioning of government than their "society-centered" colleagues.

Let us consider these four theories of local politics in some more detail. I will argue in the following summaries that each perspective is limited because of its failure to understand the nature of the local State. I will try to show that, despite holding some truths about the political process, these perspectives possess only partial views. Neither society-nor State-centeredness can provide us with the total picture necessary to an understanding of local politics and the problem of governance. In the following two chapters, then, I establish the need for Chapters 5 and 6, namely, an extended discussion on the State itself and theories that address the nature of local politics, despite the voluminous material already written on these subjects.

Public-Choice Theory

The heart of public-choice theory is its assumption that local governments harbor a pluralist State (Dahl, 1961). It is assumed that political forums aggregate citizen preferences effectively, and that they work to integrate demands in the formation of public policy. This assertion is coupled with the classic paper by Tiebout (1956) arguing for a pluralistic view of local citizen preferences. According to Tiebout different income groupings have qualitatively separate patterns of policy needs. Each group has a corresponding service and tax package that suits it best. In a large urban environment interests that are in the minority tend to be saddled with the preferences of the majority. Consequently, the existence of pluralist preferences argues for the proliferation of a number of separate municipalities that can specialize in catering to different policy packages.

As articulated in its dual sense of pluralist policies and municipalities, public-choice theory links up strongly with neoconservative perspectives on municipal regional fragmentation because it supports the existence of large numbers of autonomous local governments. As indicated in Chapter 2, analysts are split between defenders and critics of fragmentation with the issue of regional efficiency in the supply of services still unresolved. Clearly, no one can deny the extent of racial and income segregation in the United States. What is at issue in the debate on equality and fragmentation is whether or not metropolitan reforms leading to consolidation and centralization are better suited to the elimination of inequities in public-service provision than the present pattern of metropolitan fragmentation. In this debate, critics of the status quo have been labeled by Neiman (1975: 5) as "reformers," while those arguing against the reformer's solution of governmental consolidation have been labeled "revisionists"; however, I prefer the term "conservatives" because they defend the status quo.

The argument for consolidation and against the public-choice affinity for many small governments was perhaps summed up best by Hill (1974: 1, 557), who suggested that "political incorporation by class and status into municipal enclaves is an important institutional mechanism for creating and perpetuating inequities among residents in metropolitan communities in the United States." Public-choice theorists support fragmentation because they prefer small governments to large ones. In a pluralist world they assume the former will be more responsive to citizen preferences than big cities run by large, impersonal bureaucracies. This assumes that government is essentially a neutral instrument catering to a pluralist spectrum of local preferences. While public choicers acknowledge the low level of citizen participation, they feel that it does not reflect badly on the quality of political culture. In fact, participation is always at just the right level for decentralized politics to function.

Thus public-choice theorists rarely question the nature of government itself, except by examining the efficiency performances of different size. In contrast, reformers hold a different picture of local government, one that is more parochial in its outlook because of its more homogeneous constituency. In fact, the central assertion of reformers is not that fragmentation is bad per se, but that well-off people use their local government as an instrument to prevent the less well-off from either moving into their city or laying claim to their local resources. It is this instrumental view of the local State, that has been called the "social-stratification/government-inequality thesis," and which is most clearly stated by Neiman (Neiman, 1982; see also Ostrom, 1983). Reformers claim that on balance the wealthier classes prevent others from enjoying an equitable quality of life through metropolitan segregation and under cover of governmental fragmentation.

Public choicers are opposed to this reformist position. According to recent public-choice research, reformers hold an inaccurate picture of metropolitan governance. On the one hand, they subscribe to a city-suburb dichotomy, which contrasts the large minority population living in cities or clustered in suburban ghettos with the proliferation in recent years of lily-white suburban residential enclaves. On the other hand, they hold a "horizontal" picture of the government infrastructure, which can only envision the local State as the source of resource distribution within the metropolitan region. Both of these assumptions have been challenged successfully by conservatives. First, conservatives point to evidence that central-city white areas are no less restrictive in keeping out minorities than their suburban counterparts. Indeed, cities today are significantly stratified by race and income (Taeuber and Taeuber, 1965; Johnston, 1971). Second, they point to evidence that most suburbs have a relatively balanced representation among various income groups although significant racial exclusion still exists (Williams and Eklund, 1978). In fact, a study by Logan and Schneider (1981: 26) found that as much variation in family incomes existed within suburbs as among them. According to Ostrom (1983: 97) the very wealthy and the very poor are the only two groups living in homogeneous isolation, while the vast majority of suburban residents reside in communities that are balanced by income group. This may be so, but the fact that the poor also tend to belong overwhelmingly to either Black or Hispanic minority groups seems to have escaped integration into the approaches of Ostrom and Logan and Schneider. Thus, the focus on the regional distribution of income groupings alone misses the important dimension of racial segregation that reformers and those concerned about the interplay between family income and exclusionary zoning wish to overcome.

The second thesis of horizontality in the structure of governance has also been challenged successfully by conservatives. According to Ostrom (1983: 100), "Within a federal system having at least three levels of overlap (county, state and nation) above municipalities, wealthy families—wherever they live in a metropolitan area—can contribute to tax revenues that are redistributed to poorer jurisdictions."

Thus while local governments may be constrained in their ability to support redistributive public services, intergovernmental transfers can play that role. This assertion is also supported by the empirical analysis of Logan and Schneider (1981: 30), which found that suburban communities with a greater proportion of poor residents also had higher expenditures on services than wealthier areas. In fact, they found that middle-income communities spend comparably less than both the poorer and wealthier suburbs on services.

As already suggested, the central assumption of public choicers is that small, decentralized local governments work better than larger, centralized ones. They point to the growing number of studies suggesting that public bureaucracies, especially in large cities, may be an *inefficient* way of providing services (Levin, 1976; Lewis, 1982). If problems exist regarding inequities in the supply of services and in redistributive social planning, their answers must be found in mechanisms lying *outside* the nature of political fragmentation. For example, at the conclusion of Ostrom's (1983) survey of the government-inequality thesis, she asserts that fragmentation by itself does not cause inequality and that reformers should more fruitfully inquire into specific programs or economic processes, such as the housing market, for their policy effects. As she suggests,

> If discrimination in the housing market is the source of major inequities in the distribution of urban goods and services, let us identify that problem as the public policy problem to be addressed rather than municipal fragmentation [1983: 107].

Thus public choicers see the interest of reformers in attacking the nature of decentralized local government itself as a false issue.

There is an area, however, in which public choicers do advocate reform, namely, the supply of social services. It is at this juncture that this approach links up with conservative views on the interventionist State. According to public-choice theory, State provision of social services is both inefficient and unproductive. In almost all cases, people would do better to switch provision of services from local government to the private sector. There are several aspects to this argument (see Savas, 1983).

First, State provision of goods and services, it is believed, always leads to their oversupply in comparison to what individuals would demand on their own. Public provision is wasteful. The costs of goods and services should be linked more closely with public demand so that the real burden of what is supplied becomes apparent. Second, whenever possible private contractors should be used to supply city services so that wasteful government bureaucracies can be eliminated. Third, the real costs of government could be recovered, in the event that only public provision for a good or service were feasible, if user fees were charged. Thus both business and private citizens would pay for the costs of service according to the benefit they receive.

Finally, due to pluralist mechanisms of governance, it is asserted that special interests always push for public programs benefiting themselves, thereby saddling others with the tax burden in support of them. Consequently, services should be provided only by the smallest jurisdiction that includes the beneficiaries. In short, more local government decentralization, not less, is better. In the next chapter I shall examine these proposals from the context of fiscal crisis adjustment. While some of the reform prescriptions of public choicers have been tried, not all of them have worked in the manner that this theory has predicted. Improvements in efficiency and savings in costs have both been highly overrated by calls for privatization. At the same time, conservative policies have uncovered an ability of the local State to respond to fiscal problems by a retreat of its intervention, thereby also exposing weaknesses in the neo-Marxist tradition.

Public-choice theory's reliance on a pluralist view of local government qualifies it as a society-centered approach. This treats the State as a neutral mechanism of public provision that merely translates public sentiments into policies. To be sure, public choicers possess a sophisticated view of local politics understanding as they do the nature of the democratic process.

They admit that politics does not always involve a clash of equals and that powerful interests can on occasion prevail over more democratically representative sentiments. However, they view State officeholders and bureaucrats essentially as public servants caught in the constraints of local government. According to public choicers, pluralist democracy counts for its representational effectiveness on the competition for votes. Yet, when it comes to State provision, too much democracy can lead to ill effects (see Buchanon and Wagner, 1977). Politicians seeking reelection respond to special interest demands and trade active State intervention for votes. According to public choicers, because city populations are dominated by poor and minorities, this has led over the years to the massive expansion of the State-welfare apparatus. That is, outcomes over the years have accumulated in favor of the less affluent rather than big business. In short, because the democratic electoral process translates aggregate demands into votes and then into policy responses by the local State, government programs are driven detrimentally by insatiable citizen demands, especially those of the working class.

This society-centered view has been critiqued effectively by incrementalists and State managerialists alike. On the one hand, incrementalists view public-choice theory as committing the fallacy of the responsive State (see McDonald and Ward, 1984). It is not at all clear that elected officials in competition for votes acquiesce wholesale to citizen demands. Once in office, public officials tend to act as fiscal conservatives, regardless of their political persuasion. The best predictor of future government spending, according to the classic paper of incrementalist theory (Davis et al., 1966), is the level of the previous year's spending. To be sure, the incrementalist approach is not without its own critics who suggest that while it predicts budgetary spending in toto, it tells us nothing about the quality of decision-making choices constituting the lifeblood of local politics (see Padgett, 1980; Leloup, 1978).

Consequently, incrementalism cannot explain changes in public policy over time. Nevertheless, it is not possible to square public-choice theory's emphasis on the role of democratically manifested demands with the structural limitations on local government deriving, not from society, but from State-centered sources, in the incrementalist determination of public policy.

In the second case, public-choice theorists fail to account for the prominent role played by the local State in the pursuit of its own interests. I shall say more about this in the next chapter when we will consider neo-Weberianism. Basically, pluralist assumptions regarding democracy fade away once the full understanding of the State's role in the determination of political phenomena is accounted for. Some conservative arguments that have themselves attacked pluralism, such as Shefter (1977), have also taken the role of the State into account. For example, it is because politicians must be reelected, according to these views, that they manipulate municipal employment and policies to buy votes. This is clearly a State-centered interest but it is not what neo-Weberians and State managerialists really have in mind when they discuss their approach (see Nordlinger, 1981). One could just as easily counter the assertions of public choicers in this context with the well-documented history of government corruption. In neither case would the nature of State-centeredness be addressed.

Both the substantive virtues of public-choice theory and the exposure of its limitations have emerged recently in two different academic debates that are very pertinent to this discussion, namely, adjustment policies to fiscal austerity and the problem of equity in the supply of social services. However, this approach is not alone in this regard. Let us, therefore, consider the remaining society-centered approaches before we build upon a comparative analysis.

The New Political Economy

The new political economy as a means of understanding urban politics came into being because of the commonplace observations that city regimes are implicated directly in the promotion of growth and the management of the economic-adjustment process. Local governance, therefore, is a "political economy"—a marriage between politics and economics as the best means of supporting the local quality of life. It is simply incorrect, however, to go along with functionalist Marxists who suggest that identification with growth is a political manifestation of the needs of capital accumulation alone (see, for example, Harvey, 1973; Molotch, 1976). On the one hand, the ideology of growth and support for development cuts very deep into American society. On the other, local areas do not pursue growth blindly, they manage it hoping to avoid its negative consequences. The question of growth always pre-supposes its opposite, namely, the question of no growth or regulated growth. In fact, the agenda of local politics and much of its contents can be specified in terms of the social confrontation between growth and no growth (see Gottdiener, 1985a). On a more theoretical level the differences between policies promoting development and those managing it are specified by Marxists according to the twin processes of the production of social relations and the reproduction of those relations. While much of the recent interest among neo-Marxists has been focused on the latter, it is important to consider the observation of Lefebvre (1973) that reproduction of social relations requires their production first.

The progrowth emphasis of place does not represent the interest of the capitalist class alone. As Aglietta (1978) has observed, support for growth represents the historical mode of addressing the situation of capitalist development in the United States. American capitalism grew out of the marriage between laissez-faire capitalists and a mode of surplus-value generation that exploited the particular attributes of the United States, namely, extensive natural resources and cheap immigrant labor. These elements were combined in a manner that promoted rapid development as the destiny of place instead of alternatives that might have provided a more intensive emphasis on building up the productivity of both labor and fixed capital within specific centers. This globalizing "frontier principle" enacted a democratic vision of empire wherein every city and town could aspire to economic greatness. This same ideology has also been exported successfully (principally by global banks) to Third World countries such as Brazil, which also possess immense natural resources and large, poor populations. For local areas caught in the spell of this ideology, civic-mindedness and public initiatives wedded themselves to the vision of development in an ideological union that remains with us today. The promotion of economic growth, therefore, is the primary public interest in America.

As we have learned over the course of the years, urban development carries with it costs as well as benefits. Localized political needs of neighborhoods that have been affected by changes in the economy are one manifestation of the fruits from the union between civic and business interests. Consequently, the State is placed in the contradictory position of having to ameliorate through public programs the negative social effects of its growth-inducing activities. Employment, transportation, environmental and housing policies, to name a few reproductive tasks, are merely the flip side of State intervention promoting growth. Such policies address themselves to the reproduction of social relations and they enable capitalism to survive as a system. The fundamental contradiction of the capitalist State is this structural requirement that forces it to play the roles of both the promoter and the manager of capitalist development.

In a simpler time, the relation between economic growth, or the general increase in value of the volume of goods and services produced within an area, and the quality of life as symbolized by progress, was more direct than today. Growth is no longer synonymous with local well-being because of forced spatial transfers of value enacted by the nation-State and by the multinational world-system of capital (Gottdiener, 1985a). In the past, systems of local taxation, urban-government policy, and the regulatory powers of the State combined and were able to capture generated economic wealth for the benefit of local areas. This situation has been drastically and even tragically altered today, to the detriment of local everyday life, as discussed in Chapter 1.

The new political economy has been essential in pinpointing the specific changes that have restructured the relation between local areas and the functioning of the economy. The issues addressed and the subjects studied differ greatly from the focus of public-choice theory. Whereas the latter seems to implicate ordinary people in the negative changes affecting local democracies, through the failures of pluralism, the new political economy directs attention to the role of the big firms and government policies as they affect that same process. Two structural changes, in particular, seem most central to the new political economy: the way that transformations in monopoly capitalism have affected the relation between localities and business; and the way that new financial arrangements between localities and business have restructured the nature of democratic institutions in the running of cities.

Big Firms and Global Capital

According to this perspective, every major dimension of city life today is related to the shifts produced by changes in investment deriving from a hegemonic, global system of capital. The elements of this system include the following. First, since World War II there has been an accelerated increase in the concentration of capital in all sectors. This has

produced phenomenal forms of the capitalist enterprise summed up by the growth of multinationals (Hymer, 1979;
Mandel, 1975). Megalithic corporations spanning the globe
have been joined by giant financial empires that channel
investment through banking between domestic markets and
the most remote foreign places imaginable. The surplus value
generated by place is virtually free for the taking and can be
channeled across the globe by finance capital toward development projects at the discretion of the capitalist investors alone.
This has placed each town or location in a fragile position that
contrasts greatly with past times when capital was less mobile.

Second, greater concentration of wealth and economic
resources has led to a greater rationalization of economic
processes in production, marketing, and finance. On the one
hand, technological innovation has been accelerated and now
articulates with every aspect of the economy producing both
increased profit margins and the liberation of the business
enterprise from dependency on place. Economies of scale, the
mixing of infrastructural organization according to centralized
or decentralized arrangements, and the manipulation of production according to least-cost strategies now prevail in the
decision-making practices of large firms. Using the benefits of
increased rationalization, corporations can split effectively
their operations, locating administration, marketing, research
and development, and production in separate places. This
rationalizes the operation of the entire enterprise by minimizing
the locational costs of each of its units. Third, multinational
firms have themselves become footloose and have rationalized
the extraction of surplus value itself so as to enjoy "super-
profits." Firms can move investment and operations in and out
of areas with a minimization of incurred losses. They have
adopted cost-effective labor strategies drawing upon world
markets of cheap workers in what has come to be called a
"global labor-sourcing" approach. Multinationals, therefore,
can exploit to the margins options that were unknown to

business in earlier phases of capitalist development, which tied corporations more concretely to specific places. These also include: disinvestment in subsidiaries to the benefit of the whole, selective strategies of plant closing and production cutbacks, and the disciplining of labor through the breakup of union power and selective job loss.

The sum total of global capitalist changes have affected, in the most fundamental way, the relation among local places, the State, and business activities. Severe economic decline can occur merely by a shift in investment flows. Tax structures are now pitifully inadequate to the task of recovering expropriated surplus wealth from multinationals so that government revenue no longer matches the expenditure demands placed upon it. The stability of labor markets oriented toward specific local enterprises has been shattered in the general shift away from manufacturing and toward highly particularized services and specialized industrial tasks. Because of the prolonged recession touched off by the shock of the oil crisis in the mid 1970s and the municipal nightmare of the fiscal crisis a few years later, the power of corporate and financial capital has increased to dwarf that of the State and the collective demands made by ordinary people at the place of work or, as voters, at home. As Judd and Smith (1983: 12) suggest, "The social redistribution rationale once needed to legitimate capital accumulation in cities is no longer heard. . . . In the absence of a countervailing voice, the accumulation process itself masquerading as costless economic growth, has become its own legitimation."

Local places find themselves today in the precarious position of having to support publicly the well-being of large firms or suffer the disastrous consequences of economic decline. This has caused public policy to shift 180 degrees since the 1960s from a concern with the general conditions of development involving social- as well as business-oriented schemes, to an almost exclusive emphasis on providing for the private sector.

The close connection between business interests and the

government of cities has a long history. It is intertwined with
the ideology of growth that views development as a panacea for
social problems. What is new and different today is the manner
by which the power of concentrated capital has altered the
relation between the State, the polity, and the business
community for its own benefit by using the three scare tactics
of the new world-system order: potential mobility, disinvestment possibilities, and locational freedom. With regard to
the new relations of local public administration, several
changes have occurred since 1970 that place average citizens
and local political culture at a great disadvantage including a
shift in the tax burden, a sharp drop in electoral control over
public finance, and the scraping of the social mandate by local
government in favor of promoting a proper "business climate."

Shifts in the tax burden. During the halcyon days of the
1960s, urban renewal and redevelopment programs sponsored
by the federal government provided local areas with large
amounts of money to promote growth. By the 1970s, however,
with successive changes in national administrations involving
policies that deemphasized urban-area support, federal spending was sharply reduced. According to Blair and Nachimias
(1979: 12), for example, federal urban aid dropped from $3.9
billion in 1960 to $2.6 billion in 1970, or a decline of 33%.

By the mid-1970s the lack of funds available to support local
development declined even more as the economic recession
and the austerity programs of the fiscal crisis made their
impact. Lacking the substantial funds once present from the
feds, local areas fell back on their own devices in an effort to
prod urban growth forward. Among those options available,
tax relief of some kind to business proved to be the most
exercised. Tax breaks to business include: abatements, income-
tax reductions, rollbacks, sales-tax exemptions, and depreciation allowances.

The single most important effect of local government
provision of tax incentives is to shift the burden of taxation

from business to average citizens. If business fails to pay its fair share of taxes, there are few options left. In fact, citizens are asked to subsidize through taxes economic development in a second way, namely, by tax-exempt public borrowing for business. Because of the very same squeeze put on local areas during the mid-1970s, local and state governments were forced into a borrowing frenzy that eventually led to a fiscal crisis in some areas. In 1960 local government borrowed between $13 and $15 billion a year, but by 1980 that level had jumped to over $50 billion (Sbragia, 1983). Because the interest on monies loaned to municipalities is tax exempt, the federal government cannot claim returns on this type of investment. Until the 1960s such tax-exempt borrowing went to support the local quality of life in the form of infrastructure improvements, loans to civic institutions and the like. By the mid-1970s, the swing to public subsidization of capital development affected this municipal activity as well. Local areas began shunting borrowed funds to the private sector in a direct subsidization of business through the public's authority to assume debt.

According to Sbragia (1983: 68), in 1970 only $100 million in loaned monies went for private-development projects. By 1980, this figure had increased almost 100 times to $9.5 billion. As Sbragia suggests, "state and local borrowers are, therefore, borrowing not so much to build capital facilities for their own use as to allow others to build facilities for theirs" (1983: 68). Municipalities not only borrow in a tax-exempt status but also at interest rates significantly lower than prevailing market levels. For this reason, local areas have become a conduit of "cheap money" to the private sector. This activity costs the average tax payer most dearly. In fact, it has siphoned off a major source of federal funds and has so affected internal-revenue collections, that the federal government has stepped in with alarm to oversee and restrict its practice. This is especially the case for a new breed of cheap money giveaways called Industrial Revenue Bonds. As Smith and Judd (1984: 9) note,

Ordinarily governmental jurisdiction uses the proceeds of an IRB issue to purchase or to construct an industrial or business facility. The facility is then leased and eventually sold to a private firm in exchange for payments to cover the cost of the bond issue. The lease agreement is usually written in such a way that the leasee is able to receive all of the federal tax credit and accelerated depreciation allowance.

The sum effect of municipal brokerage of cheap money and tax breaks to the private sector in order to promote growth has shifted the burden of tax revenue to citizens in a rather marked manner. According to Smith and Judd (1983: 23), in 1950 business paid 20% of state and local taxes but by 1983 its share had dropped to 8%.

The disappearance of electoral control over finance. Because some localities use financial or tax incentives to attract new business, all localities must use them. Consequently, a decade of privately sponsored progrowth activities has made it commonplace for firms to require subsidies whether they need them or not. Local government courtship of capital is often institutionalized in specific developmental agencies. These are quasipublic corporations that have an autonomous bonding capacity. Development agencies do not have to ask the public, nor answer to its concerns before (or at any time, for that matter) they engage in a project under quasipublic auspices. Their efforts, therefore, are removed from the electoral process and democratic mechanisms of decision making. In no small measure their presence contributes to the decline of political culture.

Over the years the dependency of places on the subsidization of growth has led to intense, internecine competition among local areas for new business-location decisions. Ironically, even shockingly, there is virtually no evidence that financial incentives can affect significantly the location decisions of firms. Two recent surveys seem to find little support for tax differentials, in particular, as a factor in location choices (Wasylenko, 1981; Moriarity et al., 1980). Such results have not stopped the growth in number and power of quasipublic developmental agencies whose sole task is the public subsidization of the private sector. According to Sbragia (1983: 71), borrowing without public approval by quasipublic agencies currently comprises the bulk of local indebtedness accounting in 1979 for almost half (45.5%) of all new bond sales. Sbragia concludes her survey of this phenomenon with the following observation:

> The ability of special districts and public authorities to obtain credit separately from city or county government has fragmented power within the metropolitan area, and within city boundaries, to the point that merely understanding the distribution of formal authority, much less influence, has become a gigantic task . . . . Insulated from the public (because their boards are usually appointed rather than elected) and autonomous in policy-making, these authorities shape the entire urban area; as a result city officials are often unable to exercise even coordination, much less control, over their operations [1983: 99-100].

Under pressure of local competition, economic recession, and the power of the global capitalist system, all areas are forced to subsidize growth. The techniques used shift the tax burden away from business and onto citizens, as we have seen. Yet, these same techniques have not been found actually to influence location decisions in any significant way as other, more important factors, such as labor costs, marketing considerations, and the like, hold precedence over available subsidies. The most prominent social effect of municipal underwriting has been its surrender of democratic control over the societal-growth process. Such a shift is legitimated at the street level by the ideology of growth. Signs of progress invade the urban milieu and turn the place of deterioration into a

landscape of utopian promise sanctioned by the marriage
between local government and big capital. It is only recently,
when the fruits of this union have failed to materialize, that the
"tale of two cities" created by uneven development has
penetrated the sign of progress to question the validity of
progrowth ideology (see Gottdiener, 1986). Correcting the
damage done to local democratic mechanisms, however, is yet
another matter that today remains unaddressed and seemingly
intractable.

The abandonment of the social welfare mandate. The social
programs once characteristic of cities that were judged not on
their collective contribution to profits or revenues but on the
needs they fulfilled in sustaining the social quality of life, have
been severely cut back over the past decade. In part, this is
another consequence of changes in federal programs that
seemed to have scrapped urban social initiatives in recent
years. In part, however, this phenomenon is the effect of the
switch from voter-mandated programs based on tax revenues
to the new fiscal arrangements in support of growth. Precisely,
because the latter are more hidden, for the reasons outlined
above, resources have been canalized by the State in a manner
that assumes the appearance of austerity, but is, in reality,
merely a shift in social priorities away from the welfare
mandate assumed by government during the depression. As is
well known, the present federal administration, which prided
itself on austerity and fiscal conservatism, has brought national
levels of spending and debt financing to unprecedented
heights. Thus, the quality of austerity, rather than its most
visible signs of account cutbacks and reductions, demands our
attention in a conjuncture where ideological mystifications
play as great a role in the actions of government as do its real
effects.

The abandonment of the social welfare role for local
government and the canalization of local resources toward the
subsidization of growth brings with it a logic of government

decision making that contrasts distinctly and qualitatively with that of the past. Quasipublic agencies, for example, evaluate their programs according to their rate of investment return. In the calculus of profit taking, social programs have no place. The dependency of city financing on the bond market, a major change in the source of funds for municipalities since the 1960s, also throws the administration of the city into a dollar-conscious mode that figures monetary returns over social benefits. The hard facts of fiscal crisis, another factor in this change, adds to the dilemma of officials caught in the squeeze between economic decline and the scarcity of government revenue sources.

Mounting problems produced by uneven development, however, and the failure of past welfare policies to upgrade the ability of depressed population segments to compete in the new conditions of production and labor marketing, still require public initiatives in the search for solutions. Cities once played a central social role as laboratories where such solutions were sought through civic initiatives sanctioned by progressive leadership. Present conditions no longer support such a role, and thus the very nature of urban politics is played out against structural arrangements that simply trivialize the impulse to make public discourse into a meeting ground integrating the needs of all citizens. This qualitative change is one dimension of the decline of political culture.

The shift in political priorities and the change in the role of local government under the influence of the new power of business interest heightens the fundamental contradiction of the local State, namely, the need for it to manage as well as promote conditions of development. Although analysts have recently acknowledged this dilemma, its understanding has been hampered greatly by the ideological mystifications surrounding the actual role of local government and the social commitment to growth. For this reason, the approach of the new political economy has helped in providing us with a clearer grasp of the structural position and functional dilemma of local government. I can illustrate this by considering the results and argument analyzed recently by Paul Peterson (1981) and known as the "city limits" perspective.

The Dilemma of Local Government

The dilemma of local government is its relative ability to serve capital as a subsidizer of growth and its inability today to engage substantively in its historical role as the promoter of redistributive policies that alleviate the burdens of development. According to the ideologically proposed solution to this dilemma, the wealthier an area, the better able it will be to provide for the quality of life. A good business climate means, according to this conception, eventual trickle down benefits for all.

Paul Peterson (1981) suggests that, because of the structural constraints operating presently on local government, such a state of affairs cannot be altered in a manner that will improve the ability of local government to pursue redistributive policies. According to Peterson the critical determinant for the success of local public policy is an exogeneous factor lying outside the municipality, namely, the "structural arrangements of the federal system" (1981: 13). In particular, because of the current mobility of both capital and people in choosing places to reside, local areas must guard against overtaxing (quite literally) their local bases of revenue. In fact, the essential feature of the federated system of governance in the United States is the limited means of generating revenue provided to local areas. Thus, the local State is constrained severely in its ability to pursue public policies without the aid of external auspices. In short, the wealthier the area itself, the greater will be the sum total of revenues generated by property taxation, virtually the sole means of support delegated to the local State, and, therefore, conversely for poorer areas. This makes the quality of life for communities requiring State intervention highly correlated with its economic well-being. It also means that the uneven nature of economic development deploys itself in space according to this same dependency of local government on private-sector resources.

From this premise, which is quite correct, Peterson develops an argument that is conservative in its implications regarding the role of the local State as an agent of social change. According to Peterson, public policy, because of the structural constraints on available resources, is forced to pursue economic development and refrain from engaging in the types of redistributive measures that correct for the inequitable nature of growth. As he states,

> The interests of local government require that it emphasize the economic productivity of the community for which it is responsible. Because they are open systems, local governments are particularly sensitive to external changes. To maintain their local economic health, they must maintain a local efficiency that leaves little scope for egalitarian concerns. These limits on local government . . . require that local governments concentrate on developmental as against redistributive objectives [1981: 69].

In short, Peterson's approach implies that the structural division of administrative governance in the system of federalism has left to local areas the principal task of aiding economic development. Local States are not mandated only to pursue this function, rather they are constrained by the evolutionary process of the division of powers in the United States to be most successful if focused on intervening in the interests of private-sector development. This implication does not mean to preclude the pursuit of social change for local political regimes, however. Peterson makes clear that the relative success in engaging in such practices is a function of the ability of local government to afford them.

Despite agreeing with the fundamental premises of the "city limits" argument, other conclusions can also be drawn, which view the need to pursue social change on the part of the local State in a more optimistic light. To begin with Peterson utilizes a notion of fiscal responsibility that is equated with the concept of "efficiency" in neoclassical economics. This assumes, quite wrongly, that social benefits are merely aggregates of individual benefits and also, quite wrongly, that there exists some cost-benefit calculus by which individuals can judge for themselves the effects of public policy. Such assumptions are fallacious staples of neoconservative welfare economics and, by Peterson's own admission, they lead to regressive revenue-generating policies as the most attractive ones for the local State. In contrast, Peterson implies that only the federal level of government, with its ability to control the nation's resources as a whole, can pursue progressive policies based on the ability to pay without generating the kind of capital flight envisioned by Peterson as afflicting local areas.

Such an analysis supports the view that, to paraphrase Coolidge, the business of *local* government is business, while only the federal government is best suited to pursue public policies affecting social change. Reasoning of this kind commits the following fallacies. First, the entire calculus of cost-benefit analysis is called into question because of Peterson's emphasis on the individualistic nature of welfare to the exclusion of its collective determinants. Among the social priorities necessary to public welfare, the empirical relation between individual deprivation and social pathology ranks as most important. For example, there is a strong relationship between unemployment and crime, including property theft as well as violent street crime (Blau and Blau, 1982; Berger, 1980). Crime is particularly costly to city dwellers. Consequently, it is in everyone's interest, even the business community, to support public programs aimed at reducing crime, even if individuals are taxed for programs that do not benefit themselves directly.

Peterson would not deny the importance of preventing social pathology for the well-being of cities, only that those political regimes are the ones best able to support programs aimed at its alleviation. In this he underestimates the willingness of private capital to be taxed for such measures, as he also underestimates the ability of businesses to move to pathology free zones. The relation between individual deprivation and the community quality of life implies that, in addition to the individual welfare function Peterson uses in his analysis, there is also a social-welfare function taking into account that one individual's benefit at another's expense may raise the overall well-being of both. In reality, because of the uneven nature of capitalist development, the business community has always faced a three-way choice in this country between paying for social pathology by absorbing its costs directly, such as in being victimized by crime, or managing the ill-effects of pathology by containing it through public measures of social control, or finally, by supporting redistributive public policies which cure its root causes.

It is simply not true that local governments have been forced to ignore such policy issues at all for fear of driving out business. Rather, the historical record shows that the private sector has used the State over and over again as a means of force to control conflict while professing to alleviate its causes (Boyer, 1978; Duncan and Goodwin, 1982). This is the crux of the ideological battle over the determination of redistributive public policies rather than the structural constraints argued for in Peterson's analysis.

Second, Peterson's failure to employ a more sophisticated welfare analysis based on the social context of benefits is most in evidence by his handling of poverty as a measure of redistributive need, because he again relies solely on individual welfare measures. This approach neglects the social context of poverty, which is gauged best by comparative measures of inequality, such as the census's "GINI" coefficient. Once comparative indicators are employed, the need for redistributive policies can be shown to be *more* appropriate to places that Peterson claims need them the least (1981: 64); that is, inequality is severest in places with the wealthiest fiscal bases, namely, the large central cities. By neglecting socially contextual measures of inequality, Peterson overlooks the fact that those areas with the most affluent resource bases may also be the places with the greatest extremes of wealth. Consequently, by asking the federal government to be responsible for socially redistributive programs, local areas with fewer resources who also have a comparatively *more* equitable distribution of income are called upon to help pay for programs that the comparatively wealthier areas can afford themselves. This is a result that is the exact opposite of the one obtained by Peterson and it implies that redistributive allocations distort efficiency criteria the least by having local areas with the greatest need pay for programs. Such an assertion makes sense when comparative measures of social need are used, such as the GINI measure for inequality, rather than the absolute indicators used in analyses such as Peterson's.

Finally, Peterson's argument fails because of the biased view it has of the wholesale benefits of private-sector development for local communities. This ignores the significant *costs* of growth, which are summarized by the concept of "external diseconomy." It is quite simply wrong to equate community well-being with economic development and the evidence to strike down this view is legion. As Liu (1976) observes, the overriding enigma of urban dynamics highlighted by analysts such as Forrester (1969) is the discovery that "new technology and a high rate of income growth fail to diminish social pathology and improve the overall quality of life" (Liu, 1976: 5). In fact, Liu argues convincingly that economic development is only one of five measures of community well-being, which also include psychological, health, educational, and politically related factors (1976: 50). Consequently, public-policy analyses, such as Peterson's, which succumb to the ideology of growth, fail to consider the deleterious effects of capitalist development on the quality of community life. As Liu (1976: 14) remarks,

> Economic indicators have been the traditional principal measures of overall national prosperity and social well being. Not until recently did the risks of economic growth and the social costs associated with such growth call sufficient attention to the need for reexamination of national goal setting and policy making [1976: 14].

Thus if the local area is an inappropriate place to pursue redistributive policies because of the structural limits placed upon its resources, then it is also an inappropriate place to pursue developmental policies. Arguing otherwise merely reinforces the status quo, one in which special interests restructure local environments for private benefit, while the social costs of development are borne by the society as a whole. The local polity, in particular, has meager legal means at its disposal to renegotiate the inequitable costs of capital accumulation. Redistributive programs are viewed as external to the calculus of private business life only because of the ideological mask that blinds us to the way in which the private sector passes on the costs of growth to the society as a whole. In the past, for example, it was easier to ignore the environmental bill for uncoordinated development than it is presently or will be in the future.

The issues raised by the discovery of structural limits to local public policies are more profound than analysts like Peterson would have us believe. In effect, redistributive interventions by the State are needed because of the very nature of capitalist uneven development. The debate over which level of government is best able to meet this need is merely an ideological smokescreen for the fundamental way in which private capitalists pass on the costs of development to the public at large. This fundamental mechanism of capital accumulation will be considered in more detail in the next chapter, as it involves State intervention in the reproduction of capitalist social relations. Clearly, the study of public policy requires that attention be paid to the ways in which the differential apparatus of governance itself affects outcomes, yet it is wrong merely to accept this deployment as the determining conditions for framing local urban policy. Such a view ignores the very nature of the relation between the State and society in the present phase of development within which powerful capitalist interests have convinced the majority of Americans that the public destiny is married to the fortunes of monopoly capital under the sign of growth.

The lack of strict accountability for the costs of development by the private sector and the failure to present society with a true range of alternatives to present patterns (see, for instance, Alperovitz and Faux, 1983) can be ignored only if we believe in the ideological assertion that capitalist development automatically enhances community well-being. This belief is compounded by subscription to a second ideological notion, namely, that public policies targeted toward alleviating social pathology are redistributive in nature while those geared toward subsidizing economic development are not and are, instead, socially neutral in their effects. The limited historical ability of this society to amass enough public support to pursue policies that alleviate the root causes of social pathology merely indicates the inherent difficulty of effecting any type of social change in America. It is this issue that compels us to reject the conservative defense of metropolitan fragmentation and that forces us to explore ways of overcoming the present decline in structural importance for municipal politics.

While local governments are certainly limited in their ability to pursue social change, it is a mistake to let relative comparisons obscure their persisting involvement in providing use values necessary to the functioning of society through public means. Despite the recent austerity programs that are in place at every government level and the implementation of privatization in many city budgets, cities remain vehicles for the channeling of billions of funds supporting health, education, police activities, and the like. Such intervention demonstrates the importance of local government in sustaining the general conditions of the community quality of life. Two additional theories of local politics address this function of government in a more theoretical manner than the previous perspectives we have just considered. One, the neo-Marxist approach to the welfare State, will be discussed next because it is dominated by a society-centered orientation, although it contains a limited State-centered sensitivity. In the next chapter I will consider the State-centered approach of neo-Weberianism, which also addresses the same topic as the neo-Marxist theory, namely, the relation between the welfare State and local urban politics.

Neo-Marxism and the Socialization of Capital

Interest in the welfare State almost exclusively focuses attention on the national level and usually within a comparative context with other nation-states (Flora and Heidenheimer, 1982; Cameron, 1978; Gough, 1979; Shalev, 1983; Wilensky, 1975). Discussions specify the link between sociopolitical processes and State intervention as a phenomenon of national politics and parties. Consequently, little distinction is made between levels of government and public provision (for exceptions see Devine, 1983; Cockburn, 1979; Savas, 1983). Robust theories from several perspectives, however, have arisen to account for the increasing reliance on public intervention in modern capitalist states. These vary from structural accounts to more voluntaristically premised ones. The former study the relation between changes in capital development and welfare policies, such as in the transition from a competitive mode of capitalism with little government regulation, to an advanced capitalism including a State actively involved in market-replacing as well as -regulating activities (Wilensky, 1975; O'Connor, 1973; Habermas, 1975). A more voluntaristically cast approach, in contrast, concerns itself with the relation between public spending and political conflict. For the case of class conflict, analysts view welfare Statism as a means of social control (Piven and Cloward, 1971; Isaacs and Kelly, 1981). Others consider policies as a response to political-party competition for votes (Reich and Edwards, 1978; Hibbs, 1977; Buchanon and Wagner, 1977).

More recently, neo-Marxists have integrated both voluntaristic and structural perspectives, considering them as separate dimensions in the growth and modulation of welfare intervention according to the needs of capitalist development (Griffen et al., 1983; Gough, 1979; Hicks et al., 1978). By and large, however, welfare State theories have not been tailored to an understanding of policy formation at the local level and for the context of city politics. Some exceptions have already been discussed as approaches to politics that extend themselves to cover the phenomenon of State intervention in the provision of use values. Thus public-choice theory, for example, hypothesizes that certain market and political mechanisms aggregate effectively citizen preferences for public goods, while also hypothesizing that the State itself functions by being responsive to expressed demands. Government welfare policies, according to this perspective, are a direct result of the participation and influence in local politics of the less affluent. In contrast, the new political economists view the local State as having to cater principally to the demands of capital as a kind of "fiscal welfare" for business. As we have seen, growth is less a desire of all local governments than a need created for them by constraints from increasingly complex structures of State and economy. This approach, however, leaves aside the formidable involvement of the local State in the sustaining of everyday community life through the provision of public goods and services, a subject that is addressed by public-choice theory.

The neo-Marxist perspective that appeared in the 1970s, called the collective-consumption theory, focused specifically on this gap by relating State intervention to conditions of local politics. The approach called collective consumption was formulated by French sociologists to cover the involvement of the local State in the provision of public goods and services as a specific means of characterizing the uniquely *urban* nature of the city's functional role in society. Despite its popularity as a fashion and the elements of self-promotion and advertising that went along with the propagation of this view by urbanists, the critical weaknesses of the collective-consumption theory have caused it to be abandoned (see critiques by Theret, 1982; Mingione, 1981; Pickvance, 1982; and Gottdiener, 1985a). In what follows, therefore, I prefer to use the term *socialization of consumption* to specify State intervention in the provision of use values in order to relate our discussion to a broader theoretical framework within which neo-Marxists have studied this phenomenon after the abandonment of the collective-consumption perspective.

THE SOCIALIZATION OF CONSUMPTION

Neo-Marxist theories of the relation between the State and society base themselves on the assertion that capitalism, by itself, is so swamped by the contradictions of its mode of production that it cannot reproduce the conditions of its existence. Hence, the necessity for State intervention as the *reproducer* of capitalist social relations. More specifically, according to neo-Marxism, maturing aspects of monopoly capitalism, such as the appearance of concentrated forms of capital like the big firms and super profits, have thrown society into a multileveled crisis that it cannot resolve on its own involving problems with maintaining the supply of labor power and sustaining its ability to purchase commodities at a high level of consumer demand, as well as forms of intervention in production designed to attenuate the falling rate of profit. Consequently, the State is called on to intervene increasingly to solve the problems of capitalism's crises and ensure its survival, or "reproduction." Those aspects of neo-Marxism focusing specifically on State intervention in welfare policies associated with the reproduction of the labor force addressed what can be called the "socialization of consumption," thereby relating Marxian theory in general to the conditions of local politics.

Without question, the starting point for an understanding of the socialization of consumption is O'Connor's theory of the fiscal crisis of the State. Reanalyzing the Keynesian intervention of the 1920s, O'Connor asserts that the contemporary State/economy relation can be explained best by the phenomenon of the socialization of capital. Over the years public resources have been utilized more and more by the private sector so that much of the activities of capitalists are, in fact, socialized by State expenditures. O'Connor notes that this transformation is manifested in three distinct ways. On the one hand, sectors of private industry are the recipients of a wide variety of State supports including subsidies, tax breaks, and outright transfers of funds. Virtually all of this support goes to the monopolistic sector of the economy, which is characterized as capital intensive and technologically advanced. O'Connor calls this aspect the "socialization of investment" (1973: 8). On the other hand, the public sector has assumed progressively more of the burden for collective good provision, such as housing, education, health care, and cultural activities or facilities. O'Connor calls this aspect of intervention the "socialization of consumption" (1973: 8). He also notes a third category, which predates the more advanced aspects of capital's

socialization, called "social expenses capital," or, the use of
State funds in the hegemonic project of maintaining social
control, such as by providing for police protection and welfare.
In this way O'Connor specifies theoretically the relation
between the State and the economy according to the three
crises of contemporary capitalism: the crisis of the falling rate
of profit, of underconsumption and the realization of capital,
and of legitimation. O'Connor's theory is, quite simply, that as
monopoly capital develops, contradictions heighten at every
level, thereby forcing increasingly more State intervention,
also at every level. Public spending in the reproduction of
capital is, therefore, eventually pushed to its social limits by the
three streams of socialization acting in concert. The State,
finally, enters into a crisis of its own, this time a "fiscal crisis" of
the budget.

O'Connor's approach addresses the general relation between
the State and society. In France a group of neo-Marxists took
over aspects of this work as it relates specifically to State
intervention in the reproduction of labor. The most fashionable
variant of this perspective was the Althusserian approach of
"collective consumption" (see Lojkine, 1976; Castells, 1977),
or, the *direct* intervention of the State in the reproduction of
the *urban* labor force. According to collective-consumption
theory, the issues and problems associated with State provision
of welfare constitute the unique contents of urban affairs,
especially urban politics, as distinct from other academic
inquiries, such as regional, rural, or national political problems.
This approach, however, was not the only one in the neo-
Marxist camp, although its supporters in the United States
have popularized it above other neo-Marxist perspectives.
Addressing the same issue of labor's reproduction, a second
school of thought, called Fordism (now neo-Fordism), even
predates O'Connor (Gramsci, 1971: 277-318). Neo-Fordism
focuses on the relation between capital and labor with regard
to the former's needs in reproducing the latter without the

Althusserian compulsion to specify uniquely the contents of an "urban" system (Aglietta, 1978; Davis, 1984; Hirsch, 1983; Lipietz, 1982); I shall come back to this perspective later. Finally, in the United Kingdom a third alternative was developed, which rejected Marxian structuralism in order to follow Weber, but retained an emphasis on the role of the State in the provision of consumption goods specifically within "urban" environments. This perspective, called neo-Weberianism, has already been mentioned, and like neo-Fordism, it has a separate view of capitalist crisis theory than that based on O'Connor.

Theories of the socialization of consumption, such as neo-Fordism and collective consumption, emphasize the way in which the State has assumed a progressively greater role in sustaining the quality of life for the *urban* working class in the face of constant threats to that quality by the actions of private-sector growth processes. However, this concept does not connote a simple mechanism of government benevolence, but can only be grasped as the outcome of a complex process involving the maturation of the State/private sector relation associated with the late capitalist phase of modern society. It is propelled on the one hand by the articulation of needs, the sources of which are both local working-class politics and capital's desire to avoid crisis, and, on the other, by the structural constraints on city budgets and the progressive ability of capital itself to shift the burden of the costs of development into the public domain.

State involvement in the reproduction of labor is the result of the following historical changes in capitalism: first, the penetration by private enterprise itself into areas of limited profitability as a consequence of capital concentration and monopoly control in other sectors, so that services such as sanitation, health care, and education become domains of capital investment and development; second, the historical growth of organized bargaining power among workers in the class struggle, which has elevated the standard of living and changed the concept of "need both qualitatively and quantitatively" (Castells, 1978: 16); third, the effect of technology, which has simultaneously enhanced the ability of the capitalist system to provide services, such as medical care, at a respectable level, and which has also changed the quality of work to require greater sophistication and training on the part of the labor force. Finally, as certain services become melded to the requirements of labor power in an increasingly more fundamental way, especially as elements in its extended reproduction among workers across the generations, demand for them outstrips the ability of private capital to supply adequate amounts. Over the years capital has avoided this labor crisis by successfully shifting its burden to the State, thereby transforming the responsibility for the reproduction of the labor force to State intervention at the local level. As Saunders (1981: 189) remarks,

> The potential for a crisis in the provision of commodities necessary for the reproduction of labor power is inherent in the nature of capitalist commodity production. The reason for this is simply that production is concerned with exchange value while consumption is concerned with use values. There is no necessary reason why what is needed will also be what is most produced. The state must intervene to regulate the production of use values.

In sum, both public choicers and neo-Marxists have a theory of local State intervention and its link to the quality of life. The former follow a public goods argument asserting that government must intervene because the private-sector market cannot supply adequate amounts of all goods. Indivisibility problems associated with such things as protection from crime, problems in the market allocation of recreation, and so on, constitute the referents in debates among analysts of public provision over the ability of the market to function as an efficient and equitable allocator of public goods. The need here is to determine theoretically what goods and services could or could not be privatized if special interests were kept out of government. The level of social welfare most pertinent to the needs of labor is then explained, more specifically, by public-choice theorists as determined by the level of organized demand of the labor force itself *without* connection to the needs of capital or the function of the State in the general reproduction of social relations.

In contrast, neo-Marxists focus on the way in which the socialization of consumption is an outcome of the changing nature of the relationship between the local State and private capital. The needs of capital both to control the demands of labor and also to fight the historical decline in the rate of profit require it to assign to the State an increasingly greater role in the direct management of society and the quality of everyday life. Neo-Marxists, therefore, find explanations in the deep-level relation between capital and the local State, which changes over time, while public choicers have a less complicated, ahistorical perspective focusing as they do on the relative efficacy of the market and the open-ended political decision-making mechanisms of pluralism.

The essential aspect of agreement between the two approaches is that over time the public realm has assumed a progressively greater responsibility for social functions that were carried out in the past by more personalized aspects of private life, such as the care of the elderly. Accompanying this shift to State administration of private-consumption practices and personal-use values has been the increasing rationalization of intervention embodied by large public bureaucracies. In the course of time this has served to remove from public discourse the entire series of issues that are generated by the relation between social development and the quality of life, such as the quality of education, health care, provision for the elderly, support for family problems, and so on. The new political discourse pits local users of State services against the public bureaucracies staffed by career professionals, which supply them. Political life and the autonomy of local associational responses to the exigencies of everyday life has suffered accordingly and local political culture declines.

The new theories of public provision, including neo-Fordism as well as collective consumption and the mainstream public-goods approach, all suggest that along with greater State intervention comes increasing rationalization and bureaucratization. Political activities are no longer located in democratic public forums, which concern themselves with the needs of a changing society; rather they now focus on State provision itself and pit the working class, as "user" social movements, against the State. As this process of intervention and rationalization takes hold of local everyday life, earlier forms of decision making located in cultural and political modes of association die out; democratic political culture soon does, too. Local politics has become little more than a mad struggle among special interests for pieces of an ever-dwindling government-resource pie.

The neo-Marxist approach to public provision in the city has not been without its own critics. As already indicated, for example, the theory of collective consumption as formulated by French sociologists has been abandoned following several formidable critiques. As pointed out elsewhere (Gottdiener, 1985a), the suggestion that urban government can be specified as the agent managing the reproduction of the labor force is obviously false for the case of the United States. In addition, the assertion by neo-Marxists that the State always intervenes in a functionalist manner is excessively rationalistic and fails to account for the limitations and contradictions of State intervention that exacerbate rather than resolve the reproductive needs of capital (see Offe, 1984).

Third, according to Pickvance (1982), the concept of State intervention in the long-term interest of capital lacks any effective analytical usefulness, thereby undercutting neo-

Marxist attempts to specify theoretically the nature of State intervention. Pickvance (1982) also raises doubts about the efficacy of collective-consumption theory's approach to urban politics. It is most unlikely that the whole of urban political activity can be specified in terms of user movements. A more fruitful line of inquiry is the one suggested by the present discussion, namely, to focus on issues involved with sustaining the quality of life manifested as socially and spatially constituted conflicts.

A fourth limitation concerns approaches to State intervention based on O'Connor's theory of the fiscal crisis, which would include most neo-Marxist work in the United States. The present and successful retreat by the State in socialization, such as reprivatization or recommodifiation, challenges the very heart of neo-Marxist crisis theories. The issue here is not so much the reversal of the phenomenon of socialization by such mechanisms as recommodification, but rather the *successful* management of the urban fiscal crisis itself, which includes forms of State retreat (see Gottdiener, 1986). Successive cutbacks, the tempering of municipal union power, privatization and the switch to user fees, shutdowns of physical plants, and austerity management practices have all been utilized successfully to control budgets *without* creating the kind of political unrest or backlash that might be predicted by neo-Marxist theories of social control. Recent evidence, therefore, suggests that the relation between capital and the State is much more fluid and variable than supposed by fiscal-crisis theorists.

The importance of the neo-Marxist approach to the socialization of consumption is that it provides a more accurate picture of local politics, one that is characterized by conflict and contradiction rather than the harmonious responsiveness of public-choice mechanisms. Inequities of public provision create the social conditions for new forms of urban political conflict by mobilizing the users of services regardless of class membership. This helps explain the diminished importance of class-based interests in contemporary political struggles at the local level. Yet, this "new" mode of politics is not without its own internal conflicts. The very act of State intervention relates the State to problems associated with everyday life. Therefore, intervention intensifies political interests and enlarges the scope of concerns expressed as political. In this way interests that may have been acted out in the past in economic class conflict at the place of work, have been transformed into community issues framing uniquely urban questions at the place of residence. Because this globalization of conflict is not class specific, the number of groups, issues, and interests that the local political agenda comprises proliferates until the entire polity is pulverized into a large number of separate cleavages that crisscross the local population in an increasingly dense manner. The outcome of State intervention in the socialization of consumption, then, is an urban politics that is progressively more fractionalized, spatially localized, and classless in nature. At the same time, however, the urban crisis is deeply felt because it is essentially a crisis in the system's ability to sustain the quality of everyday life. Accordingly, the content of urban politics both with regard to its concerns and the nature of its intervention is typified by issues involving the State's provision of goods and services necessary to reproducing the quality of life.

The three perspectives on local government discussed in this chapter each consider urban politics according to its limitations despite different theoretical reasons for doing so. They also share a second feature, namely, a society-centered view of the relation between social demands and public policy. Public choicers consider government as a neutral mediator of special interests. In contrast, neo-Marxists consider the State to be driven by class conflict and its policies as reflecting the balance of power in society. Welfare interventions are offset by the servicing of capital's needs, so that the struggle over local

public resources becomes a complex game with hidden subsidies as well as publicized initiatives. In each case, however,
the local State acts in some way according to the interests it
serves. In contrast, State-centered approaches focus on the
interests generated by and within government itself. In addition
to considering this perspective in the next chapter, I shall also
evaluate each of the approaches to urban politics in order to
assess their comparative values and to shed some light on the
more basic issues associated with State intervention including
the determination of public policy, the fiscal crisis, and the
question of equity in the supply of social services.

CHAPTER 4

NEW THEORIES OF
URBAN POLITICS—PART II

As we have seen, local public bureaucracies and governments
are funnels for massive amounts of capital that flow through
the State in its sustenance of the quality of life. Despite the
limitations of local government, its forms of administration
wield great power to affect individual life chances and the
quality of business interaction. The components of the State do
not simply spring into motion in order to satisfy the demands
of the society. Historically, the State has always manifested an
interest of its own, one that can be identified as seeking to
preserve its conditions of existence relative to private needs.
This separate and autonomous interest defines a State-
centeredness in the relation between society and the State.
Approaches to policy determinants that focus on this interest
and the actions of State managers in affecting urban political
outcomes are the subject of the present chapter. They define
the perspectives of noe-Weberianism and State managerialism, which are much needed correetives to society-centered
approaches.

Neo-Weberianism and State Managerialism

Neo-Weberians take issue with neo-Marxists because of the
latters' one-dimensional view of the State. Following the structuralist work of Althusser and Poulantzas, it matters little to

Marxists that the arrangements of governance possess wide variability across capitalist social formations. Neo-Weberians, in contrast, seek to understand the nature of the State as a distinct, nonreducible presence in social processes. For example, commenting on the reductionist approach to public provision by French socialists, Pahl (1978, 1979) observed that, while capitalist societies certainly engage in such activities, they are not the only types of societies to do so. In particular, communist countries devote considerable resources to the same task. If collective consumption is so specific to the reproduction of the labor force according to the needs of capital, then how can we explain its role in communist countries except by calling into question the functionalist presuppositions of neo-Marxism?

There is, therefore, sufficient evidence worldwide to suggest that a more generic phenomenon is at work in *all* industrialized States, regardless of mode of production which relates the State itself to the reproduction of everyday life—a subject considered by the present discussion.

Questions raised by neo-Weberians regarding the variable manifestations of State intervention point towards the need for a comparative analysis of societies according to their patterns of "access" and the role of political processes in decision making (see Pahl, 1977a). Once this becomes the focus of research it also becomes clear that State managers and the effects of political parties both play autonomous roles in the determination of public policy. This discovery of State centeredness balances the one-sided neglect of the State itself by other approaches. The neo-Weberians, for example, have focused on the autonomy of State managers in government decision-making processes. This effort has been matched by those analysts following the State managerialism perspective in the U.S. Work along these lines has isolated several significant sources of variability in local public policies that cannot be explained by society-centered approaches.

Neo-Weberianism:
The Autonomy of Local Public Bureaucrats

Neo-Weberianism in the U.K. acquired a theoretical status with the work of Pahl on the "urban managerialism thesis" (1975, 1977b). Taking his cue from a previous study by Rex and Moore (1967), Pahl focused on the fact that public services played a role in the life chances of individuals because they were essentially income transfers operating through State subsidized consumption. Consequently, localized populations being serviced by large public bureaucracies represented distributive groupings with an acquired social status combining location within the work force and location within the urban residential array. Under Pahl's direction it was the latter feature combined with its variable relation to local government policies which came to define the neo-Weberian project because public services are resources that can aid the life chances of every individual and, when played properly, can overcome many of the social constraints on mobility. In short, public bureaucracies represented systems of distribution for resources independent of the labor market. Furthermore, according to Pahl, considerable variation in the supply of social services existed within any city and this pattern could be traced directly to access problems and locational opportunities. Consequently, the very life chances of local residents was a function of differential access to public services.

For Pahl, urban resources possess two features which produce localized access differentials. They are allocated in space—they have a specific physical location, and, they are bureaucracies—the delivery of services is subjected to a process involving a bureaucratic staff and structure. As he indicates,

The access to any scarce resource or facility could be seen as comprising two elements: the *spatial* element, which could be expressed in terms of time/cost distance, and the *social* element, which included on the one hand, the rules and procedures which defined access for populations, defined in both social and spatial terms, and on the other hand, the interpretation and administration of these rules and procedures by local managers or gatekeepers [1977b: 50].

In the United States, Williams (1971) has spent some time on the first of these aspects thereby helping to introduce a spatial sensitivity to the analysis of public service supply. Over the course of his discussions, Pahl came to focus more on the second of these aspects because it highlighted a specific property of the State itself. This second aspect is very much like Katznelson's "city trenches" (1981), and no doubt the latter had Pahl's work in mind. Yet, Pahl's formulation is much more specific than Katznelson's, confining its emphasis to public bureaucracies alone rather than to all of local politics, consequently it is much more easily studied. In particular, Pahl focuses on the role of bureaucrats as possessing discretionary power in the allocation of social services. This results in a cumulative effect of decision making favoring those localized populations who are best able to meet local bureaucrat processing criteria with a minimal interactive effort. Furthermore, because bureaucracies function with a formalized set of procedural criteria, differential access to services is also a function of the relative ability of localized populations to conform to structural categories of public administration. In short, the urban managerialist thesis transforms bureaucracy into an intervening variable of great importance in the understanding of urban political administration. Variability in the supply of public services among cities can be explained in part by variation in the structure of their individual service bureaucracies. In addition, differential access to such resources on the part of localized populations living within cities can be explained by the very same thesis and as due to variations in the practices of local bureaucrats.

Ever since its original formulation, Pahl's approach has met with stiff opposition from neo-Marxists (Norman, 1975). In the main "urban managerialism" has been criticized for its focus on the "middle dogs" while the "top dogs," presumably the capitalist class, responsible for the fundamental social inequities go unstudied. Rather than viewing differentials in access to social wealth in terms of the broader structural forces in economics and politics, urban managerialism encourages a more particularized approach that focuses alone on the variable effects of bureaucracy. Consequently, the Weberian sensibility is critiqued for its exclusion of the role of class conflict in determining urban public policy outcomes. As Dunleavy remarks,

> The built-in focus on mediating institutions in urban manager-
> ialism thus generates a possibility of seriously misleading
> conclusions in which broader structural constraints and deter-
> minants of the local or regional context are lost to sight, and
> excessively individualistic and voluntaristic accounts of urban
> management are given a one-off, non-cumulative basis [1980:
> 42].

The Marxian critique of neo-Weberianism has been taken to heart by Pahl himself who has acknowledged the limitations of his approach (1977b). The question which remains unresolved, however, is whether a purely Marxian approach can explain all the issues associated with the determination of local urban politics. As Katznelson has observed (1981), it is incumbent upon urban political analysis to explain the inherently classless nature of political conflict. Yet Marxism does no better than Weberian approaches in meeting this challenge. In fact, Katznelson, who has raised this as an issue, must resort himself to a rather strained argument about the nature of class in Weber and Marx in order to demonstrate that his "city trenches" is a phenomenon unique to capitalist industrialization (1981: 197-210). In the end this argument is so generalized and the concept of "trenches" so ill specified from a Marxian viewpoint that is nonfalsifiable and, therefore, little help in explaining the classless nature of local politics.

Similarly, in the U.K. debate between neo-Weberians (Saunders, 1978) and neo-Marxists (Dunleavy, 1979) over the nature of urban classes and their relationship to urban political conflict also remains unresolved. Dunleavy, in particular, strains to show that the differential political postures of housing groups are mediated by the State so that they are really manifestations of collective consumption. That is, the seemingly classless nature of local political conflict is in reality a product of the interventionist State, which always operates in the best "long-term interests" of the capitalist class as a whole. We have come across this assertion before as it is a familiar one in Marxist analysis. Dunleavy means to imply here that urban politics is a production of a class structured society even if the appearance of State intervention is classless. However, as Pahl observes about this argument,

A "theory" which claims that the state ultimately serves the interests of the dominant classes is very hard to falsify. Such a theory claims, for example, that whilst on the one hand the state supports the long term interests of capital, in the short term, the specific interests of a certain fraction of the dominant classes may not be served. Thus, whatever the state does must be in the interests of the dominant class. Similarly, the state may *appear* to serve the interests of the subordinate classes by channeling resources into various public goods and services, which appear as "concessions" given in response to the apparent power of organized labor; in fact, it is claimed, such provision is a subtle bribe to incorporate the organization of the subordinate class into the capitalist power structure. Alternatively, such provision may be characterized as a form of social control or as a way of reproducing and providing docile, healthy, and well trained workers. Whatever form of Marxist theory one chooses to take,

the ultimate goal is always the accumulation and reproduction
of capital [1977a: 9].

In sum, Pahl rejects neo-Marxism's dependency on functionalist accounts of the State's role in the study of urban
public provision. His focus on the intermediate role of local
bureaucracy as a determinant of public policy outcomes
cannot be explained away by Marxian analysis. In fact, in the
U.S. Lipsky (1976) has made good use of this emphasis in his
study of street level bureaucrats. These are defined as "those
men and women who, in their face-to-face encounters with
citizens, 'represent' government to the people" (1976: 196).
Consequently, Lipsky's work supports the urban managerialist
thesis within the specific context of its neo-Weberian frame.
Recent empirical work testing citizen evaluations of city
services provides substantial evidence for the role of personal
contacts in explaining satisfactions over against other approaches (see Hero and Durand, 1985).

We can appreciate Lipsky's line of reasoning, or what has
come to be called in the U.S. the "bureaucratic decision-rule
hypothesis," while retaining an acknowledgment of Marxian
criticisms leveled against all analyses that concentrate on the
"middle dogs." Street-level bureaucrats possess three distinct
role characteristics that affect urban policy outcomes. First,
they have considerable discretionary powers in performing
their work. Second, they have limited control over clientele
behavior. That is, because they deal in city services, voluntarism
plays a great role in the response of the public to the
performance of their jobs. Finally, there is great difficulty in
"measuring job performance in terms of ultimate bureaucratic
objectives" (Lipsky, 1976: 197). For example, social workers
may be asked to carry a certain case load, however, this burden
has little to do with effective job performance for each case,
except to alter the ability of the social worker to pay attention
to client needs. According to Lipsky, as a consequence of the

peculiarities of their job situation, street level bureaucrats operate in a highly stressful situation. For this reason certain on-the-job mechanisms are innovated to deal with this stress. These are structural as well as interpersonal and they tend to characterize the bureaucrat-client relation. As Lipsky observes,

> In order to make decisions when confronted with a complex problem and an uncertain environment, individuals who play organizational roles will develop bureaucratic mechanisms to make the task easier [1976: 201].

Lipsky concludes from his study that the very nature of public service bureaucracies produce the kinds of discriminatory patterns that are perceived by their clientele, because of bureaucrat adaption to work within a stressful situation. This is especially exacerbated by minority groups who have little to like about the way in which all of urban politics is managed, and who have difficulty playing the bureaucratic game. Consequently, Lipsky believes that only structural reform and an elimination of the current environment within which bureaucracies function can address the problems of urban minority populations.

The study of street-level bureaucrats has uncovered a structural constraint to the adequate performance of public bureaucracies. Because it has been formulated outside of a critical awareness it can only lead to implications that are reformist in content. However, it still provides one additional explanation for the variable reception accorded the functioning of city services by urban populations. If it does not address the big picture, it nevertheless demonstrates the complex nature of the local State/society articulation. In this sense we can take issue with neo-Marxists, such as Dunleavy, who wish to dismiss entirely the significance of voluntarism on the part of State bureaucrats as an explanatory variable of urban policy outcomes. At some point when a full accounting of case study material is assessed we must acknowledge through sheer weight of evidence the importance of State managers as an autonomous factor in public policy. To be sure, it is debatable whether Lipsky's bureaucrats enjoy real freedom from the constraints of their institution's functional roles. This issue, however, is beside the point made above. At the place of provision discretionary powers exist for urban managers which are produced by the nature of their work and employment and which are responsible for differentials in resource deployment in the city independent of class-related factors. It is this autonomous aspect of public service provision which deserves study on its own terms. Considerable empirical evidence in the U.S. exists to support this "decision-rule" hypothesis (Lineberry, 1977; Thomas, 1982; Hero and Durand, 1985).

State managers not only have effects on the efficient and equitable supply of social services, but taken together they also labor in line with an historical interest identified as the State's autonomous position in society. This aggregate State interest and the role of State managers as historical subjects in promoting it is the subject of our second variant of State-centeredness, called "State managerialism."

State Managerialism and Relative Autonomy

The access and equity problems deriving from State practices all point to explanations of public policy outcomes which stand outside mainstream Pluralist and Marxian approaches. On the one hand, policy outcomes cannot be understood through the traditional terms of pluralist analysis such as party conflict, ethnic constituencies, electoral competition, and the like (Dye, 1976; Peterson, 1981). On the other hand, differentials in the distribution of public goods and the conflicts which at times occur over public resource deployment are neither products of capitalist interests nor necessarily functional for the reproduction of capitalist relations. Consequently, a neo-Weberian emphasis on the role of State administration as a separate source of variation in the performance of the local State is a healthy corrective to extant perspectives. Yet, as developed in the literature, neo-Weberianism and neo-Marxism both commit the idealist fallacy by ascribing to State intervention an overly rational content.

For example, both neo-Weberianism and neo-Marxism start from the theory of collective consumption. According to this perspective State intervention is functional for the maintenance of the capitalist system as a whole. In order to accomplish this task, neo-Marxists hypothesize that political processes are "relatively autonomous" of the direct interests of the capitalist class and, as we have already discussed above, operate in the best "long-term interest" of capitalism (i.e., the nonfalsifiable claim of system maintenance). This view has been criticized not for its functionalist premises but because it remains a form of economism, that is, it still reduces State practices to class relations. Recently, a second version of functionalism has come to replace the notion of relative autonomy, namely, the functional autonomy of State managers. As Block remarks,

> The difficulties with relative autonomy suggest that this formulation might not be, as Poulantzas suggests, the final destination of the Marxist theory of the State. It appears rather as a cosmetic modification of Marxism's tendency to reduce state power to class power . . . because state power is still conceived as entirely a product of class relations. . . . The starting point of an alternative formulation is the acknowledgement that state power is *sui generis* not reducible to class power [1980: 228].

I am in agreement with the spirit of this observation, although the separation that Block proposes between class power and

State power is too simplistic. This is in keeping with the desire to force an either/ or choice between State and society centered views. In the next chapter I shall try to overcome these limitations while preserving the observation above, or, as Jessop (1982) suggests, appreciating the *under*-determination of political outcomes by economic relations.

According to Block, State managers represent a separate, autonomous interest in society. Because the State is a separate source of power, State managers can use it to pursue interests of their own or expand the control of the State over the rest of society. This has come to be known as the thesis of State managerialism. As Block observes,

> State managers take advantage of the changes in the structural context to expand their own power and to pursue policies that they perceive as necessary to strengthen the nation's position in the world system and to preserve internal order [1980: 223].

To be sure, the interests of State managers must be accounted for in the relation between the society and the State. Yet, while not precluding the possibility that such intervention acts *at times* in the functionalist manner that Block assumes, this is not always the case. There is a critical difference between the autonomy of State managers and the alleged autonomy of the State itself. State managers possess degrees of freedom from the interests active in the private sector so that it is possible to speak of their autonomy from them. However, there can be no analysis of the local State that does not account for the dynamics of society and the relation between the State itself and the private sphere. Thus, for example, according to Block, State managers can only be *relatively* autonomous of society because their actions are hemmed in by the class contexts within which the exercise of State power takes place (1980: 218). Indeed, all Marxists would no doubt agree with the assertion that the State cannot defy the collective interest of the capitalist class, if only because the former relies on the resources of the latter, especially in the process of capitalist accumulation. However, the theory of relative autonomy proposed by Block asserts that under certain historical conditions the functional needs of the State in acting always to preserve the society can conflict with the needs of capital, and social upheavals then occur that are often led by elements of the State rather than those of the working class or of capital.

Nordlinger (1981) is correct to criticize this notion as too limited an understanding for what is, in reality, a structural, everyday feature of society, rather than one which appears during social crises. Yet, the view that invariably gets presented in arguments over the role of State managers persists in ascribing to their actions an idealist version of functional rationality. The extreme example of this approach comes from Wirt (1983) who identifies the interest of State bureaucrats as the ethos of professionalism. Thus, over the years, it is asserted, there has been a growing consensus produced by the institutionalized training of public administrators around specific techniques of social management. This technical knowledge forms the core of a professional mode of expertise which is presently characteristic of State managers, and, in fact, can be identified as their interest (Wirt, 1983: 21). This approach ignores all those actions of State managers that do not follow technical rationality, such as in the common practice of corruption, nor does it explain why, given so much expertise, the contradictions and limitations of State intervention abound.

The thesis of urban managerialism following from this argument is that bureaucratic professionalism combines with State autonomy only in an uneven manner thereby creating contradictions of intervention that reflect the power struggles between separate social interests. At certain times the need of the capitalist class for State intervention is so great that the antagonisms between private and public control are overlooked, and the interests of the State are pushed onto society at every opportunity. At other times, however, capital is in such a powerful position that it can renegotiate its relation with the State to its benefit. This latter aspect seems to be illustrated best by the restructuring taking place in response to the fiscal crisis. In short, once we explore fully the implications of State-centered approaches, we are forced to consider society again, especially the relation between the State and capital.

By failing to develop a balanced perspective on the relation between society and the State, the new theories of urban politics discussed in the last two chapters remain limited. State-centeredness and society-centeredness are each one-sided perspectives that lack a unified conception of that relation. The issue is not, however, to be eclectic and to try and include all approaches in a kind of grab bag urban theory. This need for eclecticism in order to resolve the clash between Marxian and Weberian perspectives is false but should not be underrated (see Saunders, 1983; Pickvance, 1984a; see also Chapter 5). Rather, it is necessary to achieve balance through a deeper understanding of the manner by which power relations operate in society and through the apparatus of the State. Such a concern will occupy us in the next chapter. One way of assessing this need at present is by comparing the relative abilities of our alternate theories of urban politics to illuminate some of the central issues of that subject, including the determinants of public policy, the nature of the fiscal crisis and the question of equity in the supply of social services.

Determinants of Public Policy

State-centered approaches are limited in dealing with the determinants of policies. Perhaps this is one reason why they have only recently been recognized as pertinent to local politics. A State-centered view is tailored more towards explaining how government functions once a policy is proposed or initiated than towards how it is determined. Thus, the

outcomes of initiatives are said to reflect the role of State
managers in modulating and channeling needs expressed by
the society. Following the work of Pahl and Lipsky, this effort
concentrates on showing how State managers intervene
through public bureaucracies to affect the patterns of service
provision in the city. This bureaucratic "decision-rule hypothesis" claims many adherents and is meant to cover off as well
as on-cycle situations. According to Ostrom, for example,

> This hypothesis—that the allocation of all urban services
> results from the use of myriad little decisions made by street-
> level public employees—has become the dominant explanation
> for the distribution of urban services [1983: 104].

Most State-centered analysts suggest that it is the development of professionalism and the availability of trained managers that rely on a corpus of sophisticated administrative
techniques (see Wirt, 1983; Ostrom, 1983) that has led to a
managerial referent in the determination of policy—a factor
that is independent of others in the relation between social
interests and public policy. Yet, recent research testing this
theory points to a separate dimension of managerialism, one
that is perhaps more obvious from case study research on the
delivery of city services. Personal contacts and the informal
relation between bureaucrats and certain clients seems to be
the determining factor in the evaluation of service provision
regardless of other differences in patterns of delivery (see Hero
and Durand, 1985). This supports Lipsky's early work and also
lends credence to the position of public choicers regarding the
limitations of the large, impersonal city bureaucracies. The
presence of personal relations between managers and clients
does better as an explanation of client evaluations than other
approaches, such as those focusing on differential spatial
access by location, and, the effects of unpatterned inequalities
(see Thomas, 1982). In short, State managerialism provides

information on the functioning of local government as an intervening variable between policy determinants and their outcomes at the *implementation* level of public provision.

A second State-centered aspect that plays much the same explanatory role as the above is the importance of considering variations in forms of local government on policy. Following the early work of Lineberry and Fowler (1967), political efficacy can be measured according to whether reformist structuralist changes actually advance or impede the democratic process. Changes in the forms of representation, such as the switch from ward politics to at-large constituencies, for example, may have mixed results on urban democracy. The former form has been singled out by grass-roots mobilization as restricting the ability of minority and less affluent residents to exercise a voice in local politics. In a recent study of successful political mobilization that brought about the structural change from at-large back to district elections (Christensen and Gerston, 1984), it was found that such reforms improve the ability of local government to attend to the "little" things involved in the quality of community life. However, economic elites can still control growth for their own benefit, despite successful grass-roots mobilization for changes in political representation (Christensen and Gerston, 1984: 499).

Centralized as opposed to decentralized arrangements of local governance can also play a role in affecting political outcomes. In contrast to the views most expressed in the metropolitan fragmentation debate, there is no simple choice between these two forms (Gottdiener, 1977). Aiken (1970), for example, found that decentralization leads to greater community activism in the pursuit of federal funds. In contrast, centralization is more efficient for the supply of nonseparable goods, such as fluoridation, to the community itself (Lyon and Bonjean, 1981). Thus, depending on the issue, the source of support or funds, and the kind of decision required, different arrangements for local government provide different results.

In a review of this literature, Lyons and Bonjean (1981) suggest that it is profitable to distinguish between routine decisions that are part of the everyday practice of government, and nonroutine ones that require some form of community mobilization to be passed, such as housing moratoria, police protection, or fluoridation. They found that nonroutine decisions are determined by the factors that go into community mobilization. Routine decisions, in contrast, are explained by the process of incrementalism. The latter is decidedly indicative of the discretionary power of State managers constrained by their professional role in conforming to city budgets. Much more can be said about the role of representational structures in the determination of policy, and I shall return to this topic in more detail in Chapter 7.

State-centered arguments, therefore, including incrementalist and off-cycle explanations, help us to appreciate the role that State structures play in the political process and pinpoint the manner by which local bureaucrats may affect policy. Yet, this approach leaves the nature of policy and many of its determining factors out of the picture. For this reason most analysts of public policy prefer a society-centered approach. In recent years this perspective has come to focus on the "limits of the city"—those political and economic factors exogeneous to the local area that help determine public policy (see Dye, 1976; Fry and Winters, 1970; Hofferbert, 1966). Such factors have been found to condition policy from points lying outside the composition of communities themselves.

Economic resources, for example, located within the region and the developmental needs of the private sector that can vary from place to place, have been singled out especially in recent research as fundamental to an understanding of local government policies (Dye, 1976; Peterson, 1981). This sensibility has also become the cornerstone of the new political economy, as we have already seen. By considering the way that local governments are driven to respond to private sector needs and the complexities of their operating milieu, much can be explained about the nature of public policy.

In the past, society-centered analysts studied politics according to the relation between community composition and policy outcomes. This followed from a rather simplistic, pluralist conception of governance as reflecting directly the will of the people aggregated through forms of political representation. More recently a shift has occurred away from community composition itself and towards greater consideration for the global operating environment of all urban places defined by the latter's command of political and economic resources. Thus, a more extreme form of society-centeredness has replaced the traditional approach of urban political science that concentrates on direct correlations between local community characteristics and political outcomes. As Dye observes,

> The traditional literature in American state politics instructed students that characteristics of state political systems—particularly two party competition, voter participation and apportionment—had a direct bearing on public policy. Since political scientists devoted most of their time to studying what happened within the political system, it was natural for them to believe that the political processes which they studied were important determinants of public policy [1976: 25].

Research along the above lines, such as summarized by Peterson (1981), stresses the role of economic factors in the determination of State policy. Important especially are both the level and character of resources coming from the public and private sectors in affecting the scope of programmatic initiatives carried out by local government (Sachs and Harris, 1974; Tompkins, 1975). Consequently, society-centered approaches to local government now concentrate on factors comprising the fiscal environment of cities, intergovernmental juris-

dictional differences, and the class composition of the population—especially its median family income.

As in the approach of the new political economy, researchers
seem to be finding an increasing array of previously hidden
factors outside the realm of what passes for local political
activity that function to hem in and determine the behavior of
local government. The overwhelming weakness of local government is perhaps the single feature that explains the current shift
in empirical emphasis. Local politics itself has been put on trial
and found to be somewhat irrelevant to the current functioning
of city regimes. Both the death of politics and its incremental
possibilities for promoting social change can be illustrated by a
discussion of the next issue, the urban fiscal crisis. Before
proceeding, several observations about the nature of research
in urban political science can be made at this time.

First, the study of policy determinants is very much a
mainstream activity of urban political science. Hence, it is
hampered by the general limitations of that mode of inquiry. In
particular, a major drawback of policy determinant research is
its preponderant dependency on statistical analysis. Most
often this amounts to a blind exercise in correlating background community factors with political effects, as if the State
operates as a perfectly neutral mechanism aggregating political
sentiments. Stone, Whelan, and Murin (1979: 175) point to the
misleading results obtained by aggregate data analyses, such as
Clark's (1968), that correlate outcomes of public policies
directly with community characteristics. Unfortunately, this
method prevails even today without an adequate understanding
of its limitations simply because positivism and statistical
modes of research dominate academic production.

It is not possible to study public policy solely in this manner
because of the importance of intermediate factors in the
political process that mediate the route from organized
interests to political outcomes. Such a realization has surfaced
not only in the critique of incrementalist theory (Padgett,
1980), but in the call for case studies by historians of public

policy in order to supplement quantitative analyses (see McDonald and Ward, 1984). The hidden dimension of politics shows up in studies of the new political economy and in case studies that document the effects of party leadership, political corruption, exogenous structural limits on local government, the power of special interests, the influence of State managers on policy, and the profound but highly subtle effects of State regulations on social behavior. The presence of this hidden dimension calls for an abandonment of positivism and its relacement in the epistemology of urban political science with the realist theory of structuration (see Chapter 5) as the only means of understanding the State (see Jessop, 1982).

Second, the study of policy determinants shows up the inadequacy of all one-sided approaches such as society- or State-centeredness. Each perspective emphasizes certain aspects that would be handled better in combination and interrelation. City limits arguments that focus on exogenous structural constraints to political decisions cannot illuminate the manner by which public officials and State managers maneuver within those limits and according to the power of a variety of interests, including their own. By the same token, State-centered approaches are best suited to the administration and the implementation phase of politics. They have comparatively little to say about determinants except when studying the role of forms of representation and the effects of decision-rules such as in off-cycle policy implementation. In the next chapter I will argue for a unified approach to local government. More importantly, I will show that without an understanding of the nature of the local State itself, the study of urban policy proceeds blindly.

The Fiscal Crisis of the City

Simply put the fiscal crisis concerns the municipal cash-flow problem caused by the outpacing of revenues by expenditures. While New York City remains the most spectacular example of this crisis, requiring billions of federally guaranteed loan dollars to avoid bankruptcy, it is often forgotten that a city as large as Cleveland, Ohio, actually defaulted in 1978 (Swanstrom, 1985). Urban areas such as Buffalo, St. Louis, Detroit, Philadelphia, and Baltimore continue to receive half their revenue from the federal government and would also fall into receivership if this funding level were to cease. Such cities currently share with large private corporations like Chrysler, Lockheed, U.S. Steel, and the Penn-Central railroad a history of avoiding bankruptcy through the infusion of massive amounts of federally guaranteed loans. The last observation is an important one, because, while relatively easy to describe, the global nature of the fiscal crisis is grossly misunderstood. Mainstream political analysis is most responsible for this misconception because it treats political events in a compartmentalized manner without playing them against the backdrop of the larger society. Thus the linkages, brought to attention by neo-Marxists, between the political context of deficit spending and the progressive dependency of American corporations on public subsidization has been largely ignored. Furthermore, the fiscal crisis has somehow come to personify the ailing cities of the Frostbelt. Yet, many areas of the country have recently experienced budgetary problems as have also the higher levels of government, including counties and states. In short, the theoretical significance of what is apparently a free-floating shortfall of financial means at various levels of government and social organization has escaped mainstream concerns in favor of a more localized approach focused on individual cities themselves.

Since the spectacular advent of crisis a second fundamental element of this subject has introduced itself. Urban areas like New York have managed fiscal problems successfully. Techniques and structural changes that have been put in place to forestall or recover from municipal bankruptcy have managed well in steering ailing cities through a decade of potential financial collapse. The success of this effort throws into question all explanations once advanced for the fiscal crisis, especially theoretical approaches that considered crisis inevitable and intractable. The topic of fiscal crisis, therefore, is a fertile area for the evaluations of rival theories on urban politics.

In the main, conventional analysts seem content to describe the variety of factors that have made municipalities less able to raise necessary revenues without resorting to high levels of deficit financing. Lineberry and Sharkansky, for example, point to five separate sources of fiscal crisis (1978: 65-67). These include the fragmented nature of metropolitan government and the demographic shift to the suburbs; the socio-economic shift to the Sunbelt and the decline of the Frostbelt industrial base; inflation and its effect on municipal expenditures; the exhaustion of property tax and other local revenue sources; and the increase in demand for services despite declining population due to compositional changes in central city residents. Such factors describe supply and demand pressures quite well. However, they do not grasp the underlying reasons for why changes in such pressures, no matter how intense, have produced financial problems for cities at the particular time that they did. Even more important, why is it that by 1985 the fiscal crisis of American cities had largely disappeared? Surely the structural factors outlined above by conventional analysts have not simply vanished.

With the help of collaborators, I have examined these issues of fiscal crisis elsewhere (see Gottdiener, 1986). This material can be summarized although the reader is referred to this more extensive discussion and its bibliographic references. It is most profitable to review this material by way of assessing our four approaches to urban politics. To begin with, the fiscal crisis theory of most repute, that of O'Connor (1973), seems to have been largely refuted both by the nature of urban fiscal crisis itself and by its successful management. O'Connor's theory envisioned a general crisis of society that related Marxian economic theory and problems with the falling rate of profit to a hypothesized progressive and growing socialization by the State of social activities. Yet, we know now that there is no direct relation between economic and political crises of the budget, nor is there any general tendency of socialization pushed by the needs of monopoly capital in every social sector. Evidence suggests that the fiscal crisis of the 1970s was fundamentally a *political* event, despite its economic aspect (see Swanstrom, 1985). This observation is backed up by historical analysis on fiscal defaults that sees the recent past as not as statistically significant when compared with the profound crisis of public finance occurring in previous periods of economic depression (see Monkkonen, 1986). In addition, the economic crisis of capital popularized by Marxian crisis theorists in the 1970s was highly overrated. Recent evidence demonstrates the inherent vitality of the economy, and, in particular, the robust economic well-being of most city economies that were once cast in pictures of gloom and doom (see Ganz, 1986). Urban areas, even those located in the Frostbelt, maintain their economic dominance because of the strength of the activities that remain located there.

If neo-Marxist fiscal crisis theory has been abandoned, elements of that approach have proved most accurate in isolating the determinants of urban fiscal strains. Friedland (1980), for example, explains the genesis of crisis by showing how local State subsidization of corporate growth, while not matched by a general conjuncture of progressive socialization of social activities as O'Connor had suggested, nevertheless, became the main factor in producing the fiscal strains of urban areas in the 1970s. This result refutes noe-Conservative explanations of crisis that blamed pluralist politics for working too well in the promotion of special interests and which translated into prohibitive demands on services. It is *not* the burden of competing for votes by buying off constituencies that causes severe fiscal strain, as Shefter (1977) has suggested, although this no doubt is a secondary factor, but the burden of local State subsidization of growth that, according to Friedland (1980), figures as the main cause. Such an assertion is also backed up by the recent research of new political economists who document graphically the hidden dimension of State socialization of growth, as we have seen above.

Recent research on the fiscal condition of cities points out the surprisingly successful management of strain under new conditions of austerity. This not only involves new management techniques (see Matzer, 1986), but, also a withdrawal of State intervention reversing the socialization of consumption that once formed the heart of neo-Marxist collective consumption theory. The study of privatization or recommodification is quite new and only limitedly assessed, however, it validates assertions by neo-Conservatives that private sector mechanisms have a greater role to play in the supply of services than once supposed (see Savas, 1983), even if the result of reprivatization often does not support the claims of public choice theorists (see Marlowe, 1985; Rubin and Rubin, 1986).

The neo-Marxist perspective did not envision the quick response by public policy in renegotiating the socialization of wages at the expense of workers. At present austerity budgets are successfully in place in most American cities (Clark, 1978) and the growth of local expenditures has been brought under control, even if the costs of borrowing remain quite high (Clark and Ferguson, 1981). Evidence suggests that management has gone forward not only by installing new administrative techniques of budgeting, but by social control of protests against cutbacks (see Gottdiener, 1986). Ideological mechanisms that prevent the effective channeling of citizen discontent have demonstrated a formidable ability to control city governance under austerity (see Henig, 1986). The emergence of this previously ignored dimension of local politics and the State's powerful ability to canalize and block citizen demands will be considered in greater detail in Chapter 7. Thus, on balance aspects of both neo-Marxist and public choice theories have been borne out by the fiscal crisis and its aftermath. However, both theories also fail to account for, in the former case, the more fluid relation between the economy and the State involving the political nature of intervention, and, in the latter case, the hidden dimension of State subsidization of development under the ideological sign of growth.

State-centered views of the fiscal crisis are not only relevant but can be assessed in the same way as other approaches by the record of austerity management. According to State managerialism, economic crises are a particularly opportune time for the State. During these periodic moments the State moves to acquire greater control over the rest of society (Block, 1977). The fiscal crisis does not represent a crisis of this type. Rather, it is political in nature and involves the effort of capital to reclaim part of the ground lost to the State in previous economic crises. Consequently, just as the State moves periodically to gain greater power, capital moves at other times to temper this effect. Because the local State is dependent directly on finance capital, in the short run at least, this fraction is often the segment of capital that becomes the leading agent in the restructuring of the relation between the State and the economy in favor of business interests. As Block suggests,

> The recycling of traditional free market ideology with its emphasis on monetary restraint and balanced budgets was more a useful ideology to attack the state than a serious set of policy proposals [1980: 237].

For State managerialists, like Block, the current status quo is merely an impasse in the conflict between the interests of public bureaucrats and those of the capitalist class. Because capital needs active State intervention to unleash the productivity of its social relations, according to Block, the present forced retreat of the State in certain areas will aid in the heightening of new crisis potential and eventually lead to a new round of expansionary government intervention. So far, however, this has not occurred (for a critique of all theories that are based on the necessity of State intervention, such as managerialism, see the next chapter).

Recently, O'Connor (1981) has advanced an alternate explanation for retrenchment from within the Marxian tradition that is opposed to Block's theory and which also takes a more dynamic view of the relation between capitalism and the State. In particular, for O'Connor, current policies are not directed at the level of State involvement at all, as Block maintains, but at the working class itself through the medium of the State. According to O'Connor (1981: 46), if socialized consumption represents a forced payment to the working class through State regulation of capital, then present policies have reversed this tendency calling on labor to pay capital back by covering more of the expenses for its own reproduction directly from the wages fund.

Marxists, therefore, have some evidence for suggesting that the restructuring that took place as a consequence of the fiscal crisis, which affected social welfare programs greatly while leaving State subsidies to capital alone, may be a new form of the class war. If this has inadvertently attenuated the power of State managers by constraining local expenditures, this is an epiphenomenal effect of the class struggle itself. That is, capital has not moved against the State because its managers are the "dangerous class," rather, it has used the present social conditions, however complexly constituted, to move against its historical enemy, the working class by renegotiating the socialized component of wages. It must be pointed out that successful management of the fiscal crisis without the need for new State interventions of crisis management seem to lend support for the revised neo-Marxist position rather than the thesis of State managerialism.

In short, the argument between neo-Marxists and State managerialists over the significance of recent restructuring away from progressive levels of intervention centers on assessing which of the factors, the power of State managers, or, the class conflict between capital and labor over the welfare State, are an epiphenomenon of the other. Only a demonstration of which set of power relations is more basic to the overall relation between the society and the State can settle this issue. As in the case of our other inquiries, such a dispute requires greater understanding of the nature of the State.

Equity and the Supply of Social Services

Our final comparative topic is the question of equity. This issue relates the State directly to the fundamental issue of sustaining the quality of life. For this reason, the nature, extent and inequalities of public provision have become in recent years a major topic of urban political science.

From its beginnings, scholarship concerned with urban public service provision found that, while an aggregate measure for the quality of community life could be arrived at, such indicators hid glaring inequities in the supply of State resources to the disadvantage of lower-income areas. Recent research has tended to corroborate the presence of inequities in such resources as the supply of education (Sexton, 1961; Oakes, 1985), health care (Alford, 1975) and police protection (Nardulli and Stonecash, 1981). Studies of this kind have fed an already alarmed consciousness about the demographic patterns of racial and income segregation discovered by urban sociologists and demographers. A picture has emerged that depicts local public policies as reinforcing the spatial patterns of segregation in society produced by uneven capitalist development by an overlay of fiscal discrimination in favor of the wealthy and the white. Because life chances are a partial function of public resources, this meant that social stratification was reproduced intergenerationally and, furthermore, that local governments in the Unites States play an important role in perpetuating this pattern. Thus, while sociologists in the 1960s lamented the difficulties in achieving a racially and economically balanced community through residential choice, political scientists in the 1970s called attention to the role of local government in reproducing the inequities of segregated neighborhood location. Disputes over public service provision, therefore, have supplied the contents for much of local political activity in cities. In fact, these issues have multiplied as a consequence of the fiscal crisis.

Most recently, analysts of urban services have questioned the very possibility that the local State can be an effective policy instrument in the fight against societal uneven development. More specifically, the argument that municipalities possess culpability in aiding racial and income inequities has been attacked in certain specific ways. Several political scientists have assailed the view that local governments supply public services to residential localities in an inequitable fashion. Mlandenka and Hill (1977), for example, observed that park and recreation facilities were generally distributed in a uniform manner and, although some cities contained a major park near the wealthier areas, others had theirs located near the poorer sections of town. In addition to recreation, researchers observed that the supply of police, fire and sanitation services were equitably distributed in most metropolitan areas of the country. Finally, according to Megret (1981), while public liability for social service inequities had been substantiated in several court cases, there are also many important legal battles that have been lost on these same grounds. In short, the case against city administrations and their role in reproducing the system of social stratification is not as clear-cut as is the sheer weight of demographic evidence that substantiates the existence of racial and income residential segregation. Apparently in the United States there are a number of important *private* sector mechanisms, such as real estate industry "steering" and the dependency of lifestyle on personal income, that are also at work. As Ostrom suggests (1983), because political systems are not responsible for private sector inequities, they can hardly be considered their cause.

At present the question of inequity in the supply of public services is a highly debatable one, with several bones of contention yet unresolved. This is unfortunate because without a clear understanding of the proper role local government can play in social welfare policy, the uneven development produced by the private sector and the inequities produced by the social costs of growth cannot be resolved. For example, Coleman (1976) observes that the entire concept of what is meant by "equity" needs to be reexamined. A distinction can be made between the equitable supply of services per se or "input equality," and the supply of services in order to make up for the effects of sociospatial segregation, or "output equality." In the latter case it may be necessary to supply services inequitably in favor of lower-income and racially segregated areas. That is, it might be necessary for local government to be inequitable in order to compensate for past and present inequalities, especially if they have been produced by the uneven nature of societal development. As Lineberry (1977) has indicated, however, Coleman's distinction also leads to problems. In the limiting case, if all unnatural differences are eradicated, then inherited abilities or the meritocracy will rule, so that it is never possible to eliminate inequality. Furthermore, in instances where institutions have aggressively pursued policies such as affirmative action which attempt to rectify *past* histories of unequal treatment, they have occasionally been accused of conflicting with the commonly held belief that supports the meritocracy as a means of judging individual worth (see *Bakke v. State of California*). Most important for central city administrations, however, it is not at all clear that increased local spending for certain target populations and locations produces the kind of effects on deeply ingrained social inequities that are required to overcompensate for them. In fact, Murray (1984) has recently pointed out in an extended discussion that government welfare spending that is ill-advised may perpetuate rather than alleviate society's social problems. Thus, the concept of targeting for State intervention in domestic social programs in order to overcome past inequities remains, by itself, a problematic practice. As Lineberry remarks for the case of police protection,

> To achieve input equality, police department resources must be dispersed equally over the municipality; but to achieve output equality, resources will have to be clustered in high crime neighborhoods if victimization rates are to be equalized. This assumes, of course, that more police resources can reduce the crime rate, a proposition which is itself disputable [1977: 32].

Without question city supplied public goods and services are fundamental to sustaining the local quality of life and a good deal of political concern focuses on their character, quality and efficiency of delivery. Mainstream research on the use of such products as public policy instruments remains inconclusive regarding their effectiveness in overcoming past social inequities. This issue has been complicated further by the current shift to austerity budgets following the fiscal crisis of the 1970s. With cutbacks in needed services occurring at every level of government, the overall quality of life has suffered. At the same time, municipalities have been constrained severely in their ability to use policy as a means of fighting social inequities which are glaringly in evidence within our cities. This issue, however, should not be allowed to obscure the first aspect raised above regarding the nature of the local State's role in reproducing and accentuating the inequitable nature of the

American class structure. This is an issue which relates the production of uneven social development by the private sector, on the one hand, to questions involving social justice, State intervention and the egalitarian nature of democracy, on the other. In the specific case of the city, such questions resolve themselves as follows. Before municipal governments can be universally mandated as welfare policy instruments in the battle against social inequities, it is necessary to determine whether in fact they can ever play such a role, and, if so, under what circumstances. This question is addressed in Chapters 6 and 7.

In an important case study of one city, Lineberry tested standard explanations for inequality in the ecological distribution of fire, library, effluent water and park services. He found little evidence to support any hypothesis that suggests differentials systematically discriminate against the poorer and/or minority populations. In their place Lineberry's analysis uncovered the presence of differentials that were unsystematic or "unpatterned" (1977: 129). Consequently, he asserted that the most plausible explanation for existing inequities in the supply of public services is the "decision-rule" hypothesis, namely, that

> the quantity and/or quality of urban services are primarily functions of bureaucratic decision-rules made to simplify complex allocations of administrative time and resources [1977:67].

In short, Lineberry found evidence to suggest that public bureaucracies do not function intentionally to reproduce social inequities as some critics of existing State intervention suggest. Rather, their operation throws off random differentials in the supply of public goods and services which have variable effects on local populations within the city. As we have already seen, this explanation is in keeping with a State-centered perspective (deriving from neo-Weberianism), and possesses the limitations of that one sided approach. More recent research (Hero and Durand, 1985; Thomas, 1982) suggests that the perspective of "unpatterned inequalities" may not be as important to political behavior as other factors, even those, such as personal contacts, deriving from within the State managerialist tradition.

What can be learned from a generalized assessment of the topic of social service inequity, such as the one just given? Quite specifically the level of theoretical understanding with which research on this question has proceeded is critically weak. For example, according to Katznelson (1979), analyses like Lineberry's that test explanations for inequities through single case studies fail to deal with the essential significance of differentials in public service supply. Katznelson questions the selectivity with which some services are examined in this research and not others.

Thus, there is wide variability as well in the patterned supply among *all* city services, an observation that escapes bureaucratic decision-rule researchers. In particular, from the more theoretical perspective of neo-Marxism, some services, such as education are more important to an understanding of the differential reproduction of life chances than are others such as recreation. Despite this fact, however, inequities in the provision of public resources, such as education, which are paramount in the promotion of positive life chances are not the central concern of most researchers that study the process of "unpatterned inequality." In short, according to Katznelson, research which explains differentials in social service supply by focusing on selected interventions of local government alone fails to capture the interconnected role such services play in the larger system of social organization. More significantly, this research fails to examine the ways in which privileged groups protect and improve their own social positions through differential effects on the supply of collectivized forms of consumption. As Katznelson notes,

The study [i.e., Lineberry's] takes as given the provision of services by other levels of government and, even more importantly, the existing distribution of space, wealth and income. These are not normative but analytical shortcomings. The meaning and impact of the distribution of services at the municipal level can be understood only in terms of the ways in which the total package of government activity modifies market allocations for various groups. The non-findings of Lineberry's analysis are useful precisely to the degree that they reveal the impossibility of artificially isolating this or that feature of state policy from the larger mutually dependent relationships of which they are a part [1979: 272].

In sum, the issue of whether or not equality in public service supply exists at the level of local government for specific services is not as important as understanding the inter-relationships between the role of local government and the greater patterning of life chance resources by the system of social organization which sustains the quality of life. This issue is addressed most directly by neo-Marxist perspectives on the welfare State. With this realization we come full circle back to the critique of neo-Weberianism discussed at the beginning of this chapter. As Pickvance (1984a) suggests, it is only when a suitable level of abstraction is achieved that the benefits of the neo-Marxian approach to the welfare State over other perspectives can be understood.

In a real sense mainstream urban political scientists have reduced the local State's role in sustaining the quality of life to the study of concrete details regarding the pattern of public service provision. For example, they analyze services without asking themselves or their readers to understand the role of public provision in the reproduction of society's social relations. This practice seems to suggest that the quality of education functions in the same way as the supply of water or the presence of parks. If mainstreamers wish to hide behind the arbitrary definitions of subject matter that isolate urban political scientists from entertaining questions regarding economic inequities simply because they may not have a direct bearing on the structures or processes of governance, then at least students of these issues possess the alternative of neo-Marxist inquiries. It is not necessary to be a Marxist to accept the overwhelming empirical evidence that certain aspects of public provision, such as education or the biased subsidization of homeownership, differentially affect the life chances of certain privileged population groups. Nor, for that matter, is it necessary to be a mainstreamer in order to acknowledge that, at the level of government performance, the bureaucratic decision-rule mechanism explains many of the differentials in socialized consumption. The theoretical issues raised by the clash between neo-Weberian and neo-Marxian approaches can only be resolved by an analysis of the theory of the State (see also Pickvance, 1984a, for a comparative assessment with virtually the same conclusion).

The four theories of local politics discussed in the previous two chapters have all tried to assess the State's role in the larger scheme of social organization. Each of these perspectives share an underlying assumption that State intervention aims to manage the capitalist system and reproduce conditions that ensure its survival. This assumption, the *necessity* of the State, pervades the very heart of current knowledge regarding the nature of the State itself from both Marxian and more mainstream approaches. According to conventional academic wisdom, "system management" seems to be the preeminent social role of the State. This assumption runs deep, as Jones, for example, remarks: "It is not the role of the economic system to calculate the externalities generated by [such] investment flows. It is the role of the political system" (1983: 53).

It is probably for this reason that all citizens—liberals as well as conservatives, renters as well as homeowners, workers as well as capitalists—continue to look to the State as the means of sustaining the quality of community life. Consequently, it is also for this reason that aspects of State intervention constitute the contents of local politics. If by some chance the primal assumption regarding the necessity of the State's role as the manager of daily life were reexamined and questioned, a very different sort of politics might also reveal itself. Such is the purpose of the next two chapters, which not only assess the relation between the State and society, but also question the necessity of the former to the latter.

CHAPTER 5

THE LOCAL STATE—PART I:
A THEORY OF THE LOCAL STATE

In the 1950s social scientists knew very little about the nature of local government. There were small differences seen between the composition of community interests or the fate of localism expressed in social and economic terms, and the interests represented in local politics. Early studies on community life, such as those of the Lynds (1937) and of Warner (1949), provided us with a picture of political control that was qualitatively intertwined with the actions of a social and economic elite. This select group was observed mobilizing organizational resources of local government to modify the effects of social change caused by powerful forces emanating from outside the community.

As is the case today, these earliest studies document that the content of town politics is generated by the demands placed upon the local State to adjust to the uncoordinated process of capitalist development. Early forms of the power-elite view found evidence for the use of the local State as an instrument guiding the adjustment process for the benefit of capital. Such a theme preserves its continuity from the 1930s to the recent work of Domhoff (1983) among power elitists. It finds expression even in more structurally oriented accounts, such as that of Cockburn (1979), that view the local State as a mere cog in the administrative apparatus of national governance that stands in the service of capital.

It is within this context that a measure of the significance of the pluralist challenge to elitist theory can be appreciated.

Paraphrasing some well-worn synopses of this approach, pluralism asserts that there is no single power base from which local government decisions are directed. Instead, political influence is diffuse, that is, pluralistically held. Government decision making is a process of competition and bargaining among separate sources of influence. Elected officials do the best they can to resolve differences according to a commonly shared conception of equity. Pluralists maintain that while not every particular decision is resolved in accordance with this norm, over time every interest will share eventually in the benefits of public policy. Thus it is entirely plausible from within this perspective for powerful special interests to control government, as power structure studies suggest. Pluralists, however, maintain that such control is unstable and will eventually be countered by more democratic expressions of organized interest. In short, while ruling-class theorists see a concordance between economic and political elites, pluralists find a polyglot of separate interests confronting and negotiating with each other under the benevolent and neutral auspices of the local political leadership.

Since the 1950s, the debate between power elitists and pluralists has continued almost unabated. Positions first staked out in the early days have been repeatedly restated even in the most contemporary of contexts (Polsby, 1980; Domhoff, 1979, 1983). It is now apparent that theoretical discussions of local government need to resolve this issue. That is, in order to discuss the nature of local State power, it is necessary to plow through the literature on the nature of the State itself. Yet, given the terms of the debate over community power, it is not possible to resolve the differences between power elitists and pluralists as they are conceptualized because both perspectives raise an issue that they cannot resolve, namely, the specification of power in the relationship between the economy and the State. On the one hand, contemporary power elitists see the sphere of economic activity as determining the long-run interest behind local government policy because the political ruling class and the economic ruling class are united at the higher circles of State (see Whitt, 1982). For Domhoff (1971), in particular, this power elite is an operating arm of the capitalist class, which uses political control as an instrument of domination for that class. Pluralists, on the other hand, view the State and the economy as mutually independent spheres of activity. While one possesses linkages to the other, pluralism asserts the structural independence of local government from economic interests.

The banes of power-elite theory are its inability to avoid economic reductionism and its voluntaristic view of political power. While the business community plays an important role in influencing local government decisions, the analysis of that linkage and of the structural base of economic power by elitist theorists is much too simplistic (Offe and Ronge, 1975; Stone, 1976). To be sure, it is not possible to refute the findings of Domhoff, and over the years he has helped greatly in documenting the structure of the ruling class. However, analysts have asked, quite correctly, whether the discovery of this interconnected ruling class also explains the way power operates in society. As Block (1977) has shown, capitalists reap the rewards of State intervention often without the need for the kind of instrumental control that power elitists claim animates the State. In contradistinction, pluralists have their own limitations. They have traveled too far from determinacy. Pluralists reduce the State to an unbiased mechanism of community management. Their assertion that the power of interests is tempered by a political bargaining process mediated by neutral government officials within the public arena is patently false in its assumptions both about the way power operates in society and about the disinterested nature of the local government apparatus.

Perhaps the most interesting aspect of the clash between pluralists and power elitists is the fact that each camp is convinced of the correctness of their perspective despite the claims of the other, while neither feel the need to pass beyond the terms of their debate to engage the more recent work on the theory of the State. In both cases their conceptions of power and its functioning in society remain quite limited. Lukes (1974), for example, has been most insistent that both pluralists and elitists suffer from what he calls "methodological individualism" (1974: 22), namely, an exclusionary focus on the immediate, behavioral aspects of politics while ignoring the structural basis of power. As Whitt (1982: 22) summarizes, early power-structure research failed to develop an appreciation for the many faces of power. There is not only a second face deriving from the ability of powerful interests to suppress issues and set the agenda of politics (Bachrach and Baratz's contribution), there is also a *third* face that Lukes describes as the institutional bias of the State apparatus itself (1974, 1977).

For Lukes (1982: 22), the apparatus of State has its own bias that can be mobilized "in ways that are neither consciously chosen nor the intended result of particular individual's choices." Yet the apparatus of State possesses the ability to structure economic and social processes in distinct ways (see Clark and Dear, 1984). In the preceding chapters we have seen that the many faces of power make the understanding of the State's role in society a difficult task. Armed with this insight, a survey of salient issues in State theories and the many crosscutting arguments revolving around the relation between the State and society over the last few years reveals a growing appreciation for the structural aspects of power and a focus on the apparatus of government itself as a progressively more important area of analysis. Because there are three faces of power, theories of local politics based on voluntaristic, behavioral premises fail to account for the independent effects of structure.

Over the years analysts from both the pluralist and power-elitist camps have acquired a growing appreciation for the action of the State apparatus in determining political outcomes. Put a different way, whether we consider Marxists, elitist, or pluralist arguments, the line of reasoning that has become increasingly more salient in recent years is the growing use of features particular to the character of the local State itself as a central, if not independent, factor in explanations of the political process. This is not necessarily an exclusive focus on the State or the kind of "State-centered" approach discussed in the preceding chapter, where I argued that it is not proper to be forced to choose between the two alternatives that this concept suggests. Rather, the emerging sensibility combines social with State-centered factors in explaining political outcomes.

Consequently, research into the role of the local State has resulted in an increasing amount of attention focused on the State/society interface defined in institutional or structural terms. This object of analysis is the locus of an emergent problematic that I believe lies at the heart of contemporary research displacing other earlier concerns, such as the questions of equity or social justice. Instead, research supports the view that processes of local politics and preference articulation are filtered and even constrained considerably in influence by the action of the State apparatus. For this reason, the structure of governance, the interests of State managers, and the apparatuses of intervention all play an increasing role in urban political analysis.

This convergence of interest on the role of the State framework as an independent factor in political outcomes may be illustrated by the arguments of stratificationists, such as Stone (1976, 1980, 1982), who have attempted to resolve the pluralist/power-elitist debate by a careful examination of the relative success of social demands and articulated needs in being differentially addressed by the local political apparatus. Stone (1976) convincingly substantiates the variable way that features of social stratification mesh together with the discretionary behavior of government decision makers. According to

Stone, the needs of segments of the population, no matter how deeply felt or self-evident, as in the case of minority demands for slum renovation, do not automatically get addressed with critical priorities by public officials. Instead, the local government bureaucracy is highly attuned to specific features of social stratification, such as business influence, lifestyle, and organizational competence, in making decisions regarding public policy that are then carried out at their discretion. As he states (1976: 6),

> Policy results not from the mere presence of demands, but from the decisions of public officials who choose variously to alter, reject or assent to demands. Thus, while the socio-economic environment is a generator of demands for public action, this environment does not necessarily generate consistent demands. Demands give rise to counter demands, and choice making is intertwined with the forces of political struggle.

Stone carried out a case study of the variable success of special-interest implementation in urban-renewal efforts in the city of Atlanta. He found that local government possessed a bureaucratic (i.e., noneconomic) bias against the poor and in favor of organized interests from the business community. In addition, public officials were "predisposed to act favorably" on proposals from these same business interests (1976: 195). Consequently, while not dominating local government, those interests rating high in various indicators of social stratification fared best, almost exclusively so, in having their needs addressed. The principal reason for this outcome was found to reside in the operation of city bureaucracy and not through some alleged concordance of interests between local officials and business, as power elitists would suggest. Stone's analysis confirms other State managerialist findings about the power of bureaucratic discretion in affecting political outcomes. Aspects of the State, therefore, circumscribe and define the relevant research questions.

In a second example of this concordant sensibility to the study of local government, the pluralist Yates (1976) has also found the need to focus on characteristics internal to the local State itself. Arguing against the "society-centered" views of policy determinists, Yates has come to appreciate the independent effect of government officials. As he states (p. 235),

> What has been lacking in urban research to date, however, is an exploration of the urban policy-making process viewed from the perspective of mayors and high level administrators who deal with urban problems and policies on a day-to-day basis.

Yates finds local government to be essentially unguided by any overarching or unified policy perspectives. Assuming that public officials are neutral mediators of the political process, Yates locates the performance of their task within a structural context in which many day-to-day decisions are required in order to respond to variable and often conflicting public demands. Coordination of these decisions is not possible primarily because the city administration itself is fragmented. There is a horizontal division of jurisdictions between city hall and a variety of semi-independent public agencies, commissions, and boards, as well as city departments with their own entrenched public officials and perspectives. In addition, there is also a vertical division of authority among the levels of government that stratifies further the arenas of decision making. Hence, Yates (1976: 244) asserts that

> systematic fragmentation leads to a political and governmental free-for-all that makes urban policy making chaotic and unstable. More precisely, the fragmentation of urban government at every level produces an almost anarchic structure of demands and policy conflicts. It produces scores of different individual and institutional interests which "fight" over urban programs and policies in a policy-making context of procedures

and decision networks that may vary with every different "fight."

Yates calls this state of affairs "street-fighting pluralism" and claims that as a consequence of the fragmented nature of the local government decision-making process, the city itself is "ungovernable" (1977). That is, according to this view, no single constellation of interests, neither power elitist nor pluralist, canalizes the process of decision making with any overarching degree of intelligence or coordination.

As the above examples attest, the present mode of discourse on the nature of local government illustrates a greater recognition of, and appreciation for, the contingent nature of political activity and of the influence of characteristics internal to the State itself in determining policy outcomes. The manner in which this concept is articulated varies from perspective to perspective and is responsible for a proliferation of separate terms all aimed at capturing the more fluid picture of local political processes, such as "systemic power," "street-fighting pluralism," "relative autonomy," and so on. These conceptions, in turn, reflect fundamental theoretical positions on the relation between the State and society that differ from each other. However, the days have long since passed when the nature of the local State could be framed as a debate between Marxists, on the one hand, who advocated its determined control by the ruling class, and pluralists, on the other, who viewed local politics as an open-ended process of bargained outcomes. In short, a discussion of the nature of local politics must take into account the many separate theoretical perspectives on the State and somehow resolve the contentious issues they raise.

The growing sophistication of State theories is also exemplified by the clash within Marxism between instrumentalists and structuralists. Once again it is possible to show that underlying these arguments are fundamental assumptions over whether voluntaristic or structural factors are more important in determining political outcomes. According to Miliband (1969), while the State performs many functions in society its principal role is to act as a system manager for the capitalist class. The State is, therefore, an instrument of that class that is mobilized in order to ameliorate the crisis tendencies of the capitalist system (see also Habermas, 1975). For this reason, powerful economic interests, while perhaps only representing fractions of capital, mobilize control over society through the extension of State power and as a means of ensuring the reproduction of capitalist social relations, especially during times of crisis (Block, 1977: 355; Domhoff, 1971).

In a much-read debate, the instrumentalist approach was challenged by the Marxian structuralists possessed of a separate theoretical conception of the State that is opposed to voluntarism. The work of structuralists is exemplified best by Nicos Poulantzas (1973, 1975), who moved Marxian State theory away from its limited focus on the behavior of individuals. For Poulantzas, the State operates according to systemic imperatives emerging from the practices of capitalist relations and cannot be understood as something that is controlled as a "thing" or apparatus by the whims of any single group no matter how powerful. In order to grasp this structuralist thought on the State, it is essential to follow closely Poulantzas's argument, a task seldom attempted by American advocates of European theories.

Poulantzas distinguishes between relations of production, or relations between people and things, and what he called "the field of social relations," or relations among people. This concept is specific to structuralist analysis and has been accepted by Marxists following Poulantzas's approach. However, I shall challenge this distinction in the theory of the State presented below. According to Poulantzas, political processes belong to this conceptualization of the field of social relations. Because class conflict is the determining aspect of those relations in capitalism, the State is produced by the field of social relations as a condensation of the class struggle. This is the origin of the structuralist claim that politics is, above all else, a phenomenon of the class struggle. It is also in this sense that the State, understood as a structure or a shell only and located within the field of social relations, is "relatively autonomous" from the rest of society. It possesses degrees of freedom from specified social interests "vis-à-vis the classes and fractions of the power bloc and by extension, vis-à-vis its allies and supports" (1973: 256).

The State, for neo-Marxists following Poulantzas, defines a domain of activity wherein separate classes and class fractions operate as social forces in conflict with other classes and fractions. In this view political power is defined as the capacity of a social class to realize its own objective interests through the framework of politics. In this way, although power is unequally held, each class is limited by its own structural capacities to affect political change. Consequently, only the State itself possesses the ability to intervene in the interests of society as a whole. From a structuralist conception, however, State intervention can only occur according to systemic preconditions and practices so that the State itself is also limited by a certain structural capacity as well. The latter is specific to particular social formations and defines, therefore, their political limits. State intervention acts automatically as the reproducer of capitalist relations of production within its own State limits, and according to the principles that are operant in the system of social organization as a whole (Poulantzas, 1973: 245); that is, the State is a creature of the society that is tied to it.

State intervention, regardless of its content, which may favor first one fraction and then another, must follow the lines of action structured by capitalist social relations (in our society, that is) belonging to the social formation. It can never intervene by threatening the base of power belonging to the bourgeoisie. For Poulantzas, it is precisely because the State apparatus is not merely an instrument of class rule that it can operate "politically" in the field of social relations and mediate economic antagonisms so that it is relatively autonomous from economic interests. In the final analysis, the State serves to reproduce the very same type of social relations that exists in the private sphere, because it is a product of those same relations. Consequently, regardless of the specific nature of its intervention, its actions must operate to sustain the dominance of the bourgeoisie, if only in the very "last instance."

Despite the many weaknesses of the structuralist approach of Poulantzas (see Hindess, 1978; Jessop, 1982), this perspective has been retained by neo-Marxian analysis because it explains political phenomena in terms of the class struggle at the same time that it also asserts the institutional separation of the State from the economic base of capitalism and as located in the field of social relations pertinent to the social formation. In this manner, the approach of Poulantzas, known as the "relative-autonomy" argument, is deployed as the neo-Marxist perspective on the State. For example, according to Devine (1983: 608),

> recent developments in neo-Marxist theory contend that the advanced capitalist state, and its structure and practices, exhibit a significant degree of "autonomy" from the economic base (Poulantzas, 1975) and, thus, should be conceptualized as simultaneously "a product, an object, and a determinant of the class struggle" (Esping-Anderson et al., 1976: 106). That is, within certain structural parameters and according to the logic of historically specific selection processes which serve to limit options, shape policy choices and circumscribe the terrain of decision making, the state exercises relative independence from the domination of any particular class (or fraction thereof) and, thus, may act in the interests of society-as-a-whole as well as more particularistic groups [see Block, 1977; Wright, 1978].

Neo-Marxists, therefore, retain the view that the State is
separated from the relations of production and is specified,
instead, by what Poulantzas has called the "field of social
relations." In what follows below, I shall show that this concept
is fallacious because it is derivative of other deep-level forces.
Consequently, it is not possible to specify the capitalist State
solely in terms of the class struggle, as neo-Marxists believe.

Given the parameters of the debate between instrumentalists
and Marxian structuralists, they appear divided in two distinct
ways. First, instrumentalism is relatively more deterministic
because it has not developed a clear analysis of the fractions of
capital. Consequently, the State for instrumentalists is wielded
by the influence of capital "in general" in a manner conceptualized very much as power elitists conceptualize it,
namely, as a tool of the bourgeoisie defined as some monolithic
presence. In contrast, Marxian structuralists are aware of class
fractions and the often contentious nature of the relations
among them. In fact, Poulantzas assigns to the "new petite
bourgeoisie" of white-collar professionals, public employees,
and so on, a special historical role in contemporary society as a
mediating bridge between the industrial proletariat and the
bourgeoisie.

The outcomes of State actions are not as deterministically
controlled as instrumentalists assert. However, while State
intervention has more contingent outcomes, it is, nevertheless,
unified around fulfilling the needs of the capitalist class. For
this reason, Marxian structuralists locate Althusser's concept
of "determination in the last instance" as the function of the
State in perpetuating capitalist relations of production. Put a
different way, while the outcomes of public policy are contingent on the results of class conflict, State intervention is
constrained so that it cannot challenge the fundamental
premises of capitalist accumulation, but manages this process
in the interests of the survival of the system as a whole. Thus,
the State for structuralists operates as an "ideal collective
capitalist," and its relative autonomy from particular powerful

capitalist-class fractions provides it with the degrees of freedom to perform this task.

A second difference between instrumentalists and Marxian structuralists is also very important and involves oppositional conceptions of the role of human action in social processes. This difference also explains the limited appreciation by structuralists of the work of power elitists. As already indicated, instrumentalism is a "voluntaristic" theory. It views politics as played out by subjectively independent individuals aggregated into collectivities on the basis of fundamental economic interests. Capital relations are class relations stemming from the need of a social group, the capitalists, to control the production process in order to expropriate the products of labor and accumulate capital. In fact, as with power elitists as well, instrumentalists seek to identify discrete individuals holding political and economic power and try to uncover the interlocking networks between the two realms in an effort to prove their hypothesis regarding the instrumental control of the State.

In contrast, however, neo-Marxian structuralism is opposed to all voluntaristic explanations of human agency. The essence of Althusserian structuralism is its attempt to do away with human agency as a determinant of social phenomena and humanist Marxism's subjective view of class. According to this argument, individual actors are constrained by structures to behave in specific predetermined ways. Furthermore, the "laws of motion" of society are conceived of as constituting subjectivity itself—in this Althusser follows Lacan—so that human agents merely act out roles preprogrammed by deep-level processes, such as those studied by students of socialization. This perspective is completely foreign to the approach of power elitists such as Domhoff, for example (see Clark and Dear, 1984).

With regard to the State, such an epistemological perspective means that structuralists reject the instrumental view of class control by the human agency of the ruling class and see the approach of pluralism as a thinly disguised mystification of class conflict. Analysis of politics proceeds, from a structuralist position, by identifying the objective needs of classes and class fractions and by observing how such interests play themselves out as social practices operating on the featureless terrain of the local State, but, following Poulantzas, within the domain of social relations. These outcomes are not predetermined. For this reason, if the workers at a particular moment happen to possess the more formidable class capacity to realize their interests, then public policy will reflect that outcome. Alternatively, whenever capitalists are hegemonic in the public domain, their interests will be met. Usually the clash among interests effects some kind of accommodation, hence the structuralists refer to political outcomes as the "condensation" of class interests.

According to this view, while the State may possess an objective framework, it has no deterministic characteristics of its own. In fact, for Poulantzas (1973), any approach that pays attention to the differential variations in representational forms and localized policy outcomes among bourgeois societies, a practice that virtually defines mainstream political science, is merely an ideological obfuscation of the deep-level structural forces at work determining political outcomes by structuring class capacities and interests. Such a distinction is a central source of contention between neo-Marxists and neo-Weberians, as we shall see below.

It was important to trace out the differences between structuralists and voluntarists among Marxists if only because many of their ideas have crept into the vocabulary of mainstream social science. Whether or not we can accept the radical implications of antivoluntarism, it is nevertheless clear that mainstream formulations of political action have hitherto failed to resolve the issues raised in the debate between structuralists and voluntarists. Most Americans follow Weber and Parsons quite closely and view social relations from an action frame of reference. While this position can be defended, it neglects important information discovered about the ways in which ideological conditioning through socialization processes affect how individuals perceive social issues. Thus, the characteristic assumption of mainstream analysis, often only implied, is that groups can always be reduced to the autonomous individual. As such, questions about the conditioning of class or social position in personal biographies and its role in affecting political behavior are most often ignored. The fallacy of such reasoning can be illustrated by Nordlinger (1981), who defines the State purely in terms of the individuals that comprise it. As he asserts (1981: 9),

> First, the definition of the state must refer to individuals rather than to some other kinds of phenomena, such as "institutional arrangements" or the "legal-normative order." Since we are primarily concerned with the making of public policy, a conception of the state that does not have individuals at its core could lead directly into the anthropomorphic and reification fallacies.

The days when American analysts can hide their ignorance of structuralism by suggesting that it merely reifies social relations have long since passed. By such spurious arguments as above, mainstream analysts ignore the effect that the social stratification of resources plays in structuring political processes. Reducing class capacities merely to individual interests alone leads Nordlinger to the unfortunate assertion that the State can be reduced merely to those public officials in control of its framework (1981: 3, 11), a position that ignores the formidable effects of its structure. There can be no understanding of the State that does not include an analysis of its forms (see Jessop, 1982). Nordlinger's State-centered approach may be classified as voluntarist because of its focus on the autonomy of individual public officials. There are other mainstream approaches, however, that recognize the ability of systemic characteristics to influence behavior. For example, Peterson (1981) identifies what he calls the "interest of the city," an aggregate property of this sociospatial form, which helps explain public-policy outcomes; that is, cities have an identifiable interest,

> because cities consist of a set of social interactions structured by their location in a particular territorial space. Any time that social interactions come to be structured into recurring patterns, the structure thus formed develops an interest in its own maintenance and enhancement. It is in this sense, that we speak of the interests of an organization, the interests of the system, and the like. To be sure within cities as within any other structure, one can find diverse social roles, each with its own sets of interests. But these varying role interests, as divergent and competing as they may be, do not distract us from speaking of the overall interests of the larger structural entity.

Such reasoning is not structuralist, despite its tone, and cannot be defended. Peterson, in fact, has merely moved in the polar direction from Nordlinger while not escaping the dimension of voluntarism. Like the latter, he ignores the differential composition of group and class interests that are contradictory and cannot be summed up by some idealist conception. Spatial forms cannot possess a reified interest because they are themselves social products (Gottdiener, 1985a). In reality Peterson's city interest is really the interest of the dominant growth coalition in control of the city framework, which can bring development to the city, but which can also saddle the polity with the overburdening costs of growth that are not in the public's interest. Consequently, by failing to escape the dimension of voluntarism, mainstream approaches merely apply different idealist conceptions of social process that cannot help us understand local politics.

In addition to the two poles of structuralism and voluntarism, there is a third position or type of assertion that is intermediate between them. Within this space are located analysts who have argued that both voluntaristic interests and structural determinants come together to produce aspects of political behavior in a manner that involves the interaction between social processes and individual discretion. As Harrington (1983) remarks, these approaches may be called "dualistic models" because they hypothesize that local State policy is determined by the play between external pressures and the ability of State managers to act in their own interests. The best-known arguments exemplifying this intermediate view are those deriving from neo-Weberianism. As discussed in Chapter 4, this approach assigns to State bureaucrats interests of their own that they often pursue and that at times can conflict with the needs of important social interests external to government, such as those of the capitalist class. The special interest of State managers is voluntaristically manifested and is not determined by production relations. In the approach of Block (1980), State managers can act as a class in their own interests by advancing the power of the State at the expense of society, especially during times of crisis (1980: 233). This separate interest internal to the State itself is most often conceived of as based in the rational principles of public administration perfected over the years by the application of knowledge to the field of social management. As Wirt (1983), for example, argues, the autonomous interest of local bureaucrats is structured by such "professional" considerations that have their origins in the occupational-training paradigms of formal schools of bureaucratic management and administration.

The State-manager perspective is intermediate between the two epistemologically extreme approaches to human agency, because the voluntaristic freedom of bureaucrats is always viewed as constrained by the actions of social forces external to the State. Within these boundaries, defined by all dualist models, State managers are said to possess autonomy from societal interests because the courses of action that they take are dictated by the internalized rationality of professional State administration. Thus the autonomous interest of State bureaucrats is an important explanatory variable for understanding public policy and often leads to the enhanced power of the State itself at the expense of society. This theory also suggests that in certain specific historical situations it is the State managers that can act to bring about social change over against the wishes of any society-centered interest.

The basic problem with dualist models that assign to State managers the role of historical subject (see Block, 1980) is the essential rationality imputed to their actions. This orientation is exemplified by all State-managerialist approaches that explain the actions of bureaucrats according to uniform practices of State administration. Recently, a separate perspective has appeared that is antivoluntarist but differs from structuralism because it sees power itself as an independent force in society that underlies even the actions of structure. The practice of power is not as rational as students of State managerialism believe. The principal exponent of this view is Michel Foucault. For Foucault, history can be viewed as progress in a learning process of social control.

Foucault defines a generic category of knowledge and techniques belonging to society as a whole and available to any power user that subjugates the body to some social order. He calls this the political technology of the body. The distinguishing characteristics of this technology are its diffuse nature, located within the general field of power relations, and its constitution as piecemeal, incremental interventions, which operate cumulatively as an ensemble through the organizing ability of power itself. As Foucault (1979: 26) suggests,

Of course, this technology is diffuse, rarely formulated in continuous, systematic discourse; it is often made up of bits and pieces; it implements a disparate set of tools or methods. In spite of the coherence of its results, it is generally no more than a multiform instrumentation. Moreover, it cannot be localized in a particular type of institution or State apparatus. For they have recourse to it, they use, select or impose certain of its methods. But, in its mechanisms and its effects, it is situated at a quite different level. What the apparatus and institutions operate is, in a sense, a microphysics of power, whose field of validity is situated in a sense between the great functionings and the bodies themselves with their materiality and their forces.

According to Foucault, the political technology of power cannot be possessed. It is only *exercised* as a strategy of social control. Its use transforms those that are dominant as well as the subjugated. Consequently, the microphysics of power exists at the deepest structural level and relations of power are not mere phenomenal effects of other social forces. As he suggests (p. 26),

> This means that these relations go right down into the depths of society, that they are not localized in the relations between the state and its citizens or on the frontier between classes and that they do not merely reproduce, at the level of individuals, bodies, gestures, and behavior, the general form of the law or government; that although there is continuity there is neither analogy nor homology, but a specificity of mechanism and modality.

In short, the microphysics of power is a structural fact. It constitutes a field of relations that animates behavior rather than a property in the possession of individuals who then activate it. State intervention is only one type of power exercised in society. Yet, Foucault's ideas have special pertinence here. The French regulationist perspective on the State, in particular, has applied these ideas with considerable effect (see Lebas, 1982). While neo-Marxist theory bound itself closely to the premise of increasing State intervention and its fiscal crisis, by following Foucault the regulationist school was better able to explain the current retreat of the State. The study of domination through the State apparatus reveals that, unlike the State managerialist perspective, the exercise of power is not always rational nor in the interest of any specific group. State intervention cannot be explained as following the logic of capital. Rather, it responds to the force of power which, in the microphysics of the field of all power relations, binds both capital and the State together in a strategy of social control. This exercise of power tying the State to capital is called, by the regulationist school, a "regime of accumulation." It is a structuralist product and does not rely on voluntaristically perceived needs or logic by either capitalists or State bureaucrats. Rather, it is an outcome of regulation and the exercise of power that is conditioned by the interplay between the dominators and the dominated. As summarized by Lebas (1982: xviii),

> the development of the all-embracing system of regulation is not a conscious political and bureaucratic objective on the part of state and capital but rather a mass cultural movement, a slow evolution towards a consensual acceptance of being regulated, not by state and capital as two separate logics, but by an integrated capitalist-state logic which can permeate all aspects of social and private life.

In short, by focusing on power rather than the State itself, it is observed that political relations belong to a general category of power relations in society. This is a view that is at variance with that of neo-Marxism, as indicated above, because the latter locates political relations within a field of social relations without accounting for the independent effects of the will to power. The regulation of daily life structures activities according to the microphysics of power and unites capital with the State in a greater orchestration of social control within regimes of accumulation.

The main drawback with the approach of Foucault is his need to generalize the nature of power in order for him to make his argument about its structural properties. He goes too far in ignoring the way that particularized interests use the technology of control for distinct needs. Thus while he assigns a limited role to social institutions that exercise power for their own purposes, it is precisely this phenomenon that becomes most important in the analysis of social conflict. For example, in his discussion (1979) of the social history of discipline and punishment, the special tortures reserved for opponents of the State are not acknowledged even though, as in the inaugural example of the regicide, Damiens (see Chapter 1; Foucault, 1979), these cases are especially pertinent to Foucault's argument. In practice, applications of this perspective, therefore, can ignore specific interests, such as those of social classes and State managers, that provide a greater understanding of social processes than attention paid to power relations itself. As Bleitrach and Chenu (1982: 110) observe,

> Because of this research often ends up with explanations in terms of rather generalized and abstract notions of power and desire, and with a view of the state and social relations characterized by a diffusely-conceived domination rather than by classes and class-based exploitation.

Recognizing the autonomous role of power relations in society, therefore, also means recognizing the way that specific social interests use the techniques of domination to advance their own needs. Thus while it is essential to argue against the excessively rationalist view of State managers as historical subjects, advanced by the perspectives of State managerialism and dualist models of the political process, it is also necessary to agree with this approach that the State has a unique interest of its own that cannot be reduced to other ones operating in society, and against the views of both neo-Marxists and blind followers of Foucault.

Our survey of approaches to the State has ranged far afield and includes four separate epistemological perspectives on the nature of political relations: voluntarism, structuralism, dualist models, and the microphysics of power. In sum, explorations of the relation between the State and society align themselves according to two separate analytical dimensions that can help us cross-classify approaches to politics. On the one hand, there are theories that range from determinism to probabilistic contingency. The extreme case of the former would be vulgar Marxist economism and of the latter Yates's neopluralism. According to this distinction theories of urban government differ with regard to the assertion that identifiable interests in society are in possession of degrees of ability to control the outcomes of the political process. Determinists see the State as a mere adjunct of class interests, while contingent theories, such as pluralism, view this process as open ended according to underlying values of equity and the force of countervailing powers that then give it direction.

In addition, there is also a second dimension that helps differentiate approaches. Analysts also differ with regard to whether the State is comprised of voluntaristic or structurally determined actions. With the recent decline in the influence of Althusserian antivoluntarism, most State theorists now subscribe to a position intermediate between these two extremes. They grant to the State, in the form of its bureaucrats, degrees of freedom in political actions that follow interests autonomous of other social forces. Thus for neo-Marxists and neo-Weberians in particular, "autonomy" does not mean a total freedom to act independently, as it does in the voluntaristic approach of Nordlinger, rather that, although subject to social constraints, State managers possess an interest of their own that is independent of others centered in society.

These separate dimensions are summarized by the following figure, Figure 1, which also locates the separate positions of theoretical analysts. Recent years have witnessed a drift toward stances that are intermediate between the several extremes and, more important, a growing emphasis on the State itself as possessed of an identifiable and independent interest in the political process. One measure of the influence of Foucault is that by paying attention to the role of power and domination, the excessively rationalistic study of intervention, promulgated by State-centered advocates, is tempered so as to appreciate the contentious and contingent nature of political processes. For this reason the State-centered perspective cannot be subscribed to exclusively and it is necessary, instead, to synthesize this approach with society-centered theories.

Having summarized extant perspectives on the State, it is important to develop a synthetic account that can resolve the theoretical issues raised by the preceding discussion and that is applicable to the level of the State itself. The present approach seeks to improve on these perspectives by addressing several theoretical issues identified above. To begin with, political analysts of State behavior invariably conflate explanation with the causal reasoning of positivism. This is very clear for the case of mainstream Americans whose inquiries are most often guided by a search for one or two causal variables that are then claimed to determine public policy. Whether these are identified as a "city interest," the "autonomy" of State officials, the "intelligence of democracy," a power-elite interest, or the functional necessity of intervening in the interest of capital "as a whole," the fact remains that analysis most often proceeds by adopting some chain of causal determinacy as a hypothesis about the cause of State action. In this regard I differ with such reasoning and agree, for example, with Jessop (1982), who asserts that there can never be a "necessary and inevitable correspondence" between particular interests and the "policies and programmes pursued by the state" (1982: 125; see also Hirst, 1977). Explanation for State policies requires a dialectical understanding of the processual and, often, contingent nature of politics and State intervention (see, for example,

MODE OF EXPLANATION	EPISTEMOLOGY		
	Voluntarism	Dualist Models	Structuralism
Deterministic Models	Vulgar Marxism Instrumentalism	Peterson's "city interest" Power Elite Theory	Althusserian Theories (except Poulantzas)
Relative Autonomy	State Managerialism (e.g.: Block's Managers as historical subjects)	neo-Weberianism neo-Marxism	Poulantzas' Structuralism Power Theories (e.g.: Foucault)
Contingent Models	neo-Pluralist Theory (e.g.: Yates) Autonomy Theory (e.g.: Nordlinger)	Structurationist Theory (e.g.: Lukes, Giddens, Benton)	Stratificationist Theory (e.g.: Stones' "systemic power")

Figure 1: A Differentiation of State Theories by Mode of Explanation and Epistemology

Whitt, 1982). To the extent that this view seeks to specify the relation between society and the State as a whole, we encounter a mode of explanation for political activity that is qualitatively different from positivist logic.

Second, the following seeks to pass beyond the limits of functionalism and asserts, in particular, that the relation between the State and society cannot be specified solely by accounting the functions that the State performs. In this regard I agree with Badie and Birnbaum (1983), who argue that all theories of the State that focus on its functions commit the fallacy of idealism by positing that the State is an association that institutionalizes the rational mode of logic in the conduct of human affairs. Thus, my approach parts company with neo-Weberians and State managerialists, as I have already indicated in the discussion of Foucault above. In every extant theory of the State, its importance or necessity to society is supported by substantiating its role as an institutionalized "rational" means of decision making. I disagree with this notion. In particular, the idealist notion of the functionality of State intervention can be refuted by demonstrations that show how the exercise of power increases the contentious nature of society and follows its own logic, which harbors the contradictions of domination. State intervention, even the most organized kind growing out of accommodations between capital and labor, such as in corporatism and its production of the welfare State, can be shown to exacerbate, rather than resolve, the contentious nature of social relations (see Offe, 1984; Murray, 1984).

In place of functionalist arguments, I assert the necessity of differentiating between the nature of public institutions as a means of control, such as in Weber's view of the State framework as the "means of administration" (Gerth and Mills, 1946: 81), and the use of these means to further particular interests in the exercise of "State power" (see Holloway and

Picciotto, 1979; Jessop, 1982). The latter can only be understood as a process, however dependent as it is on the forms of
representation and administration. Furthermore, it is a process
that is contingent in its outcomes, which is not necessarily
functional for the long-term benefit of any particular interest,
even capital as a whole; and which cannot be understood as
constituted of separate realms, such as the "political" and the
"economic," but which emphasizes the ways that specific
techniques of domination and social control come to characterize particular regimes of accumulation at particular times
through broad structural movements in society that are
propelled less by voluntaristic system management than by
cultural adjustments of structure itself.

There is ample evidence to avoid idealism in discussions
about the State/society relation. According to Clarke (1983),
for example, and in opposition to Marxian structuralism, the
concept of the "general interest" in capitalist society simply
reifies rather than explains the concordance between capital
and the State. In addition, as Saunders (1983: 60) has observed,
there is no specific function for the State; its actions vary from
level to level as do its roles. Consequently, there cannot be any
single structural theory of the State according to its functions.
Instead, analytical focus must rest on a processual view of
politics and its articulation with State forms, a perspective I
shall develop in the remainder of this chapter. Within the
matrix of administrative State forms, it is possible to identify
certain specific practices involving the means of decision
making at each level of the State that then stand in a specific
dialectical relation with the activities of society. This means
that the State can be perceived as playing many roles and as
performing a variety of functions as well as sowing discord
through its antagonistic modes of intervention. In this way we
can then talk of a theory that relates the State to society
involved in the historical process.

A Theory of the State

The theory of the State centers on the examination of its relation with society. To begin with, it is necessary to dispel certain myths and false understandings regarding the relation between the State and society that limit political analysis through unfounded assertions. First, relations of production in the sense that Marx intended are not economic relations. Consequently, there is not, nor can there ever be, a clear separation between political relations and economic relations. Both types of actions are social relations produced by laws of motion internal to the mode of production. Thus Marxian structuralism, for example, violates the basic axioms of Marxism because it hypothesizes that political relations belong to a distinct domain of society. As indicated in the previous section, this assertion follows Poulantzas, who placed all political relations in "the field of social relations" rather than in the field of production relations. At the same time, however, current work on the State from the neo-Marxist perspective substantiates the view that political processes are relatively independent from economic ones. In some sense, therefore, a certain separation between economic interests and political activities does, in fact, exist.

This observation does not mean a complete break in the structure of society between political and economic relations. Yet in practice neo-Marxists seem either to be forced into choosing political reductionism over economic reductionism (see Mollenkopf, 1983) because of an inability to think through this dilemma, or to be so constrained by ineffectual theoretical ideas as to sow a great confusion in the Marxian analysis of local politics (Castells, 1983; see Pickvance, 1984b). To date only Block (1977, 1980) has effectively maneuvered Marxian analysis around the dilemma presented by the concept of "relative autonomy." In what follows I propose an alternate but compatible approach; one that argues that some political relations define a domain of social relations independent from production relations, while others are part of the base. This *two-tiered* view of the State will be explained below.

A TWO-TIERED CONCEPTION OF THE STATE

By rejecting the neo-Marxist approach we are in danger of falling back upon vulgar Marxist determinism, which asserts that the State is merely a phenomenal form of capitalism, that is, that politics belongs to the "superstructure" of the capitalist mode. However, in Marx's original formulation of the base-super-structure distinction, the fundamental property of the base was its structure as the site of the ownership relations surrounding the means. The formal or legal definition of property and its basic principles constitute the foundation for what Marx called the "relations of production," which also include as well the formal organizing techniques of the production process involving modes of management. As Oskar Lange (1963: 16) observes,

> The basic relation arises from the ownership of the means of production. This ownership is not mere possession. It is property, i.e., possession which is recognized by members of society, which is protected by generally respected social standards in the shape of laws and customs and which is guarded by the existence of sanctions against the violation of these social rules.

It is possible, therefore, to avoid the vulgar Marxist position by developing this distinction and including property relations of the State in the relations of production. More specifically, juridicopolitical relations establishing ownership of property are of central importance to capitalism because it is precisely those relations that produce the social phenomenon of wage labor and that ensure the separation of direct producers from their products under the entitlements and regulations of that mode of production. This is what Marx meant by the dialectical relation between the free-standing worker, on the one hand, and capital, on the other (see the discussion in the *Grundrisse*). As Jessop (1982: 114) quite rightly argues, this assertion does not imply that one can then derive the modern capitalist State from these relations. On the contrary, that involves attention to a historical process. I wish merely to assert the heretical view that certain legal and political regulations backed up by the legitimate means of coercion are part of the economic base of capitalism because they are part of the property relations at its core.

Recently, and after arriving at the two-tiered conception of the State found in these pages, I encountered a second version in the literature (see Clark and Dear, 1984). In the approach of Clark and Dear, however, they do not specify the location of tiers in the mode of production. In fact, nowhere in their account do they address this issue, something central to any Marxian analysis of the State, as Jessop (1982) demonstrates. In sum total their treatment of tiers is confined to the following suggestion:

> Without entitlement to the surplus products of labor, there could be no continuity in capitalist accumulation; and without protection of ownership of working capital, labor could simply take over production itself. There is, consequently, a two-tiered political structure to capitalism; first, the determination of entitlements wherein the state must decide who benefits and who loses, and who is entitled to certain roles or outcomes; and secondly, the enforcement of entitlements, wherein the state protects those who were initially given entitlement advantages [Clark and Dear, 1984: 28].

Clark and Dear's conception confuses phenomenal forms of politics with deep-level links between the means of production and its necessary relations. Yet, they are correct to separate aspects of the State according to the principal role that property relations play in the mode of production. According to my conception, to be explained more fully below, the two tiers of Clark and Dear belong to the same level of the State, namely, the second tier, or what Jessop calls the level of the social formation.

It is my contention, in contrast, that a first tier involves solely the definition of the form of property belonging to the particular mode of production and, as Oskar Lange suggests above, the sanctions safeguarding those property entitlements; that is, the first tier consists of a generic category of property expropriation deployed within a specific mode of production, and in addition, the mechanisms of legitimation and force that protect this system of entitlements. In contrast, the second tier of the State is structured by the struggle among social groups, mainly organized according to classes of property holders, over the division of wealth. In capitalist society this consists of a three-way struggle involving the State, capital, and labor. As I shall discuss more fully in the concluding section of this chapter, this second tier does not belong to the relations of production in the strict sense. Rather the contingent outcomes of this struggle help structure those relations, while the second tier exists at the global level of the social formation. In any event, the complex nature of the State/society articulation seems to call for making the kind of tiered distinctions as above.

Thus, it is not possible to lump the entire politicojuridical apparatus of the State into some level of social relations, call it the "superstructure," or some "relatively autonomous" system of practices, if you like, which can then be analytically "particularized" or structurally separated from the base, as neo-Marxists assert. At the same time, however, I do not mean to imply that all political relations are part of the relations of production, so that at a weaker level of abstraction it is still possible to talk of forms and processes of domination and administration that are only phenomenal forms of the more basic production relations, thereby agreeing with neo-Marxian analysis. What I suggest is that previous approaches to the State fail to differentiate between two qualitatively separate aspects of the State/society relation by treating political relations as belonging to the same generic category of social relations existing at the level of the social formation.

In making the above argument it is essential to distinguish between those laws or State edicts establishing the entitlements and liabilities of capitalist private property from those that merely regulate those property relations. The latter are part of the State superstructure, or the second tier, as they are determined by the production relations and must change in conformity with those basic relations in order to reproduce them. Thus, as de Brunhoff (1978) makes clear in an analogous context, there are several important ways that the State functions as a regulator of production relations, while not being essential to those same relations. For example, the State regulates and manages both labor and money in the service of capital because these are "peculiar commodities" that require special frameworks for their reproduction outside the primary circuit of capital. Consequently, the State apparatus is assigned certain functional requirements by capital of management and surveillance that are "needed by capital" but that are not part of the property relations of the base.

For much of western Europe, State intervention of this type with regard to labor is studied as the theory of "Fordism" or the "welfare State," and constitutes the bulk of the State/society relation, while in the United States it has been more fashionable to follow the fallacious approach of collective-consumption and fiscal-crisis theory. Such phenomena have proved themselves to be quite malleable and variable in both structure and impact because they are conditioned by more fundamental forces that only work through the second tier. Attention to these aspects of State intervention conditioned by the struggle over social wealth should not obscure the fundamental fact that politicojuridical aspects of the property relation have *not* been altered over time nor has the class struggle been directed at their dissolution, except in certain specific historical cases associated with the cooperative movement toward worker ownership and self-management.

Third, neo-Marxists today consider the operation of the State as a fundamental necessity to the capitalist mode of production (see O'Connor, 1973; Castells, 1978). Put another way, in the sensibility introduced by neo-Marxism, the State is seen as a necessary component of the society, even its richest source of explanation for social phenomena, as in so-called State-centered approaches. In contrast, I wish to argue the following. Because the State is comprised of two distinct levels of social relations, only the first, or deep level, is constituted by the politicojuridical relations that are part of the relations of production. These are the historical presuppositions, which guarantee the reproduction of the wage-labor form and which are necessary to capital. They include the legitimated right to use force against the workers in times of crisis. All other political relations, however, including those that regulate both capital and labor, are phenomenal forms of the mode and exist at a secondary level of society unnecessary to, but nevertheless produced by, the contingent and contentious struggle over the division of wealth and power. Significantly, this second tier also links up with the deep-level field of power relations and is structured as well by advances in the political technology of social control.

Extant Marxian approaches to the State, while differing from each other, all treat the State monolithically without making the twofold distinction above. Thus most neo-Marxists argue for the necessity of the State in toto while those asserting more orthodox views, such as Clarke (1983) and Jessop (1982) acknowledge the lack of a need for a State in the self-reproduction of capital. As Clarke (1983: 117) observes,

> For Hegel, a state was necessary precisely to represent the general interest over against the conflicting claims of private

interests—a society based on pure egoism was an impossibility. Against Hegel, classical political economy claimed that a state was not necessary to represent the general interest. It was necessary and sufficient that there be a collective institution to guarantee the sanctity of private property—"for the defense against the poor" (Adam Smith)—for the operation of the market to secure the best of all possible worlds. Marx aligned himself clearly with political economy and against Hegelian conservatism. In Capital, Marx offers an analysis of the self-reproduction of the capital relation, within which the social relations of capitalist production are regulated albeit in a contradictory and crisis-ridden fashion, by the operation of the market.

Thus the key issue for Marxists is the need to settle the question of whether the State is necessary or not for the reproduction of capitalist relations. Before proceeding further with a defense of the two-tiered conception of the State, therefore, it is necessary to address this issue. As I have observed above, the currently dominant perspective of neo-Marxism is a "political economy" in the new sense that conceives of the State as essential to the operation of modern advanced capitalism. In both its regulatory and market-replacing activities, intervention operates to reproduce the conditions of capital accumulation in general, and of labor power in particular, which the capitalist mode of production cannot by itself accomplish. This is most often conceptualized by asserting that the State possesses the dual functions of "accumulation" and "legitimation" in accordance with the needs of capital (see O'Connor, 1973; Habermas, 1975). As should be clear to the reader, this perspective is quite different from the abstract model analyzed by Marx in *Das Kapital*. The following, therefore, will discuss the necessity of the State and redefine this issue according to a two-tiered analysis.

ON THE NECESSITY OF THE STATE

Neo-Marxists have proven themselves to be poor scientists because of their penchant for taking snapshots of the three-way struggle in society and "ossifying" these states into universal principles. Duncan (1981), in particular, shows how French urban sociology, for example, commits the ancient error of "abstract empiricism" in their account of collective consumption. So much of what has been taken in the past to be a structural feature of capitalist State intervention by neo-Marxists has proven over time to be a transitory, contingent phenomenon produced by the second-tier struggle over social wealth and power.

In the main, neo-Marxists would not disagree with the more orthodox view of Clarke above that at one time the capital/labor relation was self-reproducing. However, they assert that at present capitalism has entered a new phase in which relations are no longer self-reproducing, so that capital currently requires an institutional framework *outside* the circuit of capital, which can ensure its survival through interventions.

The difference between the two main Marxian perspectives on the necessity of the State is that the orthodox view is based on the original, abstract model of capitalism provided by Marx, while those who argue for the necessity of the State base their analysis on the new contingencies created over time by transformations of capitalist development. My view differs from these positions. For Marx, the State is only a regulative agency. I see juridicopolitical relations as both constitutive and regulative. Most neo-Marxists, especially those that have been influenced by Poulantzas, view the State as a product of the class struggle, so that its form is derived from it. As Clarke (1983: 119) indicates, for example, "if there were no class struggle, if the working class were willing to submit passively to their subordination to capitalist social relations, there would be no state." In practice this makes Marxian analysis insensitive to aspects of politics that cannot be reduced to class considerations, such as those associated with race, gender, and territory. More important, as I shall show below, neo-Marxists are also insensitive to the role of the State as a third party in the struggle over the division of social wealth and power. Alternatively, I see the constitutive aspect of the State necessary for capitalist reproduction as its property relations. Dispense with capitalist property relations and, in my view, both the capitalist State and the class struggle would disappear (although another form of domination may still arise).

In Marx's analysis of capitalism found in *Das Kapital*, the wage-labor relation is self-reproducing. Specifically, in the circuit of capital accumulation labor presents itself to the capitalist as a free commodity that can be purchased for a wage. This relation presupposes that the worker is completely separated from all the means of production, a separation produced by capitalist property relations. This presupposition means that a class of workers is created in capitalist society with no recourse to supporting themselves but to enter the labor market and sell their labor power for a wage. Yet this presupposition is dependent on an historical process of capitalist development that only occurs if certain conditions are met. Therefore, if we leave the abstract model of Marx's capitalism, it is conceivable to argue that these preconditions exist external to the circuit of capital and, consequently, are part of the relations of production lying outside the process of capital accumulation. According to Clarke (1983), however, these presuppositions, while external to the relation between the capitalist and worker, are not external to the process of capitalist production and reproduction as a whole. That is, the closed circuit of capital accumulation may be shown to establish the presupposition of the free worker without the need for social relations that force the creation of a proletariat.

By an argument that follows the Marx of *Kapital* closely,

Clarke shows that the relations of production do not include a State in any institutionalized form, and, consequently, political relations reflecting conflict over the nature of the capital/labor relation are not at the same deep level of determinacy as are production relations themselves. This is demonstrated by showing that, in fact, the status of the free worker is reproduced by the class struggle itself in which the capitalist smashes the unity of the collective laborer with the means of production taking place through "work" by purposefully fragmenting the link among workers so as to reinstate collective labor as individual labor that is divorced from the means. This is accomplished through the struggle of the capitalist against organized labor, which not only involves abstract property "rights" but a host of other social-control mechanisms. In short, through strategic intervention of the capitalist class itself, the status of the free worker divorced from the means of production is reproduced over the cycle of capital accumulation without the need of institutional relations external to that cycle. As Clarke (1983: 120) observes,

> Although the capitalist can appeal to his "property rights"—his right to hire and fire—as the ultimate sanction against in- dividual workers, more subtle mechanisms have to be used to secure the subordination of the collective laborer. Such mech- anisms include: the incorporation of the means of regulating the labor process into the means of production; the construction of divisive hierarchies within the collective laborer (especially the separation of mental labor from manual work and the subordination of the latter to the former); and the development of gender, ethnic, and cultural divisions within the collective laborer which are superimposed on occupational hierarchies.

For Clarke, it is these aspects of the class struggle vol- untaristically adopted by capitalists in their strategic fight to control the status of workers as free laborers that closes the circle of capitalist production. In effect, splits in the labor force according to gender, race, and territory are allegedly produced by capitalist relations themselves. This can be accomplished without the aid of a State. That is, the State is not necessary to achieving closure in the reproduction of production relations. Thus Clarke concludes,

> The reproduction of capital depends on the capitalists' ability to maintain the subordination of the workers in production and to limit their ability to organize as producers, creating and sharpening divisions and hierarchies within the working class in order to assert the claims of capital as the necessary agent of coordination and direction. It is only on this basis that capital, and the reproduction of the separation of the worker from the means of production and subsistence can be reproduced. Therefore, the subordination of the working class to capital is not given by the external presupposition of the separation of the workers from the means of production and subsistence. It involves more fundamentally the ability of capital to use the material, ideological, and political means at its disposal to maintain effective power over the working class in the class struggle so that the working class, in reproducing itself, is compelled also to reproduce the chains that bind it to capital [1983: 121].

In sum, Marx's theory of capital was with respect to the State supportive of the "laissez-faire" view of conservatives who also argued that capitalism could function as a social system without the State. In both cases the State is viewed as an institutional arena for the class struggle with the latter perspective viewing it as extracting wealth from the capitalist class in an inefficient manner to control such conflict. If we are to argue against Marxists who assert the fundamental self-reproduction of the capital-labor relation, therefore, we must also be prepared to argue against Marx himself, or at least against one of the incarnations of Marx, specifically the one arguing for the abstract model of capitalism in *Das Kapital*.

Yet, as Marx makes clear in that work, the self-reproduction of the capital/labor relation is an historical process. Hence, it is necessary to consult other writings of Marx in order to specify the historical process that produces the dialectical categories of capital and labor, along with the specific conditions of their self-reproduction. I do not differ then with Clarke's interpretation of the self-reproduction of labor power under capitalism as found in *Das Kapital*, only with his limitation of analysis to this abstract model alone.

Specifically, as Marx describes in the *Grundrisse* (1973: 497), at least four separate social relations must be dissolved before the self-reproduction of the capital/labor relation can be assumed. These include, first, the dissolution of "community" in which individuals have a bond to the earth and to each other in the form of use-values. Here Marx certainly has in mind the medieval community. However, he has conflated communal conditions of the towns, which are important to this discussion, and those of the manor, an error of analysis with some importance. Second is the dissolution of the relations in which the individual appears as proprietor of the instrument (Marx, 1973: 497); that is, the artistic-craft ethos that had developed culturally around labor as a use-value, as an end in itself. Third, the dissolution of communal forms of the means of consumption where one's right to be fed, for example, is not preconditioned on one's exchange value (see Bookchin, 1984 for a discussion of the historical importance of this right). And finally, the dissolution of the worker as a condition of production and the reduction of the laborer merely to an input of production, that is, labor time. As Marx (1973: 498) observes,

> For Capital, the worker is not a condition of production, only work is. If it can make machines do it, or even water, air, so much the better. And it does not appropriate the worker, but his labor—not directly, but mediated through exchange.

Clearly, the dissolution of these social relations over time required certain institutional elements outside the capital/labor relation. These are precisely ones that Marx identifies as the historic presuppositions of capital. Included here is the role of the State in channeling disposed rural residents into the status of the free worker by, for example, fighting those individuals seeking to use the land they were forced off of by branding them "legally" as criminals under the laws of trespass. Prior to that, the State was implicated in the takeover of rural property by capitalist relations of production that produced the rural exodus, such as in the passage of enclosure laws. For Marx, these historical presuppositions became internalized in the relations of exchange and then passed away as necessary preconditions of the capital/labor relation because they came to be reproduced by that relation itself (1973: 461,462). In fact, it is precisely for this reason that Marx was able to specify the relation between capital and labor in more abstract terms in *Das Kapital* which, as noted above, asserts that the self-reproduction of labor and capital proceeds without the State because both processes are contained within the circuit of accumulation in the mature stage of capitalist development.

According to the Marx of the *Grundrisse*, however, during the early stages of capitalist development the State aids in the formation of the capital/labor relation but then ceases, over time, to be necessary to it once the dissolution of antagonistic social relations has been accomplished. Marx's argument asserts that historically such closure was achieved with the rise of the industrial towns and the hegemony of "modern-landed property," which produced the "free-standing worker" devoid of any resources or social connections save wage labor. In this way, the State's powers of coercion become redundant or unnecessary to the reproduction of capital's circuit.

Clearly Marx's analysis on this account was wrong as it depends on his prediction of the future course of capitalist development, a problem, I may add, which permeates all of

Marxian theory. One cannot fault Marx in this regard; however, analysts, such as Clarke, that follow this strict interpretation today are clearly in error. As most neo-Marxists would contend, it is precisely because of the patterns of capitalist development, which have culminated today in the advanced phase, that the State has assumed a necessary role in the reproduction of production relations (see Hirsch, 1983). The error of orthodox Marxists, in contrast, lies with the teleological belief in the historical production of the fully formed capital/labor relation and the dissolution of those social relations antagonistic to it, which are vestiges of the previous mode.

In actuality, then, capitalism represents an historical process that is still in its phases of unfolding. The full circle of capitalist development has not yet achieved closure around the pure dialectical categories of social relations, which Marx abstracted in *Kapital*. Hence, the historical presuppositions that sustained the relation between capital and the worker, including those of "modern landed property," have not been made redundant by a total self-reproduction of capital. In sum, the issue of the alleged necessity of the State among Marxists rests with the question of the production of needs by the mode and the relative ability of capital to meet such needs with or without the aid of the State. There are many interpretations of this problem in the Marxian literature and it remains an issue that has yet to be resolved.

I wish to interject a separate view of the topic at this time, namely, that the question of needs cannot be specified by the capital/labor relation alone, because the preconditions for the redundancy of the State have not appeared in the historical process of capitalist development. Specifically, it is the first tier of the State and its relations of power and protection of property rights that continues to condition the relation between capital and labor. In short, the pure model of the capitalist system in which labor and capital confront each other as inverse dialectical social relations of labor power has yet to be fully constituted as a self-producing relation (see the complex discussion in the *Grundrisse*).

The question of the disappearance of the historical pre-suppositions of the capital/labor relation is an empirical one, which has, by the way, remained undeveloped and little addressed in the Marxian literature. It can, however, be addressed by particular attention to the nature of the three-way struggle at the level of the local State. In fact, it is precisely for this reason that careful case studies of the local State and its role in the changing nature of capitalism become important. I shall demonstrate this observation in the next section. In conclusion then, the first tier of the State is quite necessary to capitalism. Thus, my approach is intermediate between ortho-dox Marxism, which argues for the lack of necessity, and, neo-Marxism, or the new political economy, which argues for the global necessity of the State in the current historical period. Rather than having to choose between necessity or not, it is possible to deploy a two-tiered approach and cut through the dilemma raised by contrasting views of the problem of reproduction.

A TWO-TIERED CONCEPTION OF THE STATE—PART II

It is my contention that the essential effect of State coercion has always been to safeguard the property relation at the heart of capitalist expropriation, thus negating the unity of collective labor with the means of production that takes place at the moment of work, that is, in the process of labor itself. This form of State coercion is outside, although not insulated from, the phenomenal forms of the State and of State intervention produced by the historical struggle between antagonistic classes. For this reason, I argue that bourgeois property relations codified in a politicojuridical structure that antedates the mature form of capitalism are part of the relations of production and not merely presuppositions of those relations that are then hypothesized as withering away or as being made redundant by the development of capital. This perspective has two implications that cannot be addressed at this time. First, the role of the State in reproducing the property relation at the center of the means of production, essential to a historical-materialist theory of social development, is a universal feature of all nonprimitive, industrial societies. In particular, it helps to explain the otherwise aberrant development of the so-called communist or socialist regimes of Eastern Europe and their autocratic forms of State totalitarianism (see Nowak, 1983).

Second, capitalist property relations and their support of what Marx called "modern landed property" are essential to the reproduction of capitalism and to its development through its historical phases. In fact, the periodization of capital cannot be understood without the role of modern landed property in the reproduction of capital (see Gottdiener, 1985a). At each point of periodization, the new relations must appear in the use of land as well as that of the factory. In effect, capitalism has developed as a system by producing a space for itself, and this space alters with the development of capital because modern landed property is part of the relations of production (see Lefebvre, 1974; Gottdiener, 1985a).

Precapitalist social relations, or the "historical substratum," as it is called, articulates with the developing capitalist mode of production and produces the idiosyncratic elements that then comprise the social formation, that is, the particular historical product of such development that varies from nation-State to nation-State. Most Marxists treat elements of the historical substratum as easily integrated and converted into capitalist social relations. Thus, for example, precapitalist property relations become converted into "modern landed property." The present argument asserts that the property relations supporting the precapitalist State have never been fully absorbed by capital. These support what Weber calls the "means of administration." Thus a full understanding of the relation between the State and society compels us to entertain aspects of that relation analyzed best by Weber and not Marx.

Weber's Contribution

For Weber, the State is one of the formal frameworks of decision making in society that enables the deployment of interests through the social relation of "power," that is, domination-subordination (see Foucault for an alternate view above). Because it is specialized with a control over the legitimate use of violence, it clearly possesses more power—that is, the ability to make other interests conform with those expressed through the State—than other associations. As Weber suggests, "The state is a relation of men dominating men, a relation supported by means of legitimate violence" (Gerth and Mills, 1946: 78). Yet for Weber, the State did not only embody a social relation, that of domination-subordination, but it was also the means for the deployment of that relation of power as an objective structure, which he called the "means of administration." In the exercise of domination the State employs this physical means and the "material goods" of power that it alone legally controls. Thus the State is both a relation and a structure that is reproduced by a legal relation to society and that is comprised of a certain material means of administration. In this manner the State can be particularized as an institution from the global field of power relations analyzed, instead, by Foucault. State action follows the interests of those in control of the State apparatus backed up by its means. According to Weber,

> Organized domination, which calls for continuous admin-
> istration, requires that human conduct be conditioned to
> obedience towards those masters who claim to be bearers of

legitimate power. On the other hand, by virtue of this obedience, organized domination requires the control of those material goods which in a given case are necessary for the use of physical violence. This organized domination requires control of the personal executive staff and the material implements of administration [Gerth and Mills, 1946: 80].

In short, Weber differs substantively from Marx in seeing the productive forces of society developed through the expropriation of authority relations by bureaucratic structures of politics as well as through expropriation in the relations of production. Weber's approach distinctly specifies the operation of the State not only through the domain of power relations but also as a *material* social structure possessed of instrumental means. Traditionally, in contrast, Marxists have always placed authority relations in the superstructure by considering them part of the State framework, although Marx himself considered management as part of the relations of production. As Giddens (1971: 234) remarks,

Thus Weber expressly denies that the expropriation of the worker from his means of production has been confined to the immediate sphere of industry, and instead applies the conception to other institutional contexts. In Weber's thesis, any form of organization which has a hierarchy of authority can become subject to a process of "expropriation": for the marxian notion of the "means of production", Weber substitutes the "means of administration." Oversimplifying somewhat, it might be said that Weber gives to the organization of relationships of domination and subordination the prominence which Marx attributes to relations of production.

In its bold outlines Weber's view generalizes political relations to include all hierarchically dominated modes of action. Most Marxists, however, would view the framework of the State as a vehicle for the expression of capitalist production relations. For Marxists the play of political interests is merely a "displacement" of that more basic process, thus political interests are understood at a more phenomenal level of abstraction than are the underlying production relations and as produced by the class struggle. Weber, in contrast, does not deny the saliency of the Marxian view, in that *some* aspects of political behavior may indeed be explained in this manner. However, by elevating the relation of domination-subordination to a comparable ontological status as that of exploitation through property expropriation, which is stressed by Marxists, Weber secures for his analysis a generic category of social relation that is independent from those located at the place of work. Consequently, the play of interests through the State framework concerns the power relation as well as production relations and cannot be reduced solely to what Marxists believe are more fundamental generative processes emanating from relations of expropriation.

In sum, Weber's perspective establishes the independence of political from production relations, thereby broadening the scope of potential conflict in society. It is this fundamental assertion that distinguishes the Weberian approach from the Marxian one. However, by failing to develop a conceptualization of autonomy, Weber left himself open to the legitimate attack of Marxists that the interrelations between the State and the economy argue against a deep-level separation between political and economic forces. Let us compare briefly these contrasting approaches to autonomy. I shall argue that neither Weberians nor Marxians own the concept of relative autonomy and, in fact, as indicated in Chapter 4, State managerialists possess a better conception of this phenomenon. In the view presented here, however, I shall show that a two-tiered view of the State provides an improved way of understanding its particularization. For this reason I shall dispense with what would otherwise have to be a lengthy discussion of the concept of autonomy.

Weber and Marx on Autonomy

Weber particularizes the autonomy of the State by virtue of the historical argument outlined above, which locates the growth of the means of public administration in the fundamental role played by instrumental rationality as a progressively more ubiquitous and, in fact, imperialistic technique in the organization of social relations. Furthermore, according to Weber, administration requires both legal relations of authority, which legitimate the relations of domination in State forms, and material goods, or what he calls the "means of administration." The latter enable the legitimized relation of power, that is, domination-subordination, to be manifested in society. It is precisely the centralization of these means in the State apparatus backed up by the framework of the law and their historical expropriation from the masses, i.e., expropriation from associations of self-help, which has been instrumental in the development of modern society.

Thus while there may be "political" activity among people comprised of network interaction aimed at mobilizing a specific interest, there can be no political influence that is not aimed at the State framework itself. This is a historical result that differs from earlier periods, even in the United States, when it was believed that citizens had the right of changing their government in times when extant arrangements no longer facilitated self-management of society. Quite simply, in modern society there is only one legitimated venue of political association and societal decision making, namely, the State, so that all organized interests must come to the political arena in some capacity or be recognized by it in order to exert some political influence.

The clash between Weber and Marx, therefore, centers on the former's assertion that relations of domination are generically independent of relations of production. The legitimate institution wherein relations of domination formally reside is the State, which Marxists view as working in the service of capital, hence as determined by the class struggle and the needs of accumulation. In sum, an argument for the autonomy of the State can be articulated from a Weberian perspective provided we understand that this feature derives not from some discursive statement regarding the formal appearance of the State or even the quality of its public-policy outcomes, but rather, from an examination of power relations in society, which Weber considered independent from production relations. Weber proceeds through a genetic argument, which particularizes the separation of the State by an historical analysis of the increasing complexity of social organization under the dominance of instrumental rationality.

As indicated above, for Marxists this assertion is too close to Hegelian idealism, because it seems to suggest that a mode of thinking is the driving force of history. One important way that we can appreciate the contribution of Foucault, therefore, is precisely the manner by which he has refined Weber's analysis of power locating instrumental rationality itself within the political technology of the body that belongs not to some idealist force of history but quite specifically to the deep-level structure of power relations in society. Consequently, while it may not be possible to agree with Weber today that the State can be particularized through the operation of instrumental rationality as a historical subject, other aspects of Weber's approach to the State are quite pertinent and, when developed further by the line of reasoning introduced by Foucault on power itself, help explain the way that political relations can be considered autonomous from economic interests.

Finally, Marxian analysis, especially the derivationist school, also reaches its limits in trying to specify the nature of State particularization. As we have seen there is a tendency, following the structuralist approach of Poulantzas, to conflate explanation of the bourgeois State form with the contents of its policies, yet the two are not the same. As Jessop (1982: 125) observes, public policies can never be explained solely by some "inevitable correspondence between particular forms of economic crisis and particular policies and programmes pursued by the state." Consequently, Marxian theory based on political economy fails to account for variation in State forms and policies as well the existence of political outcomes that do not reflect the logic of capital. The Marxian approach fails in accounting for the most important need of a theory of the State, namely, the explanation for contemporary political outcomes, rather than the historical derivation of its forms. At the end of Jessop's (1982: 221) survey of Marxian approaches to the State he sums up its limitations by the following:

> While it may be necessary to refer to the specific qualities of the capitalist mode of production (CMP) and the relations between capital and wage labor in discussing the state in capitalist societies, it is important to avoid any relation of logical entailment such that the existence of the CMP necessarily implies the capitalist character of the state apparatus and/or state power. Thus, the state comprises a plurality of institutions and their unity, if any, far from being pregiven, must be constituted politically.

In effect, we must acknowledge the insight of State managerialists that political relations are sui generis and nonreducible to economic relations. In addition, reasoning from a two-tiered conception of the State, we can conclude that political outcomes are contingent because they cannot be determined solely by a "condensation" of class interests or even the needs of capital. While certain outcomes may be considered functional for capital, others clearly are not. These relations are underdetermined by economic processes. Orthodox Marxian theory tries to trivialize this contingent property by discursively labeling underdeterminacy as merely the "unanticipated" outcomes of the State/society articulation. However, the State must be understood as both functional and dysfunctional for capital just as its political outcomes are not determined by the relations of production alone.

Conclusion

To be sure, Weber's analysis is not compatible with that of Marx. In particular, Weber argued for the institutional separation of the State from society. As I have already remarked, it is not necessary to choose between the two extremes of determinism once we adopt a two-tiered approach. Because the State owns the means of administration, the political infrastructure is at once structurally separate from production relations and also homologous to those very same relations. Capital uses the historically developed institutional apparatus of the State, which it inherits rather than produces and which stands outside the circuit of capital in order to aid it in its reproduction of the free worker. Yet this apparatus is not antagonistic to capitalist relations so that the circuit of capital reproduces the autonomy of the State, instead of moving toward its dissolution. This is so because the State is based on a homologous property relation to that of capital, as Weber has shown, with the individual bureaucrat expropriated from the means of administration to the benefit of some political association called "the State." Such a relation is reproduced by the process of property expropriation. For capital this takes place in the production of surplus value at the place of labor, while for the State it takes place at tax-collection time. All that is necessary for this homologous relation is that the State enjoy some legal claim to privately held wealth.

It is precisely because of this relation that tax revolts are so important in history. They do not threaten capital, rather they strike at the very heart of the State. Marxian analysis is inadequate to an appreciation of the historical role of tax revolts and its place in revolutions, such as that of America and

France. In the contemporary case of the United States, however, it is important to distinguish collective action against the State from the ability of the more affluent to shift the tax burden onto the less powerful poor. Recent research on the tax revolt of local communities in the United States discovered that the latter is at work, so that the State is not as threatened as one might think (see Mikesell, 1979).

In the course of capitalist development the State has altered the form that its expropriated surplus wealth has taken to conform to production relations, namely, the nexus of cash payment through historical forms of taxation, just as capital has altered its relations of production to account, in part, for the forms of State intervention. Consequently, it is simply wrong to suggest that production relations determine the nature of politics even in the last instance. At the deep level of the first tier the political and the economic are dialectically related and adjust mutually to the benefit of each. Under capitalism, because the claim on surplus value produced by labor from public property is homologous to the claim on it by private property, the State and capital reproduce each other as forms of expropriation. In noncapitalist societies other means more compatible with social relations located there may be employed, such as a direct flow of surplus value to the State itself under so-called communist regimes. In fact, it can be suggested that Eastern European countries gave rise to such forms precisely because the structure of the economy reproduces the relation between the individual and the lord in the relation between the worker and the "proletarian State." In both cases, the worker must surrender his product to the autocratic authority in return for the type of social welfare practiced by benevolent despotism.

In capitalist societies both capital and the State share in the surplus value produced by labor power. This is directly analogous to the antagonistic relation analyzed quite thoroughly by Marx between industrial and finance capital. If, as

Marxists must be forced into supposing, the capital/labor relation were self-reproducing, then the State under capitalism would not be necessary. Over time the formal claim of public authority to a part of surplus wealth would have to be challenged by the capitalist class as an impediment without sufficient compensation to accumulation. This is precisely what is meant by the ideology of "laissez-faire." Yet, the historical inability of capitalist interests organized around this ideology to remove the State in every capitalist society, even the United States, which does not possess a feudal past, implies that the deep-level relations supporting the State have not been dissoluted, rather they have been reproduced in the course of capitalist development. Because the class struggle presents capital with such a danger, it is possible to argue that capital has abided the State's claim to part of surplus wealth precisely because the latter remains necessary to its relations of production.

In fact, we presently possess more State, rather than less, in every capitalist society. On the basis of what has been said in previous chapters, however, this expansion is the result of three separate factors. First, the needs of capital, second, the demands of labor, which have often been articulated not in antagonism to capital but in its absence within local government growth coalitions, and, finally, the needs of State managers themselves. In the perspective argued for here, however, this threefold expansion occurs through the State because of the deep-level, homologous relation it possesses with capitalist expropriation itself, so that the development of capital helps propel the expansion of the State.

In practice neither Marxian nor Weberian analysts seem able to explain fully the actions of the State and its policies. In recent years analysts faced with this dilemma have argued that the degrees of noncommensurability between the two perspectives remain so great that neither the Marxian nor the Weberian approach can replace the other. Instead, it is suggested that for cases where Marxian concepts apply best, usually when totalizing conditions of State power are discussed, that paradigm should be used. Alternatively, when particular aspects of State forms and the behavior of government bureaucrats seem most salient, then the Weberian approach should be applied. For example, although professing to be more sympathetic to the Marxian case because of its ability to integrate and explain more aspects of social processes, Pickvance (1984a) nevertheless argues that the Weberian approach possesses validity when certain types of questions are addressed. The latter usually involve issues where the variability of State forms and structures of intervention become most important to analysis.

Working independently, Saunders (1983) has concluded much the same thing. As he contends,

> Now it is true that unlike Marx, Weber argues for the analytical autonomy of economics and politics. . . . Such an argument does not deny the often close interrelationship between these two aspects of social life, for Weber is well aware throughout his historical works of the important influence of different types of political-legal systems on economic development, and vice-versa. What Weber does insist on, however, is that the relationship between economic and political forms has to be established at different times and places through empirical research, and cannot be deduced from any a priori deterministic general theory. Similarly, he accepts that those with economic power have often also been politically dominant, but again he insists that there is no necessary reason why this should always be the case [1983: 54].

Accordingly, Saunders advocates an approach to the State that returns social theorizing to the voluntaristic perspective of Weber's theory of action. In this way the State framework is viewed as an instrument of domination, which can then be used by various organized interests in society. While these interests can be representative of the needs of the capitalist class, Weberian analysis does not preclude the possibility that other needs might also be behind the actions of the State. Furthermore, political power operates through the State by the mobilization of specific interests. In this way Weberian analysis leaves room for the autonomy of State actions at the very same time that it also conceptualizes the contentious nature of politics in a manner similar to Marxism.

Just as Pickvance does, Saunders suggests that the clash of paradigms can't be resolved. Consequently, he advocates (1983: 57) the adoption of what he calls "theoretical pluralism" which, he maintains, "should not be confused with eclecticism." By this he means that analysts should apply separate explanations, at times Marxist, at times Weberian, to an understanding of the State/society relation. As Harrington (1983) observes, the theory of this relation then proceeds through the articulation of "dualist models" because public policies can be explained by them as "either the state's independence from or its responsiveness to external pressure" (p. 202).

The present discussion takes issue with "theoretical pluralism" and strikes a different course. All dualistic models possess an underlying assumption that classical Marxian and Weberian perspectives are still, somehow, relevant. The point is not to acknowledge the cogency of each of these explanatory paradigms, but rather to recognize that neither Marx nor Weber possessed an adequately developed theory of the State. The time has come to leave the conceptual universes of both Marx and Weber. Developing a relevant approach to the State requires that we build our models by addressing first the epistemological questions involved, and not by seeking to accommodate ourselves to the above dilemma at the level of explanation, which dualist models suggest. In this way the need for "theoretical pluralism" can be overcome. In the preceding discussion I have asserted that both the dilemma of structure and agency and that of specifying relative autonomy in the analysis of the State can be resolved by adopting the two-tiered approach. This perspective goes beyond both Marx and Weber while trying to preserve what is valuable in these traditions.

This discussion on the nature of the State has drawn to a close. Armed with a two-tiered understanding of the State framework, it is now important to explore the nature of the local State.

CHAPTER 6

THE LOCAL STATE—PART II:
STATE POWER AND STATE APPARATUS

Local government should be an important place, perhaps the principal locus, for the play of mobilized interests in the community. It also follows that the critical decisions of society relating to the needs of local community life should be addressed, if not resolved, at this level. Because political culture in the United States has died, neither of these expectations is borne out. One measure of this contention can be found in the changes that have occurred with regard to theoretical discussions about the nature of local politics. As we have seen, it no longer suffices, for example, to analyze politics according to its first face of power—the play of political interests meeting solely within the public forums of the local State. Structural considerations along with attention to the interest of the State itself have displaced thought from a narrow fix on following the drama of town politics to the study of power itself and its modes of operation. Governance and political decision making have taken a back seat to the more salient questions of sustaining modes of production through a combined orchestration of political and economic processes in regimes of accumulation.

Political culture no longer animates the local State. Town government has ceased to be a stage where democracy happens. It is an instrument through which social functions and power are exercized. Politics has passed over into the field of instrumental social relations. This change is evident in theoretical approaches to the local State. Discussions analyzing the place of local government in society most often revolve around questioning the functions it plays and examining the relative necessity of those functions for society as a whole. This emergent focus characterizes the complete range of contemporary literature from neo-Marxist (see Cockburn, 1977) to more mainstream efforts (see Peterson, 1981). In this way, theoretical discussions on the local State go over much the same ground as the material discussed in the previous chapter on the State in general. A focus on functions requires us to examine the question of whether or not the local State, at this time, is necessary to social reproduction. It compels us to consider which functions operate at deep levels of the society-State articulation and which ones are mere contingent outcomes of more fundamental processes. In sum, we need to assess the relative *importance* of local State roles in analysis that addresses the question of necessity.

The purpose of this chapter is to examine the current manner by which the local State is treated and, perhaps, find something new to say about it that does not merely replicate observations made about the State as a whole. In other words, does there exist a set of societal relations manifested at the level of the local State that is somehow unique to that level and, if so, in what ways can that uniqueness be appreciated? These questions can be addressed best by attention to debates over the functions of the local State.

Local Politics and State Functions

Contemporary analyses of the local State all seem to center on the issues involved in the role of social reproduction. This has helped to isolate a dilemma that approaches to the State belonging to the full range above seem to typify as the most fundamental contradiction of local political life, namely, the clash between the promotion of development and the issues of

reducing the reproduction costs of labor power, other factors being equal. In other words, there is a socialization of the costs of production, that is to say a lowering of variable or constant costs, i.e., of advanced capital, or a lowering of *faux frais* costs of accumulation [1982: 52].

To be sure, the local State helps the process of capital accumulation by fighting its crisis tendency of falling profit rates as well as subsidizing its costs of reproduction, as the discussion on the new political economy documented. Additionally, it can be asserted that the State is also involved in the reproduction of labor power. The issue raised by the neo-Marxian view, however, is whether activities associated with reproducing the general conditions of production comprises an *exclusive* function of the State. While early work tended to claim as much (see O'Connor, 1973; Castells, 1978), recent material criticizes this view (Folin, 1982; Lebas, 1982; Theret, 1982), especially for the special case in which the local State's involvement in the reproduction of labor power has been studied as the theory of collective consumption (Pickvance 1982; Gottdiener 1985a). In short, local politics can no longer be specified by the study of the socialization of capital alone.

Despite the serious drawbacks to viewing the local State as the reproducer of social relations, neo-Marxist thought persists in stressing this role. This is the case because of the assumption that the State as "reproducer" is *necessary* to capitalism. As Clark and Dear suggest,

Two conditions are necessary for the continued viability or reproduction of capitalism. First, the accumulation and circulation problems endemic in decentralized processes of production, market exchange and distribution must be controlled or eliminated. Secondly, there must be a constantly renewed labor force which is socialized according to the existing structure of power and domination as well as the political nature of production and exchange relations. The inability of

capitalism to guarantee its economic self-regeneration and the
continued threat of class-related political disorder imply the
need for some mediating agency.... Out of this imperative, the
state appears as the guarantor of social relations in capitalist
society [1984: 4].

As indicated in the previous chapter, while an important
function of the State, reproduction of social relations through
the State is not as essential to capitalism as neo-Marxists
suggest. A more recent approach sensitive to this limitation
does not claim necessity only that functions of reproduction
can be observed to occur through the regulation of production
relations by both public and private means. Thus, it is now
suggested that the State no longer reproduces the conditions of
capital accumulation nor reproduces the labor force, rather, it
merely intervenes and regulates both of these processes in
conjunction with capital itself. This implies a certain inter-
dependence between the State and capital, instead of an
economistic determination. The difference between the current
"regulationist" perspective and the previous approach of neo-
Marxists is the recognition that social reproduction takes place
globally in "regimes of accumulation" which involve a certain
orchestration of activities between capital and the State.
According to Hirsch, for example,

At the beginning of industrialization, capital could evolve by
growing into existing 'pre-capitalist' social structures and
environmental conditions, i.e., by exploiting and transforming
these sources of resources through an extension of the relations
of production to pre-capitalist areas.... Through development
over time these areas have been destroyed as 'free conditions.'
Consequently, at present the establishment of basic conditions
of production, of man and nature, must become a concern of
organized social regulation.... This is illustrated by the replacement of traditional forms of family, neighborhood, or community based social reproduction, such as self-help in the case

of sickness or unemployment, or the care for children or the elderly, by social security systems, pension schemes, hospitals, schools, and the whole network of commercialized or bureaucratic social and therapeutic services [1983: 78].

The dissolution of "free conditions" historically self-reproducing labor power illustrates quite explicitly the central assertion of the present argument—that Marx's historical presuppositions of the pure capital/labor relation are themselves historical forms which have yet to disappear fully from the scene of capitalist development. From the point of view of local politics, perhaps the most important effect of capital and the State has been the dissolution of community networks, especially self-help schemes, which Marx in the *Grundrisse* (1973) rightly places first among the necessary presuppositions. Such mutual aid networks were identified by Weber as the essence of urban relations specifying the classical city form and they made the State unnecessary. In fact, the medieval towns existed as a domain that sheltered such "conjutorio," or self-help societies, from feudal sources of authority.

With the progressive dissolution of self-reproducing free conditions under the onslaught of the exchange relation, the State has become increasingly more involved in society, thereby breaking down other forms of association that formed the basis of community. As both Hirsch (1983) and Mingione (1981) take great pains to show, however, this progressive socialization is not merely a form of collective consumption, that is, it is not directed principally at the reproduction of labor power. Rather, State regulation and management are required to reproduce the conditions of society itself! For example, even biological reproduction is presently threatened because of massive pollution and the threat of nuclear annihilation. In the former case, at least, State intervention has been needed to modify the effects of private sector growth costs. According to Mingione (1981), in particular, contemporary production processes involve progressively less of an organized labor force in the traditional sense. Fewer workers are needed than before in industry as the Late Capitalist economy has developed through its technological transformations. Instead, an increasingly greater number of people have been shifted to tertiary functions where they work in the processes associated with the general reproduction of society. As he states,

> The process of capital accumulation cannot be interpreted in a restricted sense as an exclusive relationship between capitalists and workers engaged in the production of goods, for it also directly involves various other social groups which have a collective role in the reproduction of capital. Furthermore, capital is also accumulated in the service industry and non-material goods sector. Secondly, the process of capital accumulation is closely linked by a series of complementary social relationships of subordination and exploitation to all the remaining social sectors. Through these takes place the general reproduction of a society founded on exploitation [1981: 10].

It is important to note that those who labor in the general reproduction of society do so in either the public or the private sectors. There is no necessary reason why they should be located exclusively within the domain of the State. In fact, it is precisely at this point that we can part company with the neo-Marxist approach. Although the State has been involved most recently in the social reproduction of society including the conditions of capital accumulation and labor's reproduction as analyzed by the theory of the welfare State, conditions in capitalist countries vary with regard to the necessity of that intervention. Arguments like Mingione's above make clear that public intervention has given capital itself time to develop sectors which perform the function of its own reproduction thereby making the State less necessary. The relation between society and the State is more contingent than neo-Marxists would like us to believe. While they claim reproduction processes are invariant State functions, it is more profitable to view them as shifting between society and the State and as culturally conditioned through regimes of accumulation.

In the United States such a perspective is especially pertinent because of both the strength of the private sector and the weaknesses of direct State intervention, which have combined, for example, to block the growth of corporatism in this country (see Salisbury, 1979). In addition, and as I have shown in the discussion on collective consumption, the U.S. is a poor case to argue for the uniqueness of the State's role in labor's reproduction or that urban politics centers around the local State's role in the socialization of capital. One cannot assert that the local State functions in a necessary sense in this capacity in the U.S. Indeed, the principal role which local governments seem to play with regard to labor is in managing the urban underclass—those segments of the population so marginalized by the march of capitalist development as to constitute a permanent population relegated to life outside the mainstream of society. While this social control function of the State is necessary and increasing in scope, it is hardly a role associated with labor's reproduction. In fact, it bears a much stronger link to the first-tier function of the State as guaranteeing the property rights of property expropriators, both capitalist and State, and the protection of expropriators from collective actions against regimes of accumulation.

In sum, current knowledge about the role of State intervention tempers earlier claims to its exclusivity in promoting the reproduction of capitalism. The local State, in particular, is viewed best as both a regulator and reproducer of production relations. Furthermore, because regulation and reproduction involve questions of the division of wealth in society, they are structured by the political struggle between capital, labor and State managers. This is an activity occurring at the second tier of the State. The contingent nature of this process implies that outcomes of policy are not necessarily functional for any particular interest and that the local State is not, therefore, simply a cog in the administrative machinery of the larger society.

Marxists generally view the political process as being circumscribed automatically by the hegemonic controls of the capitalist class which neutralize threats to the system. Yet, it is quite clear that pluralists are correct when they assert that political resources can be created through forms of representation based upon the notion of citizenship. Conceivably, the demands on the masses, if organized in a formidable manner can manifest themselves so that the surplus product may be redivided by the State in favor of noncapitalist groups in society. Such is one interpretation for the growth of welfare capitalism in Europe. In effect, once issues enter the political arena, their outcome is not predetermined by the power relations of the private sphere. Consequently, as Jessop (1982) maintains, political processes are underdetermined by the class structure of society.

From time to time, the capitalist class must intervene in the political process in order to control its outcomes for its benefit, or the benefit of fractions of capital that are concerned. Much of the time, as Block (1977) maintains, however, the system operates without such a need, even for the important case of its own self-reproduction, as Clarke (1983) also suggests. The concept of hegemony presupposes that political outcomes are contingent and susceptible to renegotiation by noncapitalist interests as well as social control by means of force or the political technology of the body (Foucault, 1979) and the new techniques of surveillance. Through the influence of ideology, however, force is rarely needed.

In the event that the State is called upon to intervene because of historical events it does so *in its own fashion*. As I have discussed, it is no longer possible to view the State, as Pluralists and neo-Marxists have done, as a mere container or mediator of social interests. When the State intervenes, it impresses its own stamp on the process most often by expanding its own power and bureaucracy (Block, 1980). At times the State can even lead the way in promoting social reforms and revolution over against other interests in society.

In short, the political process represents a three-way struggle among capital, labor, and the State that can be even further complicated by the presence of fractions within these groups and consequent cross-class alliances. This makes politics a contingent process shaped by the intersecting forces of agency and the constraints of structure. It is underdetermined by economic interests and played out at the second tier level of society.

The implication of this perspective is that State intervention at the level of the social formation can vary in both form and content according to the balance of political forces. There is no direct link between the economy and State policy at this level. To be sure, intervention is conditioned by the needs of capital which require regulation of economic processes, planning and the reproduction of production relations. At every opportunity capital seeks greater social control and the spreading of the costs of growth to the society at large through State management. Similarly, intervention is dependent upon the demands of labor that seek to extract benefits in its favor. In addition, demands from more culturally distinct worker groups, such as those of women, marginalized minorities and even the working poor of the split labor market, also enter the political arena in the struggle over surplus wealth. Such demands, however, do not automatically translate into the socialization of consumption, but can be tempered by both State and capital's interests. At other times the State intervenes dramatically and even forcefully, such as in the case of general crises. Consequently, politics at the local level is a fluid phenomenon manifesting the precarious balance of forces in society's three-way struggle over expropriation.

In the past Marxian analysis of the local State has under-estimated the role of the class struggle in shaping local policy. It has also ignored the independent effects of State managers and the apparatus of regulation in politics. The remainder of this chapter will attempt to rectify these deficits. For example, the contingent, fluid nature of local politics can be illustrated by three specific examples of recent issues that have changed the way in which we approach the local State. These are the cases of the fiscal crisis, the growth of welfare and concerns over the quality of life, and the rise of territorial or growth coalitions and the problem of regionalism. Let us consider these topics briefly as examples of the three-way, contingent struggle comprising local politics.

Fiscal Crisis

As indicated in Chapter 4, the fiscal crisis of the State is not a direct consequence of some economic crisis of capital, as Marxian approaches have suggested. It seems to be a political event precipitated by the desire of banks to renegotiate the conditions under which particular cities, such as Cleveland and New York, borrowed cash. This clash represents a power struggle over the division of wealth and, as we have seen, there have been two different explanations advanced for it. These separate perspectives illustrate the way that urban politics can be viewed as a struggle among the State, capital, and labor.

For example, State managerialists suggest that the fiscal crisis has been precipitated because capital sought to regain some of the power lost to the State over the years. From this perspective, finance capital plays the role of the whip for "capital in general" while recommodification and austerity policies reign in the State and the power of its managers. In contrast, neo-Marxists now accept that the crisis is political and that the link between the economic crisis base of capitalism and State fiscal problems is no longer a direct one. For them, however, crisis restructuring is a new form of the class war. The struggle between capital and the State does not appear to be the fundamental conflict behind the crisis. Rather, through fiscal austerity programs capital seeks to take back the gains made by labor in the past, especially in cities like New York where municipal workers have always been powerful. While empirical work so far has not been able to determine which of these explanations is most salient, clearly they both may apply, it does provide evidence for the three-way struggle lying at the heart of urban politics (see Gottdiener, 1986).

To date crisis restructuring has benefitted capital at the expense of labor. Banks have been able to extract a higher price for the financing of city budgets, while austerity does not appear to have diminished the support of development through public means. In contrast, public employees have acquiesced to reductions in salary and benefits as well as a general slowing of the rate of improvement of the standard of living, while the public at large has accommodated itself to declines in the quality of life. These have occurred without sustained or dramatic protests, although each aspect of adjustment has called forth local activism (see Susser, 1982). The State has fared better than labor, but this is perhaps due to the increased level of expertise brought to bear on the problem of fiscal strain (see Matzer, 1986; Rubin and Rubin, 1986). In any event, it is entirely possible, given the contingent nature of austerity-induced cutbacks and the recent improved condition of cities, for a new round of the class war to occur in the near future. At the same time, the State will predictably follow such actions, especially if they take place outside legitimate political channels, such as in the case of a ghetto riot, with an eye towards using crisis intervention to advance its own interests. In short, it is imperative to view both the past and the future of events like the fiscal crisis from the more fluid, less deterministic perspective advocated here.

Welfare and the Quality of Life

Welfare and the socialization of consumption have long been conditioned by the class struggle (see Chapter 3). Equally salient has been the recognized role of State power in promoting the same phenomenon, but for its own purposes (see Chapter 4). What is now clear is that modes of domination and the penetration of capital and the State into everyday life are uneven and dysfunctional rather than being a clear case of increasing rationalization, as neo-Marxists maintain. Thus the boundary lines of public provision became battle lines in the struggle among all groups in society over the satisfaction of needs—a process conditioned as much by power relations as those of class itself. As Habermas (1975) suggests, State socialization of consumption "politicizes" the economy.

Neo-Marxists, in contrast, have persisted in reducing this phenomenon to a manifestation of the class struggle over the division of wealth. In this case the demands of labor for improvements in the community quality of life are reduced solely to organized claims against capital through the State for more indirect wages. When gains were not made by labor, neo-Marxists have suggested that social movements should bypass the existing structure of the State and create new modes of collective provision (Piven and Cloward, 1979; Castells, 1983).

This approach is limited because it ignores the nature of the struggle over State provision itself. As Katznelson et al. (1982: 221) observe, the reduction of the struggle over the quality of life to aspects of class conflict overlooks fundamental differences within the working class itself over the definitions of need and the nature of adequate State provision. It also ignores the manner through which socialized consumption actually shapes the internecine conflict between all groups in the city. According to Katznelson et al., therefore,

Just as the rate at which new domains of public policy are created has varied a great deal from country to country and between policy areas within countries, so the links forged between the new policy areas and specific groups have been uneven: Groups differ with respect to the *timing* of their inclusion; and, once policy includes them, they differ with regard to the *terms* of their incorporation. Further, whether they are involved with the State's policy or not, groups have different *capacities* to affect the State's policies or to provide alternatives to them [1982: 223].

In sum, the variations in the timing of the link between group demands and their inclusion in the State apparatus of public provision as well as variation in the response of the State apparatus itself all play a role in shaping the struggle over the quality of life taking place in the local community rather than at work. These contingencies explain the importance of race in urban politics over class in the United States, and they also provide a hint of explanation for the failure of disadvantaged social groups to heed the advice of Marxian academics on the proper course for their new social movements.

Along with discovering distinct qualities of the struggle over public provision in American politics, such as the role of minority status, it is also clear that attention to the fragmented and contentious nature of public provision uncovers the formidable role that the State itself plays in conditioning this struggle. Much of what can be said about this has already been covered in Chapter 4. Marxists tend to dismiss the effects of managers as only "middle dogs" in the urban hierarchy. However, this is a mistake. Recent empirical work points clearly to the role of State managers in the quality of collective provision. Hence, urban politics is best viewed as a more fluid contest of three parties and their fractions. While this process is contingent, it does not approach the open-endedness of pluralism, as mainstreamers suggest. Please note that in the next chapter I will have much more to say regarding why it is that, despite the degrees of freedom in the political process, *underdetermined* as it is by economic relations, a consistent pattern of rewards accruing to the relatively advantaged characterizes local political outcomes. In any case, as much of this discussion has already suggested, questions regarding the management of uncoordinated growth and the quality of life, rather than the nature of democracy and a greater need to be involved in decision making about society's future, constitute the bulk of what passes for local politics in American cities and suburbs.

Territorial Needs and Growth Coalitions

The regional question has become a major concern of urban analysts in recent years, especially in countries such as the U.K. that are undergoing extensive sociospatial restructuring. Regional theorists often suggest that local areas are no longer autonomous and that their policies represent the needs of capital because that is the interest manifested through the control of space (Markusen, 1978). For neo-Marxists, in particular, local areas are merely local units in the global orchestration of capitalism. This perspective is much too reductionist and fails to account for the important, autonomous effects of local politics. In an interesting paper, Pickvance (1984c), for example, observes that political effects cannot be studied from the "top down" of global capital and the nation State. Rather, it is necessary to consider how local elements, needs and interests form a localized mix of political demands that emanate from the "bottom up" to affect policy.

Sociospatial or growth coalitions figure prominently in the type of bottom up pressures that Pickvance has in mind. A principal characteristic of these coalitions is their cross-class basis comprised as they are of elements from labor as well as capital (Friedland, 1983; Mollenkopf, 1983). Much of what consisted of U.S. urban politics in the 1960s can be classified in terms of the clash between pro-growth booster groups of a cross-class nature confronting no-growth or limited-growth groups of a similar nature (see Gottdiener, 1985a). In the U. K. the decline and restructuring of distinct regions produced a different form of local politics than in the U.S., one that was conditioned by job loss and public efforts at industrial rejuvination. With regard to the latter, Pickvance (1984c) suggests that an understanding of regional concerns requires attention to the links between capital and labor existing in distinct areas that are comprised historically and according to the global organization of capital. As he observes,

> This would lead to an understanding of class structure (i.e., fractions of capital, types of labor) in a given area in terms of two factors. Firstly, the extent to which that area has a place in the developing mode of production, and what that place is (i.e., what types of jobs will be created there); secondly, the historical precipitate of previous economic activities in the area. Thus, some areas will be attractive to multinational firms, while others will remain havens for small and medium capital [1984c: 11].

The realities of urban politics today are conditioned by fiscal strains, on the one hand, and economic restructuring, on the other. Yet, each place has its own historical legacy regarding its specialized role in the accumulation of capital, as Pickvance suggests, as well as its own idiosyncratic, unevenly developed relations between the local State and separate city groups, as Katznelson et al. (1982) demonstrate. Together the combination of unique historical factors, imperatives of growth, and the special mix of people and economic specializations combine to stamp a distinctive cast on local demands and politics. When these are articulated as policy needs, regional issues get pushed up from the local level of political concerns.

As with other aspects of the relation between the State and

society, regional issues are modulated by the needs of capital, the demands of labor and the power of the State. When it is suggested by analysts that this regional question follows from some logic of capital alone, or some more "enlightened" analysis with a greater appreciation for the role of class conflict, these efforts still miss the mark. It is only by considering the tripartite division of interests including those of the State itself that a complete understanding of the regional question is achieved, one that grasps the idiosyncratic properties of politics in a social formation with deep-level forces that produce surface events through culturally conditioned regimes of accumulation.

When considering local politics, previous approaches have been weakest in capturing the *variation* found among cities. While it is not possible to survey the range of these differences for American cities, some brief observations can be made at this time. To begin with variation exists across time. In the past cities were marked by active growth coalitions subsidized and sustained by national policies of urban renewal (Mollenkopf, 1983). Presently, with austerity affecting domestic programs, the subsidization of capital has switched to less visible techniques, such as tax relief, as we have seen. At present city political regimes vary according to both the success of renewal efforts in the past and the extent to which they are committed to subsidizing further capital development. These differences, that can only be understood as a consequence of the three-way political struggle advocated here, stamp local city politics with its own distinguishing characteristics.

Cities also differ with regard to their respective responses that have been made recently under conditions of austerity and restructuring. In the main different styles of leadership and supporting coalitions have surfaced according to separate hegemonic strategies of political forces (see above). For example, even in the case where cities are fronted by minority leadership, variation exists in local politics that involves aspects of the State as well as conflicting demands of capital and labor. Judd and Ready (1983), for example, identify four different contemporary leadership coalitions running cities today. Some repackage the mix of interests characteristic of the growth coalitions in the 1960s according to the new realities of austerity, as in the cities of Denver or San Antonio. Others are providing minorities with a greater share in municipal spending while confronting powers within the State itself in a conflict over city affairs, as in the case of Chicago. Finally, it is possible to point to innovative answers being tried in cities like St. Paul to energy and technology questions, and in cities like Boston to the problems of decentralized democracy. Differences like the latter two are also amenable to the more fine grained analysis called for by the present discussion regarding their determinants.

The contingent nature of local politics and its shaping by elements of capital, labor and the State suggests that local politics itself is understood best as a social relation. This argument is most forcefully made by Duncan and Goodwin (1982: 160), who fault approaches to the local State for their excessive emphasis on functions or institutions. Yet, it is simply wrong to reduce the State merely to a social relation. This ignores Althusser's important distinction that the State is made up of "State Power" on the one hand and the "State Apparatus" on the other (1971: 140). As summarized by Clark and Dear,

> According to Althusser (1971) state power is the authority relation mediating between the state itself and other social class forces. It is a force which is expressed in the context of state policy or action. This translation of power into policy requires a state apparatus, which is the institutional organization or bureaucracy for the exercise of state authority [1984: 16].

At a certain point, therefore, once we recognize that local politics is a contingent process of power conflicts under-determined by economic interests, we must turn our attention

to the apparatus of the State and the role it plays in political
relations in order to understand its independent effects in the
clash of interests. Precisely with this realization we address
Lukes's (1977) observation regarding the third face of power
and the need to analyze politics as the complex interplay of
both agency and structure.

The Apparatus of the Local State

An approach to the State that appreciates the role played by
its apparatus in political outcomes is closest to that of Jessop
(1982, 1983). In fact, Jessop defines the State as a form
determined social relation (1983: 225-229) involving both the
effects of representational and administrative forms and the
outcome of interplay between social interests. Jessop's theory
of the State establishes several important distinctions. First,
the State as a framework or institutional form cannot exercise
power as a form. It is animated by the exercise of State power,
"thus it is neither an essentialist, autonomous subject, nor does
it perform any essential function" (1982: 188). Thus, while the
State framework is the product of factors operating historically
and at the level of the social formation, at any given moment its
structure must be animated by voluntaristically motivated
interests which can vary within a political or ideological range.
In addition, Jessop means here to criticize all functionalist
accounts of the State, such as Parsonian or Althusserian
approaches, as well as show the limits of discourse which
objectifies the "State" as some abstraction possessed of its own
idealist subjectivity. He implies that when analysts talk about
the "State" they really are referring to the exercise of State
power according to some unspecified political process which
remains taken for granted rather than being understood.

Second, although the State framework must be animated by
organized interests, those same interests are, in turn, affected in

at least two ways by the State structure itself, namely, by its forms of representation and also by its apparatus of intervention. Thus, for example, attempts at implementing a political program through the State are affected in a variety of ways by the structure of governance and the means by which intervention is accomplished. Both of these effects are a concern of empirical analysis, as I shall illustrate below, and are not predetermined by nor predictable from the State/ Society relation, per se. Neo-Marxists by following Poulantzas dismiss variations in State forms belonging to the same mode of production because, as in the case of capitalism, they are all circumscribed within the logic of capital. Reasoning from this second aspect of the State, therefore, they are wrong. The variability of State forms is itself an important source of data for an understanding of political processes, as Weberians contend. There is a world of difference between the democracies of England, the United States and of South Korea, just as there are important differences in the play of political processes produced by different structural arrangements of local governments themselves.

Third, the State is not only an institutional ensemble of forms of representation, it is also comprised of a differentiated administrative structure. In particular, the apparatus of the State and its managers are separate factors in the equation which translates organized interests located in society into State public policies. We have already observed this aspect in the discussion of urban managerialism for the case of the local State.

In sum, the study of political processes involves attention to sources of differentiation deriving from the apparatus of the State itself. Policy outcomes are determined within the State framework by three separate structural sources of variation: forms of representation, administration and of intervention. It is for this reason that Jessop asserts that economic relations alone underdetermine the political process. As he states,

Because the state is located on the terrain of the social
formation, the determination of the variety of state forms have
as their sources a variety of determinations and not just the
dominant relations of production [1982: 196].

Thus, the three sources of formal variation: forms of
representation, administration, and intervention, combine
with the contentious nature of social interests to produce
political outcomes that are contingent and underdetermined
by economic forces in an action-structure dialectic of considerable complexity. The outcomes of this process are functional for capital only in so far as they do not challenge the
fundamental premises of accumulation itself, although they
may explicitly aid that process in more direct ways.

The theory of the local State presented here explains public
policy as the complex interplay of social interests manifested
through forms of the State. Clearly, the premises of this theory
suggest that the outcomes of this process must be determined
empirically rather than being predicted by some functionalist
argument prejudging the nature of the State/society relation
under capitalism. Most important it is precisely because of the
very nature of the relative independence of the State framework
from economic relations of production, due to its two-tiered
structure, that the State can appear to play a variety of
different roles in society, as we have already seen in previous
chapters. In short, Jessop's approach to the State, which
distinguishes between its forms, on the one hand, and the play
of interests within its framework, on the other, goes beyond
traditional Marxian and Weberian approaches to forge a new
perspective which explains better the contemporary aspects of
the State/society relation.

In sum, political processes take place in *two* separate
domains, the private and the public sphere. The latter involves
three structural forms which themselves affect political out-

comes. The intersection of interests mobilized in each one of these arenas is a contentious process with contingent outcomes. For this reason, it is necessary to speak of both hegemony and legitimation as voluntaristic aspects of social control even if such strategies are helped along by structural processes intrinsic to the capitalist relations of production. State interventions, furthermore, can be explained from this perspective, as produced by the interplay of the three separate fields of action within the State framework, while policy outcomes themselves close the circle of political activity and return the play of interests back to society. If, in agreeing with Jessop that the State is a form determined social relation, viewed in this manner, it is possible to explain public policy as the intersection between qualitatively separate interests, on the one hand, and, structural constraints deriving from social forms of representation, intervention and administration, on the other. The interests which are involved in this process include intra- as well as interclass conflict, and, in addition, those of State managers. The forms involved have four structural bases: those of economic organization and State laws legitimating property rights, forms of administration and of representation which are themselves products of historical processes at the level of the social formation, and phenomenal forms of legitimation and accumulation pertinent to the social formation (see Figure 2).

So far in the discussion of the local State I have merely specified its two-tiered framework. Following Jessop we have then seen how the second tier existing at the level of the social formation joins with private sector interests in a complex, contingent manner. It is necessary to supplement this structural analysis with one that concerns the deployment of interests in society and the manner by which organized demands on the State interact with its structure. I shall leave such considerations for the next chapter.

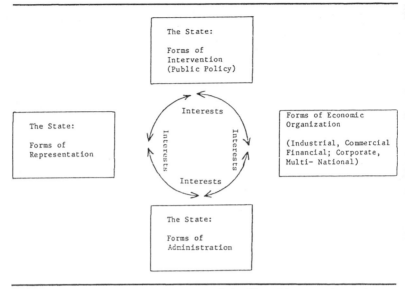

Figure 2: Forms of the State, Economy, and the Play of Interest—the Action-Structure Dialectic in the Determination of Public Policy

Conclusion

At the beginning of this chapter I questioned rhetorically whether or not anything unique could be said about the local State given its deterministically conceived role by contemporary theorists. The preceding has made the following observations.

First, whereas analysts seem to agree that the local State does not possess appreciable autonomy from either capital interests or higher levels of government, an excessively deterministic picture of its position has been drawn. Some analysts, particularly the French, find local government to be a cog in the administrative machinery of the State. In this sense its actions are destined to aid the overall systemic needs of society. Autonomy evaporates in planning directives. Other analysts, such as the new political economists, discover determinacy through the back door. They see the local State as a kind of facade of democracy. Behind the scenes, however, politicians conspire with capitalists to promote growth. Here autonomy disappears in the thickening smoke of back room meetings between bosses and businessmen.

The local State cannot be discovered through attention to the question of autonomy, as Clark and Dear (1984) suggest, for example, because that issue is pertinent not to a social institution, i.e., the State, nor to the functions it performs, but only to social process. Therefore, the real issue regarding autonomy pertains to the relative determinacy of the local political process in a milieu that constitutes limits to citizen mobilizations of will.

The preceding discussion suggests that politics is underdetermined by economic relations. It argues for an approach to politics representing a three-way struggle between capital, labor and the State, or, more voluntaristically conceived, between capitalists, workers and State managers along with all their fractions. The characteristic of politics is its contingent nature. Containing this clash are the imperatives of forces operating at the deep level—the impluse of power and its technology of domination, the necessities and contradictions of the capitalist system of expropriation and the political system of expropriation. These constitute a first tier of the State upon which the contingent, second tier emanates.

Viewing politics in this manner means appreciating it as a form determined social relation—one conditioned by the apparatus of government, historical legacy and the domain of power in struggles over need.

Secondly, functionalist approaches to the State argue for its necessity in the contemporary conjuncture called late capitalism. More fundamentally, this claim concerns the State's role as the reproducer of social relations. The preceding has called this perspective into question. The principal purpose of the local State is that of social control. This operates for the benefit of capital, to be sure, but it also does so for the sake of power and the domination of hegemonic ideology and lifestyles deriving from society as a whole. Social control is necessary to preserve legitimated claims to power and legitimated modes of property expropriation. Other functions of the State may also be important, but these can be shown to wax and wane according to regimes of accumulation. For the case of the U.S. corporatism, collective consumption, and fiscal crisis, all terms used regularly by European analysts, are phenomena that are highly overrated and debatably useful as relevant categories of functional necessity in the reproduction of social relations. It is not that such tendencies do not exist here, or that State intervention is not a formidable presence affecting the very basis of sociospatial development, clearly these phenomena are important (see Gottdiener, 1985a). However, they are conditioned by the three way struggle of politics itself. Both structure and agency limit and shape the outcome of this clash and, therefore, help define both the functions of the State and their relative necessity to historically specific regimes of accumulation.

Finally, this discussion appreciates the ideological role of the local State. It has been argued that the alleged "tension" between democracy and the absence of local autonomy is academic at best. As constituted the State and its courts under capitalism can never solve the kinds of questions regarding justice and equality raised by social process. To look to the capitalist State apparatus in this way, is to fall victim to the bourgeois ideology of democracy.

Perhaps in the past, the local State once fulfilled a democratic role by allowing citizens the right to become the social decision makers. With the death of political culture this period has long since drawn to an end. A content analysis of local politics reveals its principal concern to be issues produced by the uncoordinated nature of metropolitan sociospatial development and its agenda to be preoccupied with questions about the quality of community life. The political culture of democracy has been drowned in a sea of concerns over sustaining social well being, while the crunching jaws of today's barbarians—the fiscal crisis, violent crime, deteriorating housing values, pollution and congestion—all advance against the walls of every town carried along by the uncoordinated waves of sociospatial restructuring.

The ideology of the new bourgeois State confirms it (fallaciously of course) as the promised manager of life's quality. Perhaps in the past the ideology of the old bourgeois State functioned in a different manner, by stressing its role as the guardian of equality. Whereas the latter, however, required active participation on the part of the populace, and, in fact, a political culture, the former merely requires the advance of technical rationality in planning and the installing of professional State managers who, along with consultants, can make the rational decisions necessary for the management of growth. In place of active community debate over the *goals* of development and the nature of social life, we now possess town councils obsessed with the balance sheets of tax revenues and service costs orchestrated under the sign of growth. Trapped within this milieu the question of democracy is itself mute.

CHAPTER 7

LOCAL GOVERNMENT AND
THE PLAY OF POWER

Empirical research on the local State glimpses a phantasm. We encounter a Janus-like creature, one that can play many roles at once. Little wonder that discussions about the "nature" of the State become confusing and, at times, even circular and interminable. In Chapter 6 we have seen that when considering the State, it is advisable to distinguish between its structure, on the one hand, and the operation of agency or State power, on the other. This is in keeping with Lukes's trenchant assertion about the State that "any standpoint or methodology which ignores the power-structure dialectic is unsatisfactory" (1977: 29). According to the terms sketched out in the preceding pages, Lukes's admonition can be rephrased as "any standpoint on politics which focuses either on State-centered or society-centered explanations is incomplete." We proceed by integrating what has been learned about the role of the State itself in the determination of political behavior and public policy with those aspects of social agency pertinent to that same object of analysis. Chapter 6 has already resolved the issues involved in the first feature of State analysis, namely, the role of its framework. By following Jessop's lead we reject a monolithic conception of the State, viewing it, instead, as composed of three separate structural domains: forms of representation, of administration, and of intervention. After summarizing the place of these features in political analysis, I will then discuss the element of agency in the same way.

The Framework of State Forms of Representation

Under this heading I would include, first, the manner by which local officials are chosen and the political forums provided to citizens in order to express the *vox populi*. In the United States the main distinctions at the local level involve mayoral versus city-manager governments, and, at large or ward elections. Depending upon the arrangements chosen, the very content of local politics seems to vary according to these different arrangements (Adrian, 1961; Banfield and Wilson, 1963; Lineberry and Fowler, 1967). As Jessop suggests,

> Representation is not an expressive relationship in which representer and represented are related in a manner that guarantees the accurate representation of the views or interests of the represented. The means of representation have their own effects on the process of representation—the means of representation are themselves part of the conjuncture that determines class interests [1982: 26].

Second, local political parties and their composition in terms of both leadership and following play an important role in local politics. Despite the fact that their influence on voters has declined, the structural vehicle of party organization remains a critical variable in the equation of political influence. Representational forms constitute the opportunity structure for political expression. They can serve directly to constrain political mobilization and canalize it towards specific directions, or, they can also create political resources for groups with links to leadership. In fact, the quality of local hegemony can be understood as working through the *political* relations found in local parties, pressure groups, informal public/private-sector networks, and the like, as the early observers of local government have long suggested. Together with more visible representational forms, these elements comprise the real bases of power in the city (Sayre and Kaufman, 1960). Careful study of these relations and attention to possible alternatives, such as "little city halls," are critical elements in the equation between local democracy and public policy outcomes.

A third and increasingly interesting aspect of local politics is the extent to which initiatives and referenda, or forms of *direct* democracy, are entertained (Neiman and Gottdiener, 1982, 1985). In areas where modes of direct democracy are available the greatest impact seems to be at the state level. However, initiatives and referenda are used at the most local levels as well, just as state outcomes affect every neighborhood. Measures, such as Proposition 13 in California, have spearheaded the national tax revolt and have had a lasting impact on the nature of local politics.

Finally, social movements, if and when they occur, can also be considered representational forms. These are aspects of local politics which possess structures outside the State and other traditional institutional means of representation. Piven and Cloward (1971, 1979), in particular, suggest that in recent urban history those groups marginalized by the formal avenues of representation, such as mainstream party politics, have had to resort to informal means, such as protests, picketing, and even rioting, in order to express interests in a public way. Other urban analysts also pay close attention to such forms of political expression. In fact, French sociologists have made a focus on social movements the central interest in their urban analysis. For them only the study of social movements can explain social change, thus, academic attention to mainstream theories of local politics dooms the analyst to failure (see Castells's review of Mollenkopf, 1984). As already indicated, this assertion is false for the American case and it ignores most of what is important in the study of local politics. In fact, this approach does not even seem to hold up to empirical examination for cases elsewhere (see Pickvance, 1984b).

ADMINISTRATION

The administrative framework of the State is most associated with its bureacracy. It is through this structure that the norms of managerial professionalism and bureaucractic organization manifest themselves. All State-centered approaches begin at this point, even though forms of representation may also be pertinent to such analysis (Skocpol, 1980).

The study of administration centers on the twin themes of relative autonomy and bureacratic decision-rules. The two are related and suggest the way State managers can pursue their own interests through the function of administration. This is not as neutral an exercise of rationality and professionalism as once supposed. According to Lineberry and Sharkansky, for example,

> Matters ordinarily regarded as administrative are laden with policy implications: The cumulative effect of bureaucratic, or administrative decisions—many of which are made by the manager's subordinates in the operating units of the city government—may be as significant as any general policy selected by the mayor or council [1978: 198].

Attention to the autonomy of bureaucrats should not, however, be under the false assumption that some monolithic managerial interest prevails as a "general interest" of the State (see Block, 1980). State administration consists of a number of separate agencies, each of which may have rivalries with other bureaucratic centers of power. Although it may be in the "general interest" of State managers to expand their jurisdiction over society, when rival agencies are involved, this effort may mean internecine warfare within State administrations. Upon close examination, when State fractions can be identified, the approach of managerialism reveals itself to be just as idealist in imputing a "general interest" to the State as is neo-Marxism that imputes a general interest to capital.

Along with possible crosscutting effects produced by separate bureaucracies within a single urban administration, there is also the differentiated, hierarchical structure of State according to its governmental levels to contend with, namely, the separation of jurisdiction between the local, regional and the nation State. The influence on the local level by the higher realms of governance is by no means a trivial one. To be sure, neo-Marxists tend to dismiss the structural differentiation of the State while pointing to overarching functions that each separate jurisdiction performs in the service of capital (see Poulantzas, 1973). Even mainstream analysts of federalism argue for the substantive unity of State administration despite the structural separation of its forms (Danielson et al., 1977). Yet, recent work in public administration focusing on this topic cautions us to avoid such reductionist thinking. The interplay between levels of the State is a principal aspect of all city-limits arguments and remains a significant area of political research (Neiman and Lovell, 1980; Beckman, 1979).

Finally, forms of administration also consist of a mix between bodies of elected representatives and bureaucracies. In fact, this is probably the best way of conceptualizing these forms. There is considerable variation across nation States with regard to how this link is institutionalized and it too requires study in its own right. As with the above, neo-Marxists tend to ignore such variation and focus instead on more global, totalizing factors unifying State practice. But as Pickvance has suggested, one approach cannot simply replace the other as both involve different levels of abstraction (1984a). Consequently, in the analysis of State administration, factors determining variations and behaviors between levels as well as unifying characteristics of social life which cut across such variation are both important topics of research and analysis.

INTERVENTION

When government acts it intervenes in society. The forms this takes varies considerably from informational advice and research to regulation to subsidy, and, finally, to active partnership. Styles of planning, regulation, techniques of rationalizing social processes are all involved in and related to forms of intervention. Here too techniques of management become important objects of study. It is simply an error to confine analysis to the creation of new programs or the determination of budgets when political factors are most visible. Equally important is the study of off-cycle periods when intervention is structured by systemic sources of power from within the State and society that bypass representational forms of democracy. As Jones observes,

> Because public attention usually declines after policy enact-
> ment, the policy can be changed dramatically at the imple-
> mentation stage. Out of public scrutiny, policies may be
> modified in a manner that is not at all in keeping with the initial
> aims of the policy [1983: 31].

Most important the role of power and influence enters into the political process through the implementation stage. Groups with organized links to State managers fare better in imple-mentation than others that cannot afford the expense of constant lobbying (Eyestone, 1978).

Forms of intervention are also an important object of analysis in the evaluation of public programs. Every inter-vention of the State requires examination according to the manner by which its form has influenced and even structured its product. Such studies would include everything from State contracted defense industries (see Melman, 1983) to its social programs associated with welfare (Gilbert, 1983; Murray, 1984; Offe, 1984). As Badie and Birnbaum (1983) suggest, the State is itself an object of political struggle and so its interventions can exacerbate conflict as well as resolve it by transmitting the contradictions of society through its regulatory forms.

The remainder of this chapter concerns itself with agency and the manner by which that aspect of politics can be integrated into the model of State framework analyzed above. It is necessary to animate the bare bones of State structure by specifying the play of interests within and through it. Yet, while both the concept of "interest" and of "power" are central to the present discussion, there are serious issues in the application of these terms. In what follows I shall distinguish briefly between these two concepts before examining their interaction with structural forms.

Local Government and the Play of Political Power

POWER

When it comes to studying the manner by which interests play themselves out within the State framework, the concept of power becomes indispensable. As Althusser (1971) has argued, it is precisely through the modes of power that the apparent differentiation in the State framework and its variation from place to place can be analyzed as a unity pertinent to forms of social organization, such as capitalism. According to Benton (1982), however, separate perspectives on local politics have different conceptions of power. These conceptions operate to prejudice distinct schools of thought in the direction of obtaining results from their analysis of politics which merely reconfirm the assumptions of the perspective itself. However, some operant definition of power remains indispensable. For Lukes (1977), the place of agency in political analysis is most explicitly linked with that of power and not interest, because "power presupposes enough relative autonomy to the individual so that action is not totally determined by structural limits" (1977: 4).

Yet, what is within or beyond an individual's ability to act is a matter of some contention. In fact, this issue comprises the core of the debate on political power among urban analysts. There are several different dimensions to power depending on how carefully we examine the ability of classes and groups to affect the course of social development. Pluralists possess a "one-dimensional" view by following methodological individualism. They focus on overt decisions according to observable political issues over which there is a struggle. For Benton, this direct clash between two or more separate entities is a positivist notion which equates power and interests, "Interests, in this view, are taken to be equivalent to the express wants, preferences, choices of the actors involved" (1981: 163).

According to Benton, critics of pluralism, such as Baratz and Bachrach, have called attention to a second dimension of power. In this familiar debate, the power to prevent issues and conflicts from surfacing within political forms is just as important as the direct confrontation of interests studied by pluralists. Benton, however, finds fault with this notion because it retains pluralism's positivist view of power. As he suggests,

> The concept of interests even here retains its connection with actual wants and preferences with the requirement that though power may be exercized to prevent the political surfacing or articulation of grievances, such grievances must first exist for such an exercise of power to be identified [1981: 163].

For this reason Benton agrees with Lukes and proposes a three dimensional view of power, one that considers the structural ways by which the practices of institutions, ideology and faceless social forces constrain and canalize agency so as to restrict the very domain of freedom in society. Every social system contains this third dimension of power which patterns behavior through culturally and socially conditioned institutional practices. In this case we have a realm of nonissues as well as nondecisions produced by the anonymous forces of social structure.

In Chapter 5 we have seen that even this three-dimensional view of power is not sufficient. Power operates more subtly and pervasively in social relations and does not depend for its specificity on any single institutional framework. There is, in fact, a fourth dimension to power. Following Foucault, it is possible to demonstrate the manner by which relations of power constitute a distinct deep structure in society. Through the historical development of modes of domination according to the political technology of the body, it is possible to trace the progress of this domain of social relations. Because modes of domination work directly on individual actions or the precluding of individual action through techniques of surveillance and socialization, they constrain and canalize behavior socially and generally without any specific dependence on institutions as such. Thus, power operates through all four dimensions drawing for its energy on the deep structure of social relations patterned by control of the body itself through culture and helped along in the relation of domination-subordination by the acceptance of subordinate roles. As also indicated in Chapter 5, however, Foucault's approach is much too general and leads to arguments that cannot be falsified. With four dimensions of power virtually any political action can now be explained as the result of its operation, and this is a position that is most necessary to avoid. For this reason it is important to specify how power operates by developing analytical categories that can separate the vague, deep structure of four dimensions of power from its empirically observable forms.

In what follows, I shall apply a four-dimensional conception of power while retaining aspects of Benton's (1982) criticism of the concept "interest." More specifically, instead of using that term at all, I shall merely suggest that for every social group and every public decision there is a potential "stake in the issue" which corresponds to that group, whether or not that preference or demand is manifested empirically. Political analysis of stakes can then proceed by identifying those groups within the three domains of the economy, the State and the polity that may possess a separate stake in any given issue, rather than identification of interests themselves which are imputed to groups in a more general way and by a questionable process. In this manner we can sidestep important reservations regarding the relative existence of imputed states of consciousness which constitutes the most serious drawback to the Marxian analysis of class (see Lovatt and Ham, 1984; Hindess, 1978; Jessop, 1982). Empirically, at least, we can identify what groups actually exist and which decisions and issues may affect them, even if we cannot be sure that they possess some aggregate group interest which can be an object of class analysis.

Secondly, and with regard to power, I shall focus on the structural constraints within the present political system that unify interests around outlooks that help reproduce the capitalist system. This is a question of linking economic with political relations through ideology. Again, I shall sidestep contentious issues in the analysis of power by avoiding questions regarding its empirical identification. Instead, I will discuss the manner by which potential interests in society are circumscribed around a few central outlooks that, as Lukes and Benton, suggest, supply a third structural dimension to power. This dimension will be discussed below as constituted by the "unifying factors" operant in ideological mediations and political discourse that aid the mobilization of biases in social practices. Along with a second aspect of the intersection between power and the State framework that I shall discuss next as "canalizing factors," these two aspects comprise in the most explicit manner possible what I mean by the death of local politics.

Third, and last, I shall follow the emerging perspective of the structurationist school and, like Lukes (1977), focus on the link between structure and agency. It is possible to approach an empirical assessment of the manner by which power is deployed in society if we focus on what can be called the "canalizing factors" in political interaction. That is, given the wide range of contentious interests or demands which find their way into the political arena, why is it that time and again certain distinct biases operate in determining political outcomes. The fundamental purpose of this chapter, in fact, is to address this dilemma. Namely, why is it that, given the degrees of freedom in the mobilization of political resources, the most powerful interests in society seem to prevail time and again in the actions of the State. Analyzing the set of factors constituting this basic dilemma of democracy integrates both the study of the mobilization of demands in the political arena and the operation of structural biases deriving from State forms and the analysis of the four dimensions of power that work in concert to shape political action and policy outcomes.

In sum, therefore, I avoid an overly generalist account of the play of power within the framework of the State through the analytical deployment of the concepts "stakes in the issue" instead of "interest," and "unifying" and "canalizing" factors.

Stakes and Issues

There are three separate structural sources of stakes for any given issue corresponding to the economic domain, the political domain and the social domain of the polity. With regard to the first, it is necessary to distinguish among the fractions of capital because each has its own needs. There are differences, for example, between finance and industrial capital, between monopoly and competitive sectors, between the property sector, the commercial sector and the manu-facturing sector, and, so on. To be sure, there are important areas of overlap or concordance between the outlook of capitalists belonging to these class fractions. Such con-cordance, however, does *not* specify a "necessary" interest of capital. Similarly, we might follow some neo-Marxists and also suggest that there exists a "general interest" of capital which can even be said to characterize State intervention as, for example, in the capital logic school (Jessop, 1982; Carnoy, 1984). However, this "general interest" is an imputation to capital of a positivistically determined economic class position that is idealist and whose existence is certainly the matter of some debate (see, for example, Clarke, 1983).

The second domain, that of the State, also contains within it several sources of interest or "stakes" in the issue. State managerialists all conceptualize the autonomy of bureaucrats as some monolithic interest. As in the case of capital, some analysts assert that a "general interest" exists for the State which can be ascribed to its managers, namely, the expansion of State authority vis-à-vis society. This assertion, however, is also based on the mechanism of imputation. Ascribing a general interest to the collectivity of State managers is non-falsifiable and commits the same idealist error as asserting the structural unity of the State, a position that must be proved, not assumed.

I reject this view. Instead, it is more reasonable to suggest that there are bureaucratic fractions with each possessing potentially separate stakes in the process of decision making, without denying that each fraction may benefit by a general expansion of State power over society. Just as there can be contending bureaucracies which seek individually to enhance their own jurisdictions, there are also separate fractions among State managers within different public agencies. This is especially true for the deployment of State power among the separate levels of government, as in federalist arrangements. A second source of factionalism is intra-bureaucratic. Because the State is itself an employer, fractions are produced in public agencies that correspond to divisions in the municipal labor market. Cleavages can be produced, for example, according to the degree of professionalization required for different jobs and centering on the wage issue of comparable worth.

In the case of both capital and the State it is entirely possible that some concordance of interest might mold the fractions in each of these domains into some unified position for some specific issue. One can agree with this contingency, however, without asserting the existence of some "general interest" which can be imputed to either the State or capital. Thus, if the concept of "stake" in a given decision can be attacked as begging the entire question of the determination of interests according to the structure of classes in society, then the latter can itself be successfully critiqued for its positivist definitions of class and its use of idealist imputation to ascribe subjectivist states. It is possible to avoid the voluntarism implicit in a decision to restrict analysis to imputed class interests by specifying further the structural determinants of political outcomes, as I shall do below, that aid in the canalization of behavior.

Finally, there is a third domain which can be considered the source for stakes in any given issue, namely, the polity itself. Most neo-Marxists expropriate every source of demands outside the capitalist class to the benefit of the working class. There are two objections to this conceptualization. First, and as we have already seen, considerable problems arise when the collectivity of all workers are said by analysts to possess a single "objective interest," such as the promotion of socialism. Even among workers important fractions exist between manual and mental laborers, the skilled and unskilled, the highly compensated and the working poor, white-collar professionals and blue-collar laborers, and so on. It is just as fallacious to argue that some ideal "general interest," such as socialism, exists for workers as for capital and the State. Therefore, it is necessary to pay careful attention to fractions among the working class. The stakes in any issue are especially important to those fractions that are in contradictory locations (Wright, 1978), or in relatively weak positions of power (Susser, 1982; Piven and Cloward, 1979).

Second, political analysts of modern societies have uncovered important sources of separate demands which cannot be reduced to questions of class and which make it necessary to reach beyond Marxian analysis in order to understand them (Saunders, 1983; Pickvance, 1984a). The social bases of these include racial and ethnic minorities, women, territorial concerns and environmentalism. While some analysts might ascribe to these concerns some concordant general stake which might be called the "public interest," it is questionable whether such a position can survive the attacks of its many critics.

The preceding discussion has identified potential sources of demands which are pertinent in any political decision. For the purposes of understanding the nature of the local State, however, it is less important to argue about the nature of interests than it is to explain the empirical record of local government which finds the power and privilege of the wealthy and of influential State managers manifesting themselves time after time in the decision-making process of local government. Given the presence of relative State autonomy and the ability of the political process to generate new resources of influence, even for the most marginal groups, the existence of plutocracy in local government cannot be explained as the simple operation of some general interest of capitalists or State managers alone. The key aspects of the present chapter focus on the more subtle process involved in producing this result. This involves the constraining influence of structure, ideology, and agency summarized in terms of unifying and canalizing factors that bias the political process in specific directions.

Unifying Factors

THE IDEOLOGY OF GROWTH

Both unifying and canalyzing factors specify the relation between the process of production and political relations, on the one hand, and local contradictions of societal development and political responses to them, on the other. That is, this discussion of the local State specifies the link between the "general" level, the analysis of capitalist development in the United States, and the "particular," local political action in response to patterns of growth. The single most important unifying factor constraining political action is the ideology of growth itself and the discourse of economic progress. Because the first tier of the State and the capitalist class both require legal relations of private property ownership, the State's and capital's needs coincide at a deep level and according to the idea of progress. The local State, in particular, relies quite heavily on the activities of the private sector, especially its economic level of development. Relative well being of municipal revenue sources tends to carry the most weight in local political decision making. Ideally, according to the bourgeois theory of democratic participation, every property owner has some voice in government. The polity would include not only business interests but also the middle class. Taxes on property would provide the link between the public and private spheres. Today local government is so costly that single revenue sources are insufficient to ensure fiscal soundness. Other measures, such as the sales tax, have also been adopted. These serve to broaden the dependency of local government on the general health of business. Furthermore, dependence on growth rather than stasis, due to factors such as incrementalism in budgets and inflation, causes local political regimes to count heavily those interests associated most with development, such as real estate investors, large volume businesses and builders. Consequently, the simple "one man, one vote" equation, which democratic theory took as a core proposition, no longer applies in the local arena, as growth interests prevail in the day-to-day schemes of government.

So dependent are local governments on the well-being of the private sector, that the separation between the two realms cannot really be said to exist at the level of the town. This does not mean that economic needs determine local politics, because degrees of autonomy do exist, only that the ideology of growth circumscribes the actions of both business and the political leadership unifying them in the service of capitalist development. Even neo-Conservatives recognize this fact, viewing the State and capital as a partnership, as Novack suggests,

> Thus, the American ideal depends on an activist government which must remove impediments, lend assistance and through positive actions release the manifold energies of the private sector [1982: 9].

This structural concordance between the State and the economy, which Novack refers to benignly as a "political economy," does not prevent actions antagonistic to development from occurring, such as no-growth politics, or the more recent call by certain populists for a steady-state redistributive economy rather than a pro-growth one (see Swanstrom, 1985; Sullivan, 1985; Judd and Smith, 1983). However, it does doom such calls to failure in the long haul of daily operations over time. As in the case of Cleveland's populist mayor Kucinich (Swanstrom, 1985), for example, alternatives to government support for economic development which question the assumptions of its benefits to society are treated succinctly as threats to the society itself.

Finally, one last observation regarding the operation of pro-growth ideology can be made. The interpenetration at the

local level between economic and political interests suggests
that for most local areas, an instrumentalist, power elite view
of the State seems appropriate. Through regulation, subsidization and intervention, the State advances the well-being
of the economy at the same time as it provides for itself. This
"business as usual" ethos of the local political economy ill
equips it to deal with social problems and the contradictions of
development. Most importantly, it makes it very difficult for
alternatives to this way of doing things to ever be articulated in
public forums so that they can become the objects of public
discourse.

NEO-FORDISM AND THE QUALITY OF LIFE

A second unifying factor involves the neo-Fordist orchestration of worker and political demands by capitalists and
State managers according to its ideological mediation—a
concern about the quality of life. Recall that this theme can be
identified as providing the contents for local politics and early
chapters were devoted to detailing this assertion. We are now
in a position to explain the deep level reasons for why such a
contents manifests itself uniformly as local politics. While I do
not subscribe to Aglietta's theory specifying the material basis
for neo-Fordist organization (1978), it is clear that such a
phenomenon can account for the unity of political concerns
around questions relating to the quality of community life. As
Lipietz (1982) points out, the concept of Fordism (the term
originated with Gramsci and has undergone modulation to
become "neo") relates together two distinct phases in capitalist
development. The first, called attention to by Gramsci (1971)
refers to the application of Taylorism to the productive
process. The workers' knowledge is extracted from them
through observation of the work process and then incorporated
into machinery at the same time that the process itself is
rationalized by time-motion studies. As Aglietta points out,

this stage is confined to Department I, that of production, and leads to an increase in capital intensity along with a quantum jump in the productivity of labor. Elsewhere pre-capitalist forms dominate and the consumption of commodities is determined not by the logic of capital, but only by practical need dictated by the culture of the domestic economy. According to Aglietta, this precapitalist culture backgrounds life in the capitalist factory in the early phase of development and is characterized by

> close relationships between town and country; a rhythm of work marked by the seasons and stabilized by custom; an incomplete separation between productive and domestic activities; and a domination of non-commodity relations over commodity relations finding the conditions for their existence within the extended family and in relations of neighborhood proximity [1978: 23].

As capital develops, however, the intensive circumscription of its relations around Department I and the factory form breaks down, and, capitalist relations penetrate extensively into the domestic culture. In the United States this occurred most dramatically following the Great Depression and due to Keynesian measures to combat underconsumption or low consumer demand. A switch then occurred as production for Department II, or consumer goods, was stimulated as a means of combating the realization crisis of industrial capital. Capitalism was transformed under State auspices to a "consumer society" dependent upon the production and mass consumption of commodities as the main means of realizing surplus value. This change according to what Aglietta prefers to call the "new consumption norm" (1978: 23) broke down inhibitions to high consumption in the domestic economy just as capitalist relations in partnership with State intervention were extended to noncapitalist relations in the same domain.

Since the 1960s analysts of the social organization of
Western democracies have encapsulated their work within the
perspective of Welfare Statism. This approach has been
borrowed by American urbanists whose discourse uses the
European Welfare State literature as a referent in their own
analyses of government intervention (see, for example, Friedland, 1983; Mollenkopf, 1983; Piven and Cloward, 1971;
Wilensky, 1975). Only a few writers have picked up on the
irony of applying such a term to the U.S. case without
questioning its substance (see Skocpol, 1980). Welfare Statism
is an inadequate way of understanding the relation between the
American State and society. It has contributed to a false sense
of security enabling researchers to avoid questioning this more
basic relation while proceeding full steam in the production of
positivist analyses correlating social variables directly with
policy outcomes as a shorthand conflation of a more complicated process. Neo-Fordist theory, in contrast, is a superior
approach, although not without its own problems. This is so
because it explains the actions of the State through a deeper
level of analysis. While we have not created a Welfare State in
the U.S.—Skocpol's term for it is an "incomplete" Welfare
State (1985)—we certainly have created what Lefebvre calls the
"bureaucratic society of controlled consumption" (1971) and
Guy de Bord calls the "society of the spectacle" (1970) that
relies at a deep level on the shift in emphasis from industrial
production to regulated consumption (see Baudrillard, 1975,
for an unorthodox interpretation of this change that is also a
critque of Marxism). At present, the neo-Fordist approach is
weakened by an endemic functionalism which links State
activity with economic determinants, and I shall try to remedy
this limitation below.

Neo-Fordism is limited as an approach by its functionalist
explanations for changes in State intervention, which conventional analysts identify as either Welfare Statism or "incomplete" Welfare Statism. Neo-Fordists attribute such change

to overt policies as determined by the needs of the capitalist class. This capital logic argument is too reductionist. Instead, it is necessary to trace changes in State policy according to the separation of the second tier of the State from economic needs. Yet, the fact remains that the shift to high consumption and State welfarism *has* occurred, even if it has taken place through a contingent process mixing political as well as economic determinants. In short, my perspective integrates neo-Fordism with the State-centered approach. As with other aspects of the relation between the society and the State, this synthesis is but one aspect of the dynamic between economic and political processes in a two-tiered link between production and political relations.

Neo-Fordism forces us to consider a broader range of social changes and their implications than the simpler Welfare State approach. Some of the more important transformations in American society brought about by restructuring following the Depression include the stimulation of needs and desires and their orchestration for high consumption through mass advertising; planned obsolescence of commodities; stimulation of trade-in or trade-up mentality for such consumer durables as automobiles and houses; the almost universal extension of credit to workers so that buying can exceed income and the amplification of leveraging power for all credit risks, so life can be lived at the budgetary margin and in high debt; creation of a wide range of income transfers to marginalized workers through the "welfare State," not to reproduce the labor force, as collective consumption theorists wrongly suppose, but, in fact, to reproduce the consumer whether he/she works or not; the "predominance of monetary gain as a criterion of social success and a spur to labor discipline" (Aglietta, 1978: 25); the stimulation of suburbanization and privatization through State housing policies, not as a "welfare State" measure, but as a means of expropriating the individual or family economy of home construction to the benefit of a State regulated, capitalist housing industry; a restructuration of finance capital so as to service the requirements of a high consumption, debt-ridden society; and, finally, the transformation of family relations through the penetration of the consumption norm within households.

The above changes sketch out the borders of what needs to be an extended discussion on the transformation of American society and culture, but which cannot be pursued at this time. Instead, it is necessary to focus on how these changes have affected directly local political culture and have contributed to its decline. According to neo-Fordist theory both the new production relations and the extensive penetration of capitalism to consumption combined to consolidate a normative view of workers and capitalists organized around questions relating to the quality of life. It is precisely this effect which unifies political relations according to a discourse that constrains the possibility that alternative goals or visions for local communities will arise. First, the standard of living appeared on the agenda of all workers as a central concern in labor negotiations. Over time this standard rose dramatically in most sectors, not as a means of controlling labor militancy alone, but, because purchasing power itself had to rise, even though the range of this increase was indeed dependent upon labor's bargaining power and activism from industry to industry. As Lipietz observes,

> The realization problem, associated with the flooding of commodities into the market, had caused the great crisis of the Thirties. But after the war, "monopolistic" forms of wage-regulation linked the normal wage to both the cost-of-living and productivity, thereby ensuring that final demand would keep pace with supply. As a result of this "normalization," the life-style of wage earners underwent a dramatic change, and was even integrated into capitalist accumulation itself" [1982: 35].

The linking of labor's rewards to their relative buying power identified wage demands with a consumer's vision of the quality of life. State stimulation of suburban housing and the expansion of the automobile industry fed that same vision. The ideology of a consumer paradise circumscribed labor militancy within a narrow range of issues focusing on wage and benefit demands. To be sure other aspects of work, such as its conditions, safety and the need for more self-management, cropped up from time to time. But these demands, like the demand of no-growth politics, had a short life span in the larger flow of labor's new relation with capital organized under the sign of progress. At home this ideology produced a discourse concerned with the quality of community life that encapsulated local politics within a narrow range of issues complementing the Fordist orchestration at work. In the end the separation of home from work, which Katznelson (1981) treats as structurally distinct (see next section), became, in reality, a division of labor unified by the ideology of consumerism.

Second, if capital was open to worker demands, then so was the State. The Great Depression and Keynesian restructuring produced the "welfare State," but this worked both ways. The State itself became a new target for demands from both capitalists and workers, in fact, from any organized group pressing a special concern phrased as a matter of public policy. Government intervention under the New Deal was not intended to evolve into the management of life's quality, but this relation has progressively come to characterize the very nature of public policy as identified in preceeding chapters. Over time mediating institutions, such as voluntary associations of health care, charity and self-help, were caused to atrophy to the benefit of the State. The increasing lack of alternative institutional means available to address social problems accentuated further the turn to the State as the manager of daily life.

The confluence of social goals around the above two norms

of private progress and public welfare constitutes the second
set of unifying factors which constrain political demands and
needs. Since the 1930s, self-reproducing and self-actualizing
mechanisms of social life have been attenuated making in-
dividials more dependent upon big business and big government. Those social groups in society with the most power in
these separate venues, such as high-skilled workers and growth
coalitions, reap the greatest rewards from the system. The
affluent and the poor exist side by side in increasing polarity
with the former serviced by a rising quality of life and the latter
marginalized and banished to existence in areas isolated from
the mainstream. This uneven development is rationalized away
as the very price to be paid for progress. In this manner the
ideology of neo-Fordism encloses around work and community
even in the present moment when the relation between capital
and the "welfare State" is being altered at the expense of the
latter. If the State doesn't provide, then capital will, it is alleged
by our political leaders, so the working class waits for its just
reward first from one, then the other. Positivist neo-Marxist
analyses of public policy have done much to support this view
by showing the conditions under which labor militancy has
effected a shift in the flow of State funds to activist local areas.
What has been missed by this approach is the underlying
concordance of all State flows with the ideology of growth that
provides the material foundation for the myth of progress and
the ideological discourse centering around advancing the
quality of life.

American Exceptionalism

When compared to the industrialized democracies of western
Europe, the United States not only has the lowest rate of
participation in politics among its citizens, but also can be
characterized by a virtual absence of class related politics.
Within the context of this group of nations this characteristic is

often called "American Exceptionalism" (Shalev and Korpi, 1980).

Ira Katznelson recently has devoted himself to a lengthy discussion of this phenomenon. According to him, "What needs to be explained is not the absence of class in American politics, but its limitation to the arena of work" (1981: 10). Americans act "on the basis of shared solidarities of class at work but on ethnic and territorial affinities in their residential communities" (1981: 19).

American exceptionalism has the effect of unifying antagonistic class relations around the political values of the State while retarding the growth of class consciousness outside the workplace. The cultural conditions which support this phenomenon work not only to support the status quo, but also constitute a barrier to alternative political ideologies seeking to transform the nature of local politics towards a more radical direction.

In Katznelson's analysis of this phenomenon he suggests that the separation of community demands from those arising at work have consolidated themselves over time in a particular set of political relations. Emphasis in local politics was narrowed to concerns about ethnicity, territory, patronage, and party support. Upon these pillars arose a political culture which came to characterize urban politics. In the course of time routine politics produced institutional and cultural traits which hemmed in action and constrained the selection of alternatives. Katznelson calls these trait mechanisms "city trenches" and they possess three basic aspects: the separation of community life from work; the isolation of the working class from the dominant classes who reside outside the community; and the segmentation of the society within the territory, dividing workers from each other along ethnic lines (1981: 73).

Using the concept of "city trenches," Katznelson proceeds to explain, in a case study, how the radical militancy of civil rights activism and black community control was canalized into lines of action which became lost and defused on the terrain of city politics. The trenches became the conduits of political action keeping the latter safe from challenging the status quo and instituting structural political changes.

In a review of Katznelson's book, Castells (1982) criticizes his conceptualization on two counts, first, the misplaced emphasis on the separation of home from work, and, second, the failure to explain the operation of urban political mobilization. With regard to the first point, Castells is correct. A reading of Katznelson reveals his interpretation of the structural separation between the two realms as exemplified by his three characteristics above, which rely heavily on physical factors. Instead it is necessary to explain why the link between the physical separation between home and work was not bridged through political relations of class. In this regard Castells raises his second point and suggests that this developmental failure can be explained by the absence of working-class parties in the American political milieu. According to Castells, "In the U.S. the working class did not have any significant political representation as a class, and therefore could not generate local politics on a class basis" (1982: 448).

Quite simply this interpretation is wrong and displays an ignorance of the historical record in this country. As indicated in the previous section, the neo-Fordist transformation operationalized the material separation of home from work through a set of ideologically biased cultural relations. Prior to this change, labor parties of several denominations were quite active in local urban politics (Fusfield, 1980). The socialist party, the socialist labor party, the socialist workers party, the international workers of the world, and even the communist party were very active at the local level. Some of these radical groups may even have been, throughout the world, the most militant of their day. Socialist mayors and radical political leaders were commonplace in many parts of the U.S., especially in the

Midwest and the Northeast. In some states, such as Minnesota, socialist parties even elected governors.

Beginning with the turn of the century and following quickly after the Bolshevik revolutions, radicals in this country were subjected to an unprecedented wave of terror organized by both the State and capital (Fusfield, 1980). Capital also moved against workers through accommodations such as the highly influential peace won with Samuel Gompers and the creation of the American Federation of Labor on a platform strictly opposed to communism. In short, there are a variety of reasons for the decline of working class party activity within cities and these are associated more with a developing political culture opposed to community activism, than the absence of factors such as parties which are alleged to be present elsewhere. It is not a question, therefore, of what was missing in the U.S. vis-à-vis Europe, but of how what was present here became transformed sufficiently to canalize labor militancy towards nonthreatening directions. Katznelson is quite correct contra Castells for identifying the way of "doing" politics as a major factor in American exceptionalism. Political culture is a mixture of forms of representation, cultural proclivities, and ideological perceptions that constitute a system of trenches that constrain the direction and intensity of local political life. City trenches are an important factor in the determination of political outcomes and require operationalization in any accurate model of local city government.

At the same time, however, this is not all there is to local politics which contains some more straightforward reasons for American exceptionalism. The most familiar argument in this regard belongs to Hofstadter (1974, 1963). The prevailing openness of opportunity in America coupled with the absence of a medieval aristocracy to make politics and business closely related in the history of the U.S. Thus under cover of ideological disputes which appeared to threaten class rule lurked an ever present opportunism displayed by political leaders from Jefferson to Jackson that provided a continuity to politics and which avoided fundamental issues of class. According to Hofstadter class based party politics did, of course, exist in the history of the U.S. However, equally important was a focus on *status* deriving its power from the universal acceptance of the American dream which fueled the aspirations of all social groups. As Hofstadter suggests,

> We have, at all times, two kinds of processes going on in inextricable connection with each other: *interest politics*, the clash of material aims and needs among various groups and blocs; and *status politics*, the clash of various projective rationalizations arising from status aspirations and other personal motives. In times of depression and economic discontent—and by and large in times of acute national emergency—politics is more clearly a matter of interests, although of course status considerations are still present. In times of prosperity and general well-being on the national plane, status considerations among the masses can become much more influential in our politics [1963: 71].

Clearly, the composition of the polity is more complex than Hofstadter suggests, just as his analysis of consensus politics has been altered considerably in recent years. Yet it is still possible to agree with him that status considerations play a fundamental role in the determinants of American exceptionalism, and these are especially important in the study of suburban politics.

In sum, I have discussed several aspects of agency pertinent to local politics which constitute formidable domains of discourse that structure political action by unifying it around specific questions, tactics and processes. These canalize the potential stakes in public decision making toward directions which rarely threaten the status quo and which make it difficult for alternative visions of local government and community to surface. It is now time to relate these elements back to the structure of State forms in order to explore the central question of just how demands are constrained toward such outcomes. In a sense we require a more developed notion of city trenches, one that understands the connection between political relations and ideological modes of discourse, on the one hand, and the intersection between political stakes or needs and the forms of the State framework. This intersection is provided by what can be called "canalizing factors."

Canalizing Factors

In bringing back the forms of the State into our discussion we take a cue from Katznelson and focus on the way urban actors and institutional structures combine to canalize political behavior into normative patterns which do not threaten the status quo. Several recent contributions to the urban political literature have been concerned precisely with this object of analysis. These include the "city limits" argument of Peterson, Stone's "systemic power" approach and the analysis of "neighborhood mobilization" by Henig. In previous chapters I have already discussed the first approach, which specifies the way that constraints on public responses limit the scope and powers of the local State. The discussion below shall address the latter two perspectives which are more pertinent to an understanding of how group needs and demands arising from everyday metropolitan life are canalized by political relations into nontransformative outcomes.

Before proceeding with a discussion of the syntheses proposed by Henig and Stone, there are a number of specific canalizing factors that can only be treated briefly at this time. Two have already been mentioned in the course of this discussion: the use of force and surveillance by the State, and, the bourgeois political ideology of the capitalist class itself. First, the State always has the capacity to strike quickly and at times mercilessly with force to counter threats to hegemonic power. Marxists like to downplay this feature of the State by asserting that its primary function is rather the reproduction of production relations and not legitimized use of violence (see Chapter 3). This follows from their views on the necessity of the State (see Chapter 5). Yet, the issue of law and order and the function of social control act together to support many of the conservative democratic regimes in our cities and even in nations around the globe. Political organizations pushing for social reforms, for example, know that they must prepare themselves for self-defense even in the most stable of democracies. This act is ironically often used as a pretext by the State for moving in on them with force. Recent events in Philadelphia during May 1985 reveal that this power can be used excessively and under current conditions of an enlightened, professionally directed mode of local government. The fact that a black mayor sanctioned the use of a bomb against black radicals living within a residential black neighborhood, resulting in the destruction of the entire area, is sobering news. Generally, as with other graphic forms of social control, the threat of force is as great a deterrent as is the use of force itself; all the more so, because, when the State does act with force it usually does so to excess finding its own functionaries weakly controlled when its violent power is unleashed.

Since the 1950s the State has shifted resources to more subtle forms of social control joining the capitalist class in developing sophisticated forms of surveillance. With the introduction of computerized record keeping and telecommunications between levels of government using satellite and microwave links, the sharing of information about civilians and groups has reached a level of intensity which threatens our basic civil liberties (see Marchand, 1980; David Burnham, 1984). Public surveillance has combined with private means bolstered by electronic information processing to create an infrastructure with the potential for on-line record checks to make social control of the population for business and government purposes an essential component of every social transaction.

A second canalizing feature already discussed above involves the ideology of the bourgeois State. Specifically, the norm of citizenship operates in society to attract citizens carrying the cost burdens of societal development to redress their grievances publicly or through the courts. The myth of political equality and blind justice placates the victims of private sector inequities by trapping them in the local political process and canalizes class antagonisms away from the sources of uneven development. Behind the scenes nondecisions and the third dimension of power operate to squelch issues from ever arising work to support the status quo.

The ideology of the bourgeois State also canalizes the articulation of needs away from the private sector and towards city hall. As indicated in previous chapters, while wishing that the costs of supporting the State would diminish, local residents of every class and status group still desire it to do more as the caretaker of community life. Under neo-Fordist arrangements self-help associations and other mediating institutions that were remnants of the pre-capitalist domestic economy have socially atrophied making it more difficult to ignore the State as a resource. Thus, while the State has never been a true source of welfare for all nor the seat of rational social planning, group demands within the city seem to act as if these functions still remain immanent. Recently, neo-Conservatives and urban radicals have resurrected a call for the generation of self-help associations which can once again bypass the State as a focus for daily needs. I shall return to this development in the final chapter.

The above two aspects, that is, social control and bourgeois ideology of democratic politics, are two canalizing mechanisms which have been treated in previous chapters. A final canalizing factor has not been discussed above simply because it concerns a vast amount of material that has been treated well elsewhere, namely, the constraining role of the State through its control of space. However, a few remarks on the relation between State power over space and its effect on constraining political discourse are necessary at this time.

THE CONTROL OF SPACE

The State is a framework for power. It not only defines the legitimate use of violence, but also regulates "legitimate" forms of behavior. Government deploys its framework of power in space. In addition to its panoptic activities of surveillance and social control, the State deploys itself through forms of regulation and adjudication interposing its presence between individuals and groups to canalize behavior.

The use of space for any purpose is an existential freedom (Gottdiener, 1985a) that is abridged severely by the power of the State through the regulation of land. This social space of use values is controlled further by the surveillance function of the police, another local State activity in the case of the U.S. Regulation not only defines the categories of private sector real estate markets, as in "single family," "multiple family" and "commercial" use, but through building codes it also defines for us the very type of house we are allowed to live in. The topics of spatial use values, the local neighborhood as the space of communion, the "right to the city," and the importance of social space will not be discussed here, because they are covered extensively in previous books (Gottdiener, 1985a; Lefebvre, 1974). To sum up this argument, if the use of space through social interaction produces a "social space," then the combined actions of State power and economic activities in real estate function to pulverize, fragment and reduce social space to an abstract space of homogeneous units of domination and exchange value. Consequently, the abstract space of combined real estate activities and government regulation is the enemy of the spontaneous, generative community use of *lebensraum* and the bain of culturally manifested architectural vision.

Local government in the U.S. does not plan for growth, no matter how extensive is its planning bureaucracy, because that is uncoordinated and controlled by the private sector. But it does regulate it through a host of land use interventionist mechanisms. Building codes, zoning regulations, historical preservation, variances, and so on, are some of the forms that State control of land and space can take. Among all the powers ascribed to the local State by other levels of government, in fact, this ability is most central. Land is not only the major revenue source for many communities (but not all since Prop. 13), through property taxation, but landed interests in the private sector are invariably the major supporters of most local politicians. There is a very close connection between local government leaders, political parties and elements of the private sector speculating in, developing or owning developed land (Gottdiener, 1977).

On balance, land use regulation has worked systematically against the less affluent and the nonwhite in restricting housing choice and quality. In fact, the first zoning ordinances were passed in the 19th century precisely to control and ghettoize minorities. Mainstreamers argue that private sector activities, such as the housing market, have much more to do with the canalizing effects of land use than State regulation (Ostrom, 1983; Windsor, 1979). This is an argument typical of the mainstream approach in that it assumes a fundamental separation between the State and the economy, as we have seen in chapter three. Such an evaluation of land use regulation ignores the basic ways that State control of land *meshes* with private landed interests to form something like a real estate development corporation organized to promote growth and housing for the wealthy and the white (Gottdiener, 1977). At the local level one cannot separate public regulation from private sector activities in the development of land (Feagin,

1983, 1985; Friedland, 1983; Mollenkopf, 1983).

It is not possible at this time to survey the material on the failure of land use controls in the U.S. and its use by the local State to canalize social processes, because this literature is so vast (see Danielson, 1976; Babcock and Bosselman, 1973; Delafons, 1969; Feagin, 1983; Fellmuth, 1973). Instead, I will restrict myself to the observation that, because American communities are segregated by race and class, and, because there seems to be no present means of producing balanced community growth, especially in suburbs, local land use regulations combined with private-sector market activities constrain the demands of the less affluent in a manner that restricts their impact to minority community power bases. By combining this effect with all the other limitations of local government examined in this discussion, it is possible to appreciate how ineffectual local political culture has become as a mechanism of social justice in a society characterized by uneven development.

I must move at this time to consider the remaining two canalizing mechanisms that will be examined in more detail, because they focus directly on the play of action and structure in local politics. Both "systemic power" and "neighborhood moblization" combine aspects of economic power, State managerialism and formal constraints on political action to explain why some groups in society are consistently un-successful in realizing their needs through the medium of local politics. Given what has been said above regarding the spatial segregation of race and class in the U.S., if local government is not a vehicle for the satisfaction of needs among the less powerful, then democracy has failed at its most fundamental ideological level. For we have been told that the political system promotes equality, not that we must organize into massive power bases to have minority rights respected. The following canalizing factors help explain this failure, not as a product of some voluntaristic conspiracy by power mongers, but as an inherent quality of our political system.

SYSTEMIC POWER

According to Clarence Stone (1980, 1982), all interests are not the same once they enter the political arena. Some interests are structurally stronger than others and possess greater influence or power because of socioeconomic properties which have little to do with the qualitative merits of respective political demands themselves. In particular, Stone places the local political process within the social system of stratification and in this way can define what is meant by "systemic power."

> Specifically, systemic power grows out of the fact that as office holders make decisions, they take into account: (1) economic considerations—especially the government's revenue needs; (2) associational considerations—capacities of various groups to engage in and sustain policy and other goal-oriented actions; and, (3) social status and lifestyle considerations—especially as they bear on professional and career accomplishments [1980: 984].

As Stone indicates, the political decision-making apparatus is most receptive to interests possessed of any one or more of these dimensions of systemic power. Thus economic interests are well received not only because of the capital accumulation base of local government, but also because the ruling class, precisely because it commands successfully economic resources, can produce success in its government involved projects. That is, from the point of view of public bureaucrats, successful business interests are more prone to carry out projects with a degree of success than other elements of the community, such as a neighborhood coalition of minority residents. Second, any interest which is organized into associations possesses a greater chance of success in having its interests atttended to by local government, As Stone indicates,

> Associational influence operates when public officials favor the activities of large institutions, such as universities and hospitals,

over local residents even though their decisions are unpopular with voters. This is so because officials have an inclination to work with powerful forces that they know will succeed as a way of enhancing their usage as progressive officials. Pluralism cannot account for this outcome [1980: 985].

Finally, Stone indicates that bureaucrats are prone to work best with those elements of the community that are similar in lifestyle to them, or which possess a social status in which they have an interest. They can do so because, as the neo-Weberians point out, the process of decision making possesses a large discretionary component. Bureaucrats can utilize this degree of latitude to make judgments in line with their own personal biases. Consequently, it is relatively more difficult for minorities, new immigrants, the working class, or the relatively less educated to make an impact in the processing of citizen demands by public officials than those groups or individuals representing higher status locations.

In summation, Stone uses the three fold properties of stratification embodied in his concept of systemic power to explain the differential way in which public policy seems to work best for powerful business interests and organized institutions even though there may be considerable vocal demands articulated by other segments of the population. As he indicates,

> The logics of success and failure follow the lines of social stratification. A political alignment that has a prominent place for business interests, the directors and staffs of major institutions (non-profit as well as profit), and the upper status has promise of much success. One that consists mainly of the dependent poor, those without organizational leverage and staying power, and the lower status offers little hope of success and a high probability of failure [1982: 289].

Although Stone has advanced our understanding of the interactive nature of local politics there are several limitations to his approach which require comment. First, systemic power acknowledges the important influence of economic factors in local decision making. His approach, however, must be supplemented by an understanding of the way in which the third and forth dimensions of power operate behind the scenes to restrict the articulation of issues so that governmental concerns and solutions to problems are constrained within a narrow range of alternatives. That is, while organized interests in the business community in Stone's analysis possess a greater chance of success because of their structural position in the system of stratification, they also operate intentionally to ensure their success by controlling the resources at their disposal. Voluntarism and hegemonic strategies intersect with the more structural properties analyzed by Stone (see also Block, 1977) to effect efficient regimes of accumulation despite the promises of bourgeois democracy.

Second, Stone fails to develop a notion of fractions within social groups at the intake level and, therefore, does not explain conflict over alternate policy solutions situated outside the bureaucratic process between groups of similar systemic power. This is especially important in the analysis of political interaction within representational forms, an interest most associated with pluralist research. As we have seen, much of local politics does not involve the events studied by Stone, namely, the relative success experienced by groups possessed of differential levels of systemic power. Community studies have revealed that organized auspices are essential to most groups interested in fighting city hall (Suttles and Hunter, 1973). Consequently, many political disputes over policy options involve separate camps each with a reasonable assemblage of equivalent systemic power.

For example, in a three way dispute involving the police, the city administration and the public over increased salary and benefit demands, opposing factions might involve the police union, and other municipal unions similarly affected along with local merchants all aligned in one single camp, the political leadership and its party along with appointed city officials aligned in a separate camp and interested in blocking the desire of the union to get its salary demands, and, finally, a local polity including financial capital interests, homeowners, minority groups, and so on, concerned about the fiscal crisis and/or reform of the police department. If this example sounds familiar, it should because most political issues at the local level involve well organized constituencies that cut across the dimensions of stratification painstakingly described by Stone. Sayre and Kaufman's (1960) "islands of power" perhaps personifies the way urban collectivities operate to hold and reproduce positions of power in urban areas.

In addition, objective economic conditions, such as inflation or changes in the job structure, and political factors, such as the larger context within which local mobilizations take place make such dramas involving separate camps comprised of a mixed bag of urban groups repeat themselves over time often with different results. Thus, until the fiscal crisis municipal unions generally enjoyed much success in having their interests met in political disputes, while at present even the federal government has taken strong measures to break the power of organized government workers under the watchful eyes of national parties crediting themselves with being the "voice of labor." Consequently, the contextual political environment of parties, leaders, programs and priorities plays a great role in the local operation of systemic power.

Finally, systemic power fails to grasp the reciprocal nature of the relationship between relatively autonomous bureaucrats or political parties and the interests they serve within the larger community. These effects appear most explicitly in the forms of public policy intervention. Although Stone does mention that public officials may have interests of their own (1980: 984), this characteristic is undeveloped especially in the way in which it might cut across the dimensions of systemic power. For example, in many cases policy may be forced to go against both the wishes of local bureaucrats and of influential local interests. As we have indicated the administrative context of local government is one in which political control and private support are divided between the levels of State. Local governments and local political parties possess limited opportunities to generate political and financial support, consequently they have difficulty sustaining themselves. In part this means that local government can fall prey to powerful interests located at other levels of government, such as at the state and federal levels, despite entrenched political interests within local government. In part this also suggests that powerful business interests, such as finance capital, can withhold needed resources and constrain greatly the independence of local municipalities so that the relative autonomy of local officials and party leaders is greatly tempered, if not completely eliminated (see Newfield and DeBrul, 1981).

In a separate case, the success of public programs may be thwarted by internal corrupt practices that have no bearing on outside interests but which result when local politicians and/or bureaucrats use public office for personal gain. While corruption does not explain most public policy outcomes, it does help us to understand those events where determinations are made which seem to run counter to the influence of stratified forces such as associational or economic systemic power (Scott, 1972).

Despite these limitations, and in sum, systemic power is an approach highly sensitive to the way that constraining factors bias the institution of local government against its most ideologically sanctioned function, namely, as a means of promoting social justice.

COMMUNITY MOBILIZATION

Recently significant attention has been paid by political analysts to the process of community mobilization (Gitel,

1980; Boyte, 1980; Henig, 1982; Crenson, 1983; Castells, 1983; Lovatt and Ham, 1984). This effort traces back to the early pluralist literature on the functioning of local democracy and others' efforts at articulating a "rational choice" approach to politics (Dahl, 1972; Hirschman, 1970; Olson, 1965). The optimism of the former was tempered greatly by the pessimism of the latter. More recent work pursues the sobering theme of rational choices in an activist light by searching for those ingredients of collective political action which contribute to success.

The importance of community mobilization research is that it helps us become aware that a focus on neighborhood action alone cannot provide an understanding of local politics. Rather, mobilization must be studied in conjunction with an analysis of the effects stemming from the differentiated forms of the State—its modes of representation, administration and intervention. Thus, the urban social movements perspective is important but quite limited as it only deals with the stage of mobilization at the *pre*-intake level, mobilization as it occurs first on the street. This is an analysis that ignores the larger political context of society and the independent effect of the State framework in modulating urban movements. For example, with regard specifically to the social movements perspective of Castells (1983), Pickvance has suggested that this approach over the past ten years has been so centered on movements themselves that it has ignored more important, contextual factors in political analysis, such as the role of the State structure itself. As Pickvance remarks with regard to Castells's latest effort,

> The central flaw in the model is that it relates only to characteristics of movements, whereas the case studies show time and time again that what are equally important are characteristics of political systems. This has been a persistent weakness of Castells' work on urban movements as I pointed out in 1974. It leads to effects being attributed to urban

movements in isolation from other political movements and from political institutions [1984b: 590].

Thus, one limitation of an approach to urban politics that is focused on social movements is its neglect of the larger political context within which these movements take place, or what I call the "meso-political" level (Gottdiener, 1986). I shall come back to this point below.

A second limitation of the social movements perspective is that it ignores most of what passes for political activity in the cities of today. As Ceccarelli poignantly reminds us, the current interest among some Marxists in social movements seems excessive not only because they have died out in intensity, but also because that form of expression seems not to be the chosen political path of marginalized urban residents even when informal means are warranted. According to Ceccarelli,

Large-scale urban social movements have faded out as rapidly as they originated and no longer play the role that they did in the political process of the past decade. This is so in spite of the fact that most of the problems which at the end of the 1960's had supposedly ignited urban movements are still unresolved or even aggravated [1981: 261].

Ceccarelli is quite correct in his observation. For example, close to a decade of fiscal crisis has left us with the overpowering realization that, since the 1970s, urban affairs associated with restructuring have been met with extraordinary quiescence rather than resident mobilization (see Gottdiener, 1986). While it may be subjectively useful to indulge in the kind of wishful thinking that urban social movements encourage, the fact remains that local politics is characterized more by the death of democracy and change than by its renaissance through activism.

In contrast to the Marxian perspective on social movements, Clarence Stone's approach improves our understanding of the limits of social change because it provides a microscopic look at the intake level of politics itself. Other analysts argue forcefully that the entire framework of the State must be examined to understand the full policy determination process, especially off-cycle effects of bureaucratic decisions, as well as on-cycle demands from the street (see Lineberry and Sharkansky, 1978; Mazmanian and Sabatier, 1980). What I am suggesting then, is a model of demands or stakes intersecting with the framework of the State and as structured by the four dimensions of power that synthesize "society"- and "State"-centered approaches, as indicated in Figure 2. Within this context, Jeff Henig's (1982) work on mobilization is important because, for the case of the local level, it considers all aspects of that phenomenon from pre-intake to policy outcome.

Henig evaluates three theories of mobilization—the pluralist, rational choice and radical perspectives. Pluralists assume that mobilization is a cost free process. The needs of the community, in this model, are easily aggregated from individual resident perceptions and then just as easily translated into community action. Consequently, pluralism is not only a theory assuming the presence of a responsive State which functions effectively as a mediator of influence but also assumes that collective action is easily facilitated at the local level (Henig, 1982: 224).

In contrast, rational choice theorists focus on the barriers to mobilization, especially the "free rider problem" (Olson, 1965) and the "exit option" (Hirschman, 1970). Essentially, this perspective takes issue with the pluralists by pointing out the costs of mobilization operate as an impediment to it. Residents, especially those with more affluent means, can always move rather than fight, as Hirschman suggests. Furthermore, if they stay, they face the rationalist's dilemma of all individuals embarking on collective action, namely, the awareness that what is achieved by a mobilized community will generally benefit every resident whether they participate in political action or not (Olson, 1965). These two aspects of mobilization are formidable constraints to activism.

Finally, Henig assesses the radical literature as the third perspective. In the hands of analysts like Piven and Cloward, work has centered on the manner by which less advantaged groups *rationally* perceive the biases against them operating in local politics. According to this perspective such collectivities are less likely to become involved in routine politics and more likely, when mobilized to use extra institutional means (see Lipsky, 1970; Swank, 1983; Piven and Cloward, 1979). Furthermore, some radical analysts also make the point that the unlikeliness of political success forces marginalized and powerless people to resign themselves to the status quo rather than mobilizing at all (Henig, 1982: 218). Studies such as Stone's above help explain quiescence rather than mobilization precisely for this reason.

Using case studies of mobilization, Henig evaluates these three perspectives. He identifies three phases in the mobilization process from conditions to response: perception of conditions; evaluation of conditions; and calculation regarding what to do about conditions (1982: 50). Henig then ties together perceptual factors stimulating mobilization with the effects of State managers and structural elements of the State that either facilitate or retard the realization of political demands through mobilization. This enables him to evaluate the three perspectives above. For example, with regard to State forms he finds that, while the local structure of representation is important in mobilization, this relation is not a simple correlation between relative openness on the part of representational forms and mobilization success. Henig concludes that neither a system totally open to protest nor one completely centralized and closed off to it facilitate the relative responsiveness of city regimes to grass-roots needs. The best form of government is one situated in between these two extremes. As Henig concludes, "in a perfectly open system organized protest is unnecessary, in a perfectly closed system, it would not even be worth attempting" (1982: 175). Apparently, there is a "threshold effect" which is necessary to effective community government, if some resistance to resident demands exists from State managers, collective efforts will consolidate and become more organized to pursue greater influence thereby facilitating mobilization. This result resonates with a second case study look at community activism carried out by Crenson (1983). He found that the stereotypical view holding that tightly knit, homogeneous communities are the ones most effective in mobilization does not seem to be true in the cases he studied. Instead, a degree of contention between neighbors or activists over the goals of mobilization actually facilitates community action.

Finally, Henig also accounts for the more subtle effects on mobilization stemming from the autonomy of State managers. On the basis of his case study materials he concludes that the actions of local officials play a significant role in both the willingness to mobilize and resident perception of neighborhood influence. This effect, however, is not a deterministic one. What officials do in response to neighborhood activism is less important to mobilization than what residents perceive to be their potential response. Thus, past dealings with officials and informal network ties between neighborhoods and public officials are important for the democractic process (1982: 201). In fact, the success of community activism depends greatly on the presence of standing neighborhood organizations which constitute a recognized voice for local residents (see also Hunter, 1974).

In short, the political culture of local areas, its leadership, structure of governance and representational forms and its bureaucracy, that are themselves products of historical factors, define considerably both the conditions under which political mobilization will occur and its chances of success. The discovery of the saliency of political culture which is comprised of both objectively measurable characteristics and subtle, subjective attitudes represents a major finding of the recent mobilization literature. Crenson (1983), for example, reproduces the earlier finding of Kotler (1969) that neighborhoods are themselves political entitites when they possess a local political organization. Under such conditions they cannot be known in their effects according to the background information of the individuals who comprise them. As Kotler once suggested, it is an error to define a neighborhood in social terms because it "was never a sufficient unit for friendship and social intercourse" (1969: 9). Rather, with the presence of a political organization, the local neighborhood constitutes "The basic unit of political life" (Kotler, 1969: 9). Case studies of community activism suggest that both a balanced mix of local residents and long-standing neighborhood associations provide the infrastructure of people and institutions necessary for effective local democracy.

Henig's comprehensive case study of mobilization is most helpful. Yet, it also has serious limitations. In the main he displays neither an appreciation for the sufficient conditions that produce success at mobilization, nor, for the more global way that the current State/society relation orchestrates political demands through systemic power. In this respect, Henig's study shares the same limitation as both Stone's and Castells's (1983), namely, a failure to account for political effects arising from the contextual nature of society and an essentially nonhierarchical view of political power as it operates through the levels of the State. The meso-political level, for example, possesses the capacity to propel local mobilizations towards greater effectivity in the realization of demands. Many of the mediating factors highlighted by Henig, for example, such as the roles of bureaucratic influence, mayoral authority, even the relative perception of chances at success, can all be said to depend in part on how conducive the meso-political level is to political and social change. This is not just a question of leadership, although that plays an important role. Structural conduciveness enters into this equation as well. The roles of political parties, trade unions, city, county, state and federal programs and mandates, which comprise the hierarchical aspects of the meso-political level and which constitute the contextual milieu of mobilization, all contribute to shifting the weight of mediating factors toward different outcomes. The nonhierachically sensitive studies mentioned above take for granted the fluid nature of this higher, contextual level of politics. Class capacities and the relative success of local mobilizations are, in part, a function of this finely textured interplay between structure and agency at different levels of the State.

Attention should be paid, therefore, to the complete model of the State framework provided by Figure 2 and the play of power throughout the cycle of policy from pre-intake conditions to the final outcome of intervention. Just such an analysis would reveal instantly the fallaciousness of pluralist approaches and validate critical perspectives stressing the limitations of local government as a vehicle of democratic change.

Perhaps the main significance of neo-Marxian work, in this regard, is its underscoring of the limited extent to which the basic infrastructure highlighted by Henig for effective mobilization exists in the neighborhoods of American cities. Our urban centers each contain two cities—one for the wealthy and influential, and a second world for the poor and the powerless. Because political cultures have died out in less affluent areas, local democracy exists only for the few. Even when playing by the rules of the system, Stone amply demonstrates the biases operating against those most in need of government help (see also the case study by Susser, 1982). Caught within such a bleak political prospect, collective action outside the institutions of government becomes the only avenue of promise. Yet, as Piven and Cloward (1979) and Katznelson (1981) all remind us, it is precisely because of this marginality and the radicalism which the present system fosters upon the less affluent, that poor people's movements have little chance of ultimate success.

With this in mind, the most substantive issue facing analysts interested in social change concerns the relative quiescence of disadvantaged groups in society. As Piven and Cloward observe,

> Ordinarily, in short, the lower classes accept their lot, and that acceptance can be taken for granted; it need not be bargained for by their rulers. This capacity of the institutions of a society to enforce political docility is the most obvious way in which protest is socially structured, in the sense that it is structurally precluded, most of the time [1977: 7].

The question of quiescence is a much neglected subject, especially among Marxists, and should not be equated with consensus, as the 1950s sociologists were fond of doing. Marxists seem to be drawn to spectacular elements of political life, such as social movements and the takeover of special districts in the city by select groups with power (Castells, 1983), rather than the more sober, less glamorous everyday events of overbearing political weakness (Susser, 1982; Bleitrach and Chenu, 1982). What is clear, however, is that quiescence is a response to the death of political culture. Its roots are structural, its perspective historical. Both Stone and Henig help document rational reasons why disadvantaged groups might look with suspicion on political involvment *within* the system, even if others seek to focus on a more utopian prospect (Lefebvre, 1973). As indicated above, understanding whether one looks at the cup half empty or half full has a lot to do with gauging not mobilization itself but the larger political context within which it takes place. Both the meso-political level and leadership in Washington at the highest level play a great role, as the experience of the 1960s and the contrasting one of the Reagan years clearly show. When local political culture has died, it can only be ressurrected from outside. All other changes are doomed to be coopted within the encapsulating, totalizing logic of State power. As with the case of mobilization against capital, how one gets outside a globalizing system while being caught within it is a puzzle of some magnitude.

CHAPTER 8

POLITICS WITHOUT POLITICS

In a book that is largely critical of existing social institutions it is traditional to offer up solutions in a final chapter. When they are not forthcoming, critics eagerly pounce on such gaps in the work of authors. It is necessary, however, to bypass this issue in the present case. Solutions to the decline of political culture must be found in a public dialogue and not through academic prescriptions. What other means is there available to us to revive a culture? Capital and State move together through economic, political, and cultural adjustments accommodating themselves in regimes of accumulation and according to the deployment of power relations. Only the conscious recognition and understanding of this process by the public can counteract the ideology that legitimates it and the current social drift toward the annihilation of political discourse.

Local government in the United States is nourished currently by political crumbs falling from the tables of higher State levels. Its functions are defined by the interplay between systemic needs of the larger social structure and the actions of powerful interests that bind decision making to specific social outcomes. Democratic participation in this process has very little to do with the way this system functions.

Once we appreciate the limited way that average citizens participate in political decision making, it is possible to glance at history and acknowledge that such a state of affairs was not always the case. Over the past century in the United States the apparatus of State intervention, its regulatory and administrative activities, has expanded hypertrophically. During the same period, the democratic means of participation have atrophied. What is most surprising about this revelation is the realization that other industrialized nations are not very different from our own. In fact, most of Europe, for example, has no provision for local autonomy and the local State is reduced there merely to an administrative adjunct of the central government. Mass forms of mobilization at election time in national contests, for which Europe is most notable, are important democratic expressions, but they are no substitute for involvement in the everyday affairs of local civic life. Consequently, the reconstruction of democracy at its grass roots is a project that pertains to a number of societies, including our own.

In the preceding pages I have developed the realization that there can be no local politics without maximum public participation in decision making. Solutions to the dilemma of local governance must begin from this substantive premise about political process, and not from the idealist approach that involves issues of equity or social justice (see Rawls, 1971; Clark and Dear, 1984). Yet, suggesting that local government should include provisions for direct participation is just the beginning of the process of cultural revival. We need only to be reminded of the implementation of direct participatory schemes in Kaddafy's Libya to be drawn away from the impulse to grasp at easy solutions.

The concept of "political culture" is usually discussed among academics through a value problematic, that is, by focusing on the question of values or norms that are believed to underlie the political process (Knoke, 1981). In this case the political scientist's concept of culture is really simply a form of ideology. It expresses what ordinary people are socialized into believing by the ideological apparatuses of society (Althusser, 1971; Bourdieu and Passeron, 1970). For example, according to Almond and Verba (1973: 440), in comparison with other industrialized democracies, "the United States possesses a 'civic culture' in which individual participation is highly valued and supported by existing political structures." Such an observation seems scarcely true today. At bottom, while people may be encouraged to vote and participate, they actually are blocked from engaging in substantive involvement and with good reason they participate only marginally. Arguing against the value-problematic approach means that we cannot put the blame for a lack of a "civic culture" on its victims. Instead, I suggest that part of ruling-class ideology, which aids in the legitimation of the present system, is precisely this link between an empirically measurable belief in democratic civic culture and its absence in the everyday reality of political process. Theories of politics that define culture in terms of prevailing beliefs and norms are simply exercises in ideological obfuscation (see Banfield and Wilson, 1963).

The role of ideology in the study and analysis of politics is so formidable that without an understanding of its role little progress can be made in the reconstruction of politics. As Jessop (1978: 27) suggests,

Although bourgeois law is rooted in capitalist relations of production, it denies the existence of exploitation and establishes a juridical system of formally equal juridical subjects under the authority of an impartial and independent *Rechstaat*. Moreover, although the *Rechstaat* is a mirage, it is a mirage extremely convenient to the bourgeosie. For it replaces religious ideology and obscures from the masses the fact of bourgeios domination.

Before we involve ourselves in the "equity problematic" of mainstream reformist political analysis, therefore, it is worthwhile remembering that social justice issues can never be resolved under capitalist relations of production. The strength of Pateman's (1970) analysis of participation was precisely in demonstrating that the blossoming of political democracy at the local level must be linked to its appearance at the place of work. Put a different way, when we discuss the revival of local political culture it is essential to connect self-management in the community with self-management at the place of work. These ideas make no sense otherwise.

The volunteering of solutions to the conditions belonging to the present regime of accumulation, however, presupposes that the contemporary dilemma of local politics *without* politics is perceived by the public. It is difficult to guess today whether the sentiments behind the decline of political culture represent a genuine acceptance of alienation and the irrelevance of local public life for average citizens, or an unresolved struggle among idealism, frustration, and failure. What is clear, however, is that the political philosophy of democracy belonging to the McCarthy period that can be personified by the writings of Lipset on politics advocated an elitist ideology that ignored what is most essential to civic culture, namely, that the lack of political participation cannot be equated with social contentment. The growing academic concern now in evidence over the decline of politics only underscores this point.

From a content analysis of local political activity the issue of greater participation seems foreign indeed. Political needs are produced by the uncoordinated nature of societal growth. Citizens most require relief from the effects of sociospatial restructuring. They look to local government as a means of ameliorating the costs of change not by bringing to it some substantive vision of democratic society and egalitarian ideals; in fact, the present moment can be characterized by its lack of social imagination and vision—the loss of discourse about social engineering and alternatives to our future. Demands generated from the present lack of direct planning are most often expressed as concerns about the quality of life. Rarely is the connection made, in the articulation of needs, between threats to that quality and the nature of capitalist development. Center-stage expressions for greater State intervention in the provision of use-values do not get connected in the public's mind with the backstage activities through which the State subsidizes business and pays the costs of providing the general conditions of capital accumulation. There is no coordinated link between these two activities, only a free play of concerted interests that are organized according to two traditional ideological expressions—one advocating growth and its benefits, the other lamenting the need for equity and the redistribution of wealth for the public's benefit. The balance affected between these two collective forces changes over time and is reflected in local public policy and the spending priorities of the moment. Goals of growth, visions of the future, of appropriate modes of development and design, and images of organized everyday life in a city environment planned for use-values rather than exchange value have no place in this empty ideological discourse disguising the clash between winners and losers in the capital accumulation process.

Most of the writing on the local State follows this clash of interests and tries to explain policy according to the factors antecedent to political organization coalescing around questions of social development. Theories of urban politics seem to suggest that what local government does is largely what powerful interests or aggregate expressions of will ask it to do. But attention to a content definition of local politics *cannot* explain why such a state of affairs exists. More important, an approach located at the level of appearance fails to acknowledge the essential democratic failure of present-day political arrangements.

According to the perspective advocated here, the play of power and interests observed by analysts of the local State merely observes the second, more volatile, tier of the State's structure. At the base of governance in all societies lies the State's definitions of property rights, including those of the

State itself. In the extreme case of State communism, these State rights replace all others. The first tier works, in part, through the law, through the entitlements that structure the system of expropriation. For the case of the United States there is a capitalist component of these laws and there is a part addressing the needs of State power. One is homologous to the other and this relation defines the conjuncture of interests between the capitalist class and the State, despite the potentially antagonistic claims on expropriated wealth that both of these domains represent.

In part, the first tier of the State also works through its legitimated means of force. It possesses a framework that can exercise the techniques of power. The State not only controls decision making according to the norms of property ownership, but also deploys its framework of power spatially to control behavior itself. As Foucault (1979) observes, the regulation of social interaction does not take place through voluntaristic acts of power alone. More important is the cultural drift of society through piecemeal regulations that perfect the political technology of social control. The power of the State is exercised through a massive framework of surveillance, control of space, police force, imprisonment, and the regulation of use-values and needs. The major responsibility of local government, in the case of the United States, is precisely this regulatory function of social control.

The first-tier functions described above along with the involvement of the legal infrastructure in entitlements, property deliberations, and disputes between the capitalist class and the State over taxation are the common ground of concern between the State and capital that has shifted little over the years when compared with second-tier activity. Because the interests involved in property rights are merely homologous between the State and capital, however, the relation worked out among property expropriators can give rise from time to time to contentious clashes and subsequent changes in the differential claims among them over the division of wealth. This struggle is located in the second tier of government because it does not challenge the basic rights of expropriation itself.

Most commonly, second-tier disputes between capital and the State involve issues of taxation. In the past the State vigorously regulated private incorporation and its tax liabilities. Over the years, and with the rise to hegemony of monopoly capital, however, the tax burden has shifted away from multinationals and squarely onto the shoulders of average citizens. Present shifts in the relation between capital and the State over property expropriation have appeared in the form of debates on tax reform. Trickle-down ideologies, homeowner revolts, and flat tax limits reflect the contemporary power of propertied interests and their ability to shift the tax burden onto the working class.

These historical changes in sources of revenue support for the local State compose a principal means for understanding its current limits. In the past its ability to expropriate surplus value from capital was far greater than today. Local capital needed the State to help it expand the scale of accumulation and to control labor. Capital required public diffusion of the costs of growth and public expenditure on the general conditions of production during the early phases of industrialization. Consequently, local government had a greater control over local capital resources because of mutual needs. Today this is no longer the case. While small business is still the lifeblood of the city contributing the greatest share in new employment, the city is hamstrung in its ability to support it by the structural weakness of its resource base. Taxation burdens have shifted to workers. Outside financing is, therefore, a necessity causing the local State to be dependent on finance capital and federal funds. In sum, as the local State has lost control over its own powers of expropriation, it has gained new partners that work against the kind of activities historically most synergistic to its own growth. It plays a deadly game with finance capital and higher levels of government acquiring the help needed to stay solvent and existing as a facade of governance but without the substantive resources and control over its own destiny characteristic of past days.

If the first tier of the State concerns the structural conditions that enable wealth to be expropriated, the second tier concerns politics as it is usually observed. In this domain of power there are no boundaries, no homologous concordances, only the raw play of organized interests according to the finer details involved in the struggle over the division of wealth and power. Three parties are involved here—the State, capital, and the workers, each with their own fractions. Organized interests clash in a variety of venues including the factory, city streets, corporate board meetings, public hearings, legislatures, commissions of government, and so on. Basic premises about the nature of property ownership belonging to the first tier are rarely discussed. Instead, ideological mechanisms are deployed to support alternative claims over the management and gains of growth. This second tier houses a process of contingency. Outcomes of conflict cannot normally be predicted except by observing long-term trends in the balance of power. It is no accident that Lasswell's concise description of politics—"Who gets what, how, and from whom?"—finds so clear a grasp of government activities at this level.

Over time crises of capitalism have provided the opportunity for the State to expand not only its power but also its apparatus. When the State has been asked to intervene in society it has done so according to its own fashion. This involves the penetration of the State into everyday life through the expansion of its institutional forms and, consequently, the extension of its regulatory power. Recently, analytical attention has been drawn increasingly to this aspect of the State. Not only has the power of State managers been observed to influence political outcomes, but the structural effects of institutions themselves have been discovered to act almost like trenches in canalizing political initiatives and contending interest groups according to specific patterns of policy outcomes.

The contingent nature of political processes and the involvement of three parties—the State, capital, and labor—in public disputes make the intersection of powerful social forces at the second tier a complicated affair. For this reason a wide variety of interpretations of local politics can be found in the literature with each school convinced, through empirical work, that their picture holds the most accurate rendering of local politics. Power elitists, for example, are quite sure that an interlocking network of the ruling class exists and can demonstrate their contention through well-known methods. Pluralists, in contrast, acknowledge this concerted force but find in local decision making degrees of freedom that belie ruling control. They provide evidence for the autonomy of politics and for the possibility of a free play of interests at the local level. Both perspectives fail to account for the four-dimensional confluence of power that provides the basis for today's regime of accumulation.

The State is Janus-like. It is either friend, ally, and confidant or enemy, obstacle, and tormentor. Among the more important functions of the State can be found its roles: in improving the performance of private-sector mechanisms in the supply of use-values; as a regulator of economic activity to overcome the costs of unbridled capitalist competition; as the manager of society in the interests of society as a whole; as the third-party mediator in political disputes, especially in confrontations between capital and labor; and as the promoter of social justice through the intervention of redistributive measures and programs and through its courts. The State's myriad functions perplex accounts to circumscribe its exact nature. It has the ability to play several roles at once. For this reason the most common form of studying the State, namely, attention to its functions, cannot grasp the underlying unity of its relation to society and becomes lost in the contingent nature of second-tier processes.

Functionalist accounts of the State commit the error of viewing politics solely from a society-centered perspective. This perpetuates the myth of the responsive State (see Chapter 4). Alternatively, State-centered approaches ignore the struggle taking place outside the State that is conditioned by the development of capitalism. Both views, however, have told us much about the exercise of State power, especially its expansion far beyond apparent boundaries in the regulation of everyday life. Yet, all one-sided approaches hem in the three-way struggle over power and wealth in a limited way. The past chapters have argued for a more synthetic perspective capturing the relation between society- and State-centered forces.

The presence of the many different views of the State that can be found in the literature has been explained by the preceding discussion in terms of its two-tiered nature. Conflict, contingency, the play of pluralist interests, management and steering of economic activity, along with the self-expansion of the State's apparatus, can all be located at the second level of political interaction concerned with clashes over the distribution of power and wealth. This is a political process that is allowed an indeterminacy by system constraints provided the power of expropriation is itself never challenged. Because the State needs an efficiently functioning capital accumulation process in order to maximize its own revenues, and because capital needs the State's guidance and intervention in order to rationalize its profit taking among the class of capitalists, concordant interests operate to constrain political conflict so that systemic processes are left unchallenged and free to function. Depending on an analyst's perception, different views of this process are observed forming the foundation for separate schools of thought.

It is only when the homology between the State and capital over the sanctity of property expropriation is brought to the surface of analysis that the real limits of political activity can be determined. At this deeper level the State stands ready to respond with force against any interest that challenges this right. In every social formation, whether it be capitalist or State communist, some underlying arrangement regarding property expropriation constitutes the basis for economic and political power (Nowak, 1983). This homological relation does not explain political interaction, but it does define both its ground rules and the limits beyond which it cannot pass.

In the study of political interaction focus shifts to the division of the surplus product. The entitlements and legal claims established in the first tier become animated by the contentious clash of interests in the second tier. Here the analysis of the State shifts from a focus on its forms to that of functions and apparatus. As Clark and Dear (1984) suggest, therefore, there is an order to the manner by which analysis can grasp the State and by progressing from discussions of State form to functions and finally to its apparatus. As they state,

> A proper analysis of *state apparatus* requires an understanding of *state functions* which in turn must be derived from an analysis of *state form*. . . . The question of "form" examines how a specific state sturcture is constituted by, and evolves within, a given social formation; state "function" refers to those activities undertaken in the name of the state, that is, what the state actually does in capitalist society; and state "apparatus" refers to the mechanisms through which these functions are executed. Therefore, the proper analytical logic would begin with issues of form, proceed to derive notions of function, and end by reading off the set of apparatus [1984: 36].

These distinctions come into much clearer focus when we consider the local State. Contemporary urban political analysis is virtually equated with studying the functions of government. Such an approach is limited because it equates the State itself only with the phenomenal modes of interaction belonging to its second tier. This is a form-determined social relation, as Jessop

(1982) suggests, meaning that the apparatus of the State has as much to do with political outcomes as does the clash of interests itself. Functional aspects of State intervention are also contingent for the same reasons, that is, contingency follows from the nature of second-tier political interaction. Precisely because of this phenomenal aspect, the State appears multifunctional and Janus-faced. And, precisely because of this multifunctionality, any approach basing analysis on the State's functions fails to penetrate the phenomenal layers of the three-way relation between the State, capital, and labor in the struggle over wealth and power.

A survey of the literature on the local State reveals that among both mainstreamers and Marxists there is general agreement that reproduction functions are the most important ones carried out by the local State. Urban politics then becomes the study of interaction organized around these reproductive functions, especially as a focus on explaining public policy.

For example, collective-consumption theorists consider urban politics as literally defined by State intervention in the reproduction of labor (see Saunders, 1981; Dunleavy, 1960; Castells, 1977). In previous chapters I have argued against this approach. Although socialized modes of consumption are aspects of State intervention, they are less necessary to capital than previously supposed and appear to be determined principally by the struggle between capital and labor that is contingently played out at the second-tier level of the social formation itself.

The political nature of socialized consumption, its divorce from the crisis base of capitalism and its fluid dynamics have been uncovered by the present retreat of the local State in supporting such activities and the current reprivatization of use-values. This readjustment against labor reveals the volatility behind the three-way relation of the State, capital, and labor in the local political process. So too does the historical course of the local fiscal crisis. Until as late as the 1980s, all State analysts were convinced of its necessity. Only very recently has it been revealed that fiscal strains have been managed more successfully by local government than previously imagined.

Both the retreat of the local State into reprivatization and the successful management of the fiscal crisis cast doubts on its functional necessity in the reproduction of capital accumulation. At least for the case of the United States, analyses such as Cockburn's (1979) that ascribe to the local State the principal task of reproduction are not valid. I am inclined, therefore, to suggest that there is a distinct order to the functions assumed by local government. Highest priority goes to State intervention in social control and the legitimation of the power relations in society. As indicated in Chapter 6, this function derives from the first-tier properties of the capitalist State and its unity with the mode of production. Other functions are those that are ascribed to it by political struggle located at the level of the social formation itself and due to needs generated by regimes of accumulation. Both the conditions of production through socialized intervention and integrative activities concerned with social welfare are modulated by the three-way clash among the State, capital, and labor in a contingent manner.

According to the terms of the present discussion, this makes issues concerned with the management of the quality of community life last in the series of functional priorities ascribed to the role of the State. In Chapter 7 I indicated that such concerns derive ideologically from the Fordist orchestration of cultural values. At the same time, political concerns about the quality of life are produced by uncoordinated capitalist development. Thus, the belief in a high quality of life is continually being undermined by development itself. This frames the principal contradiction of local governance under present structural arrangements of economy and society. In turn, this helps explain, perhaps, why questions about redistribution and general social welfare are the most debated issues of local politics—so little can really be done by the local State about them. This principal contradiction is also manifested by the failure of local politics to address questions of redistribution and equity. As indicated in Chapter 7, the third face of power, structural bias, militates against the demands of the less powerful. Once the action of State managers, of the intake apparatus, modes of administration and intervention, are all taken into account, we observe that biases already in place act in favor of the more affluent and the white. Thus, even when mobilization occurs it is doomed to fail as long as people work within the system and without the aid of more powerful auspices acting at the meso-political level.

In addressing the role of the State apparatus in the determination of political effects, I have followed Jessop (1982) by conceptualizing the State apparatus according to its forms of representation, administration, and intervention. As argued, because second-tier political activities are so complex—involving as they do the contingent struggle among labor, capital, and the State—the articulation between political interests and the threefold apparatus of the State is a highly volatile affair. At the local level voluntaristic efforts at providing some overarching vision and guidance to this articulation cannot hope to succeed. The uncoordinated nature of capitalist development is matched by the inability of the separate levels of the State to pull together the disparate forces of growth and change. Little wonder that this proceeds through the process of uneven development reproducing all the social contradictions of capitalism rather than resolving them through State intervention.

With regard to the local State, in particular, the death of politics plays a pertinent role in the diminishing ability of the State to perform the task of social guidance. Management functions of government have both exploded and then shifted from control by democratic modes of decision making to other venues of State administration. Special service districts, non-elective and quasipublic agencies, joint business/State commissions and programs eminating from higher levels of government, have all taken over functions that once were administered by more direct means of public participation. As the dispersal of instrumental functions has accelerated over time, the abandonment of participation has been helped by the increasing needs of local areas to accommodate future plans to unpredictable shifts in economic growth, the vagaries of finance-capital money market, and the overburdening problem of social inequality. Quite simply local government seems in danger of giving up its ghost to other levels of the State and to the direction of powerful economic interests. There is nothing left of its democratic core except the fragmented attempts of local residents to vent their needs, which take the form of ad hoc protests dotting the metropolitan landscape.

The failure of democracy means, within this context, a failure of the higher levels of government as well. No mechanisms currently exist that can aggregate neighborhood mobilization of needs into a viable public discourse on the future state of the metropolis. Growth proceeds without regionwide coordination because the decentralization of administrative units, while perhaps no less efficient than more centralized forms, cannot provide residents with the proper framework for addressing anything but the most immediate concerns of local neighborhoods. Present arrangements, in short, trivialize politics and reinforce its ad hoc nature.

Within the present milieu, the question of citizen participation cannot be addressed seriously. Mindless advocacy of mass democracy moves us away from confronting the real issues of local politics. The system has a powerful means of coopting struggles that seek to enter into the game of politics as it is currently structured (see Gitel, 1980; Shearer, 1984; Boggs, 1983). Expansion of involvement for formerly disenfranchised groups and mobilizations targeted toward new political demands merely make the present system stronger precisely because of greater participation in it. Playing by the system no longer works because there really is no system of democratic self-realization left.

Consequently, calls for greater self-help or self-management within our urban environments as well as more participation are equally doomed to avoid the necessary transformations. Self-help schemes, in particular, are merely new ways of reducing the costs of the local State. Both self-management and self-help are old ideas that have been polished off most recently, precisely because capital and the State have each entered into restructuring phases that can take advantage of such solutions in the reproduction of the present system. For example, facing a crisis in the declining productivity of labor and the marginalization of profit rates in some industries, capital has accepted the once revolutionary idea of worker ownership and self-management. As Russell (1984: 256) remarks, "The consequence of ownership without changing the capitalist system is greater control by that system in the larger sense of having to be more responsible about propertied interests."

Worker ownership makes for better and cheaper workers. Analogously, and *ceteris paribus*, participating citizens make for more coopted and cheaper citizens. This occurs most directly when the State itself moves against other associational forms or self-help groups, placing them under its auspices or dissolving them as illegitimate forms. As Katz and Mayer (1985: 17) observe, for example, in the case of housing, "in N.Y.C. tenant self help groups were appropriated from the street level by state agencies in an attempt to restore tax and rental revenue flows from slum properties to the public treasury."

It is precisely in this light that we can evaluate the neoconservative push for mediating institutions (see Egan et al., 1981; Novack, 1982). According to this proposal, the limitations of welfare Statism are acknowledged. The need is then expressed for less State and more privately sponsored institutions that will provide use-values for society. In this way free choice is encouraged and society circumvents the growth of social control, government waste, and bureaucratic meddling.

In evaluating any self-help scheme and on the basis of what has been said in Chapters 5 and 6, the question to be asked is whether the State itself will allow any rival forms of association to exist in society that usurp State power. Clearly, the answer is no, except under specific circumstances. Mediating institutions will be sanctioned only if they work to reduce the costs of the State by absorbing and privatizing functions and *not* if they assume for themselves the right of decision making and the steering functions of society. With the formidable apparatus of the existing regime of accumulation in place, movements toward greater self-help and reprivatization may be precisely the answers searched for under current conditions of capital restructuring, solving problems of legitimacy, fiscal strain, and the need for the provision of use-values so as to mollify the call to sustain the quality of life through less costly means than State socialization.

At present our cities and suburbs constitute a vast expanse of social contrast in the quality of life. Racial and income segregation prevail. Extreme forms of wealth and the concentration of well-off capitalist industries exist alongside marginalized firms seeking any means to survive. Within this milieu the only visions of the future that enter into political discourse come from big business. The spirit of daily life, its communicative content, all emerge from the marriage between capital and the State under the new, restructured conditions of accumulation, spatial modifications, and public provision. The discourse of needs pertinent to the daily life of average citizens, their vision of community quality, their articulation of societal priorities, all hang in the air without connection to sources of power. Today one can speak realistically only of the decline of political culture, not its prospects for rebirth at some future time.

REFERENCES

ABRAMSON, P. and J. ALDRICH (1982) "The decline of electoral participation in America." Amer. Pol. Sci. Rev. 76, 3: 502-521.

ADRIAN, C. (1961) Governing Urban America. New York: McGraw-Hill.

AGLIETTA, M. (1978) "Phases of U.S. capitalist expansion." New Left Rev. 110: 5-42.

AIKEN, M. (1970) "The distribution of community power: structural bases and social consequences," pp. 487-525 in M. Aiken and P. Mott (eds.) The Structure of Community Power. New York: Random House.

ALFORD, R. (1975) Health Care Politics: Ideological and Interest Group Barriers to Reform. Chicago: Univ. of Chicago Press.

ALFORD, R. and E. LEE (1968) "Voting turnout in American cities." Amer. Pol. Sci. Rev. 62: 796-813.

ALFORD, R. and H. SCOBLE (1968) "Sources of local political involvement." Amer. Pol. Sci. Rev. (December): 1192-1207.

ALMOND, G. and S. VERBA (1973) The Civic Culture. Princeton, NJ: Princeton Univ. Press.

ALPEROVITZ, G. and L. FAUX (1983) Rebuilding America. New York: Pantheon.

ALTHUSSER, L. (1971) Lenin and Philosophy. New York: Monthly Review.

ANDERSON, M. (1964) The Federal Bulldozer. Cambridge: MIT Press.

ANTUNES, G. and K. MLANDENKA (1976) "The politics of local services and service distribution," in R. Lineberry and L. Masotti (eds.) The New Urban Politics. Cambridge, MA: Ballinger.

ANTUNES, G. and J. PLUMBE (1977) "The distribution of a public service." Urban Affairs Q. 12 (March): 313-332.

AULETTA, K. (1982) The Underclass. New York: Random House.

BABCOCK, R. and F. BOSSELMAN (1973) Exclusionary Zoning: Land Use Regulation and Housing in the 1970s. New York: Praeger.

BACHRACH, P. and M. BARATZ (1962) "Two faces of power." Amer. Pol. Sci. Rev. 56 (December): 947-952.

BADIE, B. and P. BIRNBAUM (1983) The Sociology of the State. Chicago: Univ. of Chicago Press.

BAHL, R. [ed.] (1981) Urban Government Finance. Beverly Hills, CA: Sage.

BANFIELD, E. (1974) The Unheavenly City Revisited. Boston: Little, Brown.

BANFIELD, M. and J. Q. WILSON (1963) City Politics. New York: Vintage.

BAUER, R. (1966) Social Indicators. Cambridge: MIT Press.

BAUDRILLARD, J. (1975) The Mirror of Production. St. Louis: Telos.

BECKMAN, N. (1979) "Outside the city limits." Urban Interest 1, 1: 41-48.

BEDERMAN, S. and J. ADAMS (1974) "Job accessibility and underemployment." Annals of the Assn. of Amer. Geographers 64: 378-386.

BEER, S. (1978) "Federalism, nationalism and democracy in America." Amer. Pol. Sci. Rev. 72 (March): 9-21.

BENTON, T. (1981) "Objective interests and the sociology of power." Sociology 15, 2: 161-184.

BENTON, T. (1982) "Realism, power and objective interest," pp. 7-33 in K. Graham (ed.) Contemporary Political Philosophy. Cambridge: Cambridge Univ. Press.

BERGER, R. (1980) The Social Economy of Street Crime. Ann Arbor, MI: University Microfilms.

BISH, B. (1971) The Public Economy of Metropolitan Areas. Chicago: Rand McNally.

BISH, B. and V. OSTROM (1973) Understanding Urban Government. Washington, DC: American Enterprise Institute.

BLAIR, J. and D. NACHIMIAS [eds.] (1979) Fiscal Retrenchment and Urban Policy. Beverly Hills, CA: Sage.

BLAU, J. and P. BLAU (1982) "Metropolitan structure and violent crime." Amer. Soc. Rev. 47, 3: 114-129.

BLEITRACH, D. and A. CHENU (1982) "Modes of domination and everyday life," pp. 105-114 in M. Harloe and E. Lebas (eds.) City, Class and Capital. New York: Holmes and Meier.

BLOCH, P. (1974) Equality of Distribution of Police Services. Washington, DC: Urban Institute.

BLOCK, F. (1977) "The ruling class does not rule: notes on the Marxist theory of the state." Socialist Rev. 33 (May-June): 6-28.

BLOCK, F. (1980) "Beyond relative autonomy: state managers as historical subjects." Socialist Register, 1980: 227-242.

BLUESTONE, B. and M. HARRISON (1981) The Deindustrialization of America. New York: Basic Books.

BOCCARA, P. (1973) Etudes sur le Capitalisme Monopoliste D'Etat, sa Crise, son Issue. Paris: Editions Sociales.

BOGGS, C. (1983) "The new populism and the limits of structural reforms." Theory and Society 12, 3: 343-363.

BOOKCHIN, M. (1984) The Ecology of Freedom. Palo Alto, CA: Cheshire.

BOOTS, A. et al. (1972) Inequality in Local Government Services. Washington, DC: Urban Institute.

BOURDIEU, P. and J. C. PASSERON (1970) La Reproduction. Paris: Minuit.

BOYER, P. (1978) Urban Masses and Moral Order in America, 1820-1920. Cambridge, MA: Harvard Univ. Press.

BOYTE, H. (1980) The Backyard Revolution. Philadelphia: Temple Univ. Press.

BROWETT, J. (1984) "On the necessity and inevitability of uneven spatial development under capitalism." Int. J. of Urban and Regional Research 8, 2: 155-176.

BUCHANON, J. (1974) "Who should distribute what in a federal system?," in Hochman and Peterson (eds.) Redistribution Through Public Choice. New York: Columbia Univ. Press.

BUCHANON, J. and R. WAGNER (1977) Democracy in Deficit. New York: Academic Press.

BURGESS, E. (1925) "The growth of the city," in R. Park, E. Burgess, and R. McKenzie (eds.) The City. Chicago: Univ. of Chicago Press.

BURNHAM, D. (1984) The Rise of the Computer State. New York: Vintage.

BURNHAM, W. D. (1982) The Current Crisis in American Politics. New York: Oxford Univ. Press.

CAMERON, D. (1978) "The expansion of the public economy: a comparative analysis." Amer. Pol. Sci. Rev. 72 (December): 1243-1261.

CARNOY, M. (1984) The State and Political Theory. Princeton, NJ: Princeton Univ. Press.

CASTELLS, M. (1977) The Urban Question. Cambridge: MIT Press.

CASTELLS, M. (1978) City, Class and Power. New York: Macmillan.

CASTELLS, M. (1982) "Review of City Trenches." Int. J. of Urban and Regional Research 6, 3: 447-449.

CASTELLS, M. (1983) The City and the Grass Roots. Berkeley: Univ. of California Press.

CASTELLS, M. (1984) "Review of Mollenkopf, The Contested City." Int. J. of Urban and Regional Research 8, 4: 606-608.

CAVANAGH, T. (1981) "Changes in voter turnout, 1964-1976." Pol. Sci. Q. 96 (Spring): 53-65.

CECCARELLI, P. (1981) "Politics, parties and urban movements: western Europe," in S. Fainstein and N. Fainstein (eds.) Urban Policy Under Capitalism. Beverly Hills, CA: Sage.

CHANDLER, A. (1977) The Visible Hand. Cambridge, MA: Harvard Univ. Press.

CHRISTENSON, T. and L. GERSTON (1984) "Redefining voter representation: San Jose California." Cities 1, 5: 487-499.

CLARK, G. and M. DEAR (1984) State Apparatus. Boston: Allen and Unwin.

CLARK, T. (1968) "Community structure, decision-making budget expenditures and urban renewal in 51 American communities." Amer. Soc. Rev. 33 (August): 576-593.

CLARK, T. and L. FERGUSON (1981) "Fiscal strain in American cities: six basic processes," pp. 137-155 in K. Newton (ed.) Urban Political Economy. London: Francis Pinter.

CLARKE, S. (1983) "State, class struggle and the reproduction of capital." Kapitalistate 10-11.

COCKBURN, C. (1979) The Local State. London: Pluto.

COLEMAN, J. (1976) "Liberty and equality in school desegregation." Social Policy 6: 9-13.

COX, K. (1982) "Housing tenure and neighborhood activism." Urban Affairs Q. 18: 107-129.

CRENSON, M. (1983) Neighborhood Politics. Cambridge, MA: Harvard Univ. Press.

CROTTY, W. (1977) Political Reform and The American Experiment. New York: Thomas Crowell.

CROTTY, W. and G. JACOBSON (1980) American Parties in Decline. Boston: Little, Brown.

DAHL, R. (1961) Who Governs? New Haven, CT: Yale Univ. Press.

DAHL, R. (1972) Democracy in the United States: Promised Performance. Chicago: Rand McNally.

DANIELSON, M. (1976) The Politics of Exclusion. New York: Columbia Univ. Press.

DANIELSON, M. et al. (1977) One Nation, So Many Governments. Lexington, MA: D. C. Heath.

DAVIS, M. (1984) "The political economy of late-imperial America." New Left Rev. 143: 6-38.

DAVIS, O. et al. (1966) "A theory of the budgetary process." Amer. Pol. Sci. Rev. 60: 529-547.

de BORD, G. (1970) Society of the Spectacle. Detroit: Black & Red.

de BRUNHOFF, S. (1978) The State, Capital and Economic Policy. London: Pluto.

DELAFONS, J. (1969) Land Use Controls in the United States. Cambridge: MIT Press.

DEVINE, D. (1972) The Political Culture in the U.S. Boston: Little, Brown.

DEVINE, J. (1983) "Fiscal policy and class income inequality." Amer. Soc. Rev. 48 (October): 606-622.

DOBRINER, W. (1963) Class in Suburbia. Englewood Cliffs, NJ: Prentice-Hall.

DOMHOFF, G. (1971) The Higher Circles: The Governing Class in America. New York: Vintage.

DOMHOFF, G. (1978) Who Really Rules? New Haven and Community Power Reexamined. Santa Monica: Goodyear.

DOMHOFF, G. (1979) The Powers That Be: Processes of Ruling Class Domination in America. New York: Random House.

DOMHOFF, G. (1983) Who Rules America Now? Englewood Cliffs, NJ: Prentice-Hall.

DOWNES, B. [ed.] (1971) Cities and Suburbs. Belmont, CA: Wadsworth.

DOWNS, A. (1970) Urban Problems and Prospects. Chicago: Markham.

DUNCAN, S. (1981) "Housing policy, the methodology of levels, and urban research." Int. J. of Urban and Regional Research 5, 2: 231-253.

DUNCAN, S. and M. GOODWIN (1982) "The local state and restructuring social relations." Int. J. of Urban and Regional Research 6, 2.

DUNLEAVY, P. (1979) "The urban bases of political alignment." British J. of Pol. Sci. 9: 409-443.

DUNLEAVY, P. (1980) Urban Politics. New York: Macmillan.

DYE, T. (1976) Policy Analysis. Montgomery: Univ. of Alabama.

EGAN, J. et al. (1981) Housing and Public Policy: A Role for Mediating Structures. Cambridge, MA: Ballinger.

ESPING-ANDERSON et al. (1976) "Modes of class struggle and the capitalist state." Kapitalistate 4-5: 196-220.

EULAU, H., B. ZISK, and K. PREWITT (1966) "Latent partnership in non partisan cities," in M. Jennings and L. Ziegler (eds.) The Electoral Process. Englewood Cliffs, NJ: Prentice-Hall.

EYESTONE, R. (1978) From Social Issues to Public Policy. New York: John Wiley.

FEAGIN, J. (1983) The Urban Real Estate Game. Englewood Cliffs, NJ: Prentice-Hall.

FEAGIN, J. (1985) "The role of the state in urban development: the case of Houston, Texas." (unpublished)

FELLMUTH, R. [ed.] (1973) Land and Politics: Power and Land in California. New York: Grossman.

FERGUSON, L. (1981) "Fiscal strain in American cities: some limitations on popular explanations," pp. 156-178 in K. Newton (ed.) Urban Political Economy. London: Francis Pinter.

FISCHER, C. (1976) The Urban Experience. New York: Harcourt Brace Jovanovich.

FISCHER, C. (1983) To Dwell Among Friends. Chicago: Univ. of Chicago Press.

FISHEL, J. [ed.] (1978) Parties and Elections in an Anti-Party Age. Bloomington: Indiana Univ. Press.

FLORA, P. and A. HEIDENHEIMER [eds.] (1982) The Development of Welfare States in Western Europe and North America. New Brunswick, NJ: Transaction.

FOLIN, M. (1982) "The production of the several conditions of social production and the role of the state," pp. 51-60 in M. Harloe and E. Lebus (eds.) City, Class, and Capital. New York: Holmes and Meier.

FORRESTER, J. (1969) Urban Dynamics. Cambridge: MIT Press.

FOSSETT, J. (1983) Federal Aid to Big Cities: The Politics of Dependence. Washington, DC: Brookings Institution.

FOUCAULT, M. (1979) Discipline and Punish. New York: Vintage

FREE, L. and H. CANTRIL (1967) The Political Beliefs of Americans. New Brunswick, NJ: Rutgers Univ. Press.

FRIEDLAND, R. (1980) "Corporate power and urban growth." Politics and Society 10: 203-224.

FRIEDLAND, R. (1983) Power and Crisis in the City. New York: Schocken.

FRUG, G. (1980) "The city as a legal concept." Harvard Law Rev. 93, 6: 1059-1154.

FRY, B. and R. WINTERS (1970) "The politics of redistribution." Amer. Pol. Sci. Rev. 64 (June).

FUSFIELD, D. (1980) The Rise and Repression of Radical Labor in the USA, 1877-1913. Chicago: Kerr.

GAFFNEY, M. (1973) "Tax reform to release land," pp. 115-129 in M. Clawson (ed.) Modernizing Urban Land Policy. Washington, DC: Resources for the Future.

GANS, C. (1978) "The empty ballot box: reflections on non-voting in America." Public Opinion (September-October).

GANZ, A. (1985) "Where has the urban crisis gone?," pp. 39-58 in M. Gottdiener (ed.) Cities in Stress. A New Look at the Urban Crisis. Beverly Hills, CA: Sage.

GERSON, E. (1976) "On 'quality of life.'" Amer. Soc. Rev. 41 (October): 793-806.

GERTH, H. and C. W. MILLS [eds.] (1946) From Max Weber: Essays in Sociology. New York: Oxford.

GIDDENS, A. (1971) Capitalism and Modern Social Theory. Cambridge: Cambridge Univ. Press.

GILBERT, C. (1967) Governing the Suburbs. Bloomington: Indiana Univ. Press.

GILBERT, N. (1983) Capitalism and the Welfare State: Dilemmas of Social Benevolence. New Haven, CT: Yale Univ. Press.

GITEL, M. (1980) Limits to Citizen Participation. Beverly Hills, CA: Sage.

GOLD, N. (1972) "Mismatch of jobs and low-income people in metropolitan areas and its implications for the central-city poor," in S. Mazie (ed.) U.S. Commission on Population Growth. Washington, DC: Government Printing Office.

GOTTDIENER, M. (1977) Planned Sprawl: Public and Private Interests in Suburbia. Beverly Hills, CA: Sage.

GOTTDIENER, M. (1985a) The Social Production of Urban Space. Austin: Univ. of Texas Press.

GOTTDIENER, M. (1985b) "Whatever happened to the urban crisis." Special Issue of Urban Affairs Quarterly, June.

GOTTDIENER, M. [ed.] (1986) Cities in Stress: A New Look at the Urban Crisis. Beverly Hills, CA: Sage.

GOTTDIENER, M. and M. NEIMAN (1981) "Characteristics of support for local growth control." Urban Affairs Q. 17: 55-73.

GOUGH, I. (1979) The Political Economy of the Welfare State. London: Macmillan.

GRAMSCI, A. (1971) The Prison Notebooks. New York: International.

GREER, S. (1960) "The social structure and political process of suburbia." Amer. Soc. Rev. 25: 514-526.

GREER, S. (1962) Governing the Metropolis. New York: Wiley.

GRIFFEN, L. et al. (1983) "On the economic and political determinants of welfare spending in the post-World War II era." Politics and Society 12, 3: 331-372.

GROSS, B. (1980) Friendly Fascism. Boston: South End Press.

HABERMAS, J. (1975) Legitimation Crisis. Boston: Beacon.

HADLEY, A. (1978) The Empty Polling Booth. NJ: Englewood Cliffs, NJ: Prentice-Hall.

HARRINGTON, T. (1983) "Explaining state policy-making: a critique of some recent 'dualist' models." Int. J. of Urban and Regional Research 7, 2: 202-217.

HARVEY, D. (1973) Social Justice and the City. Baltimore: Johns Hopkins Univ. Press.

HENIG, J. (1982) Neighborhood Mobilization: Redevelopment and Response. New Brunswick, NJ: Rutgers Univ. Press.

HENIG, J. (1985) "Collective responses to the urban crisis: ideology and mobilization," pp. 221-246 in M. Gottdiener (ed.) Cities in Stress: A New Look at the Urban Crisis. Beverly Hills, CA: Sage.

HERO, R. and R. DURAND (1985) "Explaining citizen evaluations of urban services." Urban Affairs Q. 20, 3: 344-354.

HIBBS, D. (1977) "Political parties and macroeconomic policy." Amer. Pol. Sci. Rev. 71, 4: 1467-1487.

HICKS, A. et al. (1978) "Class power and state policy." Amer. Soc. Rev. 43 (June): 302-315.

HICKS, A. and D. SWANK (1984) "On the political economy of welfare expansion." Comparative Pol. Studies 17, 1: 81-119.

HILL, R. C. (1974) "Separate and unequal: governmental inequality in the metropolis." Amer. Pol. Sci. Rev. 68: 1557-1568.

HINDESS, B. (1978) "Classes and politics in Marxist theory," pp. 72-97 in G. Littlejohn et al. (eds.) Power and the State. London: Croon Helm.

HIRSCH, J. (1983) "The Fordist security state and social movements." Kapitalistate 10-11: 75-87.

HIRSCHMAN, A. (1970) Exit, Voice and Loyalty. Cambridge, MA: Harvard Univ. Press.

HIRST, P. (1977) "Economic classes and politics," in A. Hunt (ed.) Class and Class Structure. London: Lawrence and Wishart.

HOCH, C. (1984) "City limits: municipal bonding formation and class segregation," pp. 101-122 in W. Tabb and L. Sawers (eds.) Marxism and the Metropolis. New York: Oxford.

HOFFERBERT, R. (1966) "The relation between public policy and some structural and environmental variables in the American states." Amer. Pol. Sci. Rev. 60 (March): 73-82.

HOFSTADTER, R. (1963) "The pseudo-conservative revolt," pp. 63-80 in D. Bell (ed.) The Radical Right. Garden City, NY: Anchor.

HOFSTADTER, R. (1974) The American Political Tradition. New York: Vintage.

HOLLOWAY, J. and S. PICCIOTTO [eds.] (1979) State and Capital. Austin: Univ. of Texas Press.

HUNTER, A. (1979) Symbolic Communities. Chicago: Univ. of Chicago Press.

HUNTINGTON, S. (1968) Political Order in Changing Societies. New Haven, CT: Yale Univ. Press.

HYMER, S. (1979) The Multinational Corporation. Cambridge: Cambridge Univ. Press.

ISAACS, L. and W. KELLY (1981) "Racial insurgency, the state and welfare expansion." Amer. J. of Sociology 86, 6: 1311-1386.

JESSOP, B. (1978) "Capitalism and democracy: the best possible shell?," in G. Littlejohn et al. (eds.) Power and the State. London: Croon Helm.

JESSOP, B. (1982) The Capitalist State. New York: New York Univ. Press.

JESSOP, B. (1983) "Accumulation strategies, state forms and hegemonic projects." Kapitalistate 10-11: 89-112.

JOHNSTON, R. (1971) Urban Residential Patterns. New York: Praeger.

JONES, B. (1983) Governing Urban America. Boston, MA: Little, Brown.

JUDD, D. and R. READY (1984) Entrepreneurial Cities and the New Politics of Economic Development. (unpublished)

JUDD, D. and M. SMITH (1983) "Economic restructuring and the politics of growth, welfare and territorial preservation." Presented at Association of Schools of Planning, San Francisco, October 21-23.

KAIN, J. (1968) "Housing segregation, negro employment and metropolitan decentralization." Quarterly J. of Economics 82: 175-197.

KAPP, K. (1963) Social Costs of Business Enterprise. Bombay: Asian Publishing.

KATZ, S. and M. MAYER (1985) "Gimme shelter: self-help housing struggles within and against the state in New York City and West Berlin." Int. J. of Urban and Regional Research 9, 1: 15-45.

KATZNELSON, I. (1976) "Class capacity and social cohesion in American cities," in R. Lineberry and L. Masotti (eds.) The New Urban Politics. Cambridge, MA: Ballinger.

KATZNELSON, I. (1979) "Review of Equality and Urban Policy." Int. J. of Urban and Regional Research 3, 2: 269-275.

KATZNELSON, I. (1981) City Trenches: Urban Politics and the Patterning of Class in the U.S. New York: Pantheon.

KATZNELSON, I. et al. (1982) "Race and schooling: reflections on the social basis of urban movements," pp. 215-236 in N. Fainstein and S. Fainstein (eds.) Urban Policy Under Capitalism. Beverly Hills, CA: Sage.

KNOKE, D. (1981) "Urban political cultures," pp. 203-225 in T. Clark (ed.) Urban Policy Analysis. Beverly Hills, CA: Sage.

KOTLER, M. (1969) Neighborhood Government: The Local Foundations of Political Life. Indianapolis, IN: Bobbs-Merrill.

LACAN, J. (1968) The Language of the Self. Baltimore: Johns Hopkins Univ. Press.

LANGE, O. (1963) Political Economy, Vol. I. New York: Pergamon.

LEBAS, E. (1982) "Introduction—the new school of urban and regional research," pp. ix-xxxiii in M. Harloe and E. Lebas (eds.) City, Class and Capital. New York: Holmes and Meier.

LEFEBVRE, H. (1971) Everyday Life in the Modern World. New York: Harper.

LEFEBVRE, H. (1973) La Survie du Capitalisme. Paris: Editions Anthropos.

LEFEBVRE, H. (1974) La Production de L'Espace. Paris: Editions Anthropos.

LELOUP, L. (1978) "The myth of incrementalism: analytic choices in budgetary theory." Polity 10: 488-509.

LEVIN, H. (1976) "Concepts of economic efficiency and educational production," pp. 149-198 in J. Froomkin, et al. (eds.) Education as an Industry. Cambridge, MA: Ballinger.

LEVY, F. D., B. MELTSHER, and W. WILDAVSKY (1974) Urban Outcomes. Berkeley: Univ. of California Press.

LEWIS, C. (1982) "Interpreting municipal expenditures," pp. 203-218 in R. Rich (ed.) Analyzing-Urban-Service Distributions. Lexington, MA: D. C. Heath.

LINEBERRY, R. (1970) "Reforming metropolitan governance: requiem or reality?" Georgetown Law J. 58 (March-May): 675-718.

LINEBERRY, R. (1977) Equality and Urban Policy. Beverly Hills, CA: Sage.

LINEBERRY, R. and E. FOWLER (1967) "Reformism and public policies in American cities." Amer. Pol. Sci. Rev. 61: 701-716.

LINEBERRY, R. and I. SHARKANSKY (1978) Urban Politics and Public Policy. New York: Harper and Row.

LIPIETZ, A. (1982) "Towards a global Fordism?" New Left Rev. 132: 33-48.

LIPSET, S. (1963) Political Man. New York: Anchor-Doubleday.

LIPSKY, M. (1970) Protest in City Politics. Chicago: Rand McNally.

LIPSKY, M. (1976) "Toward a theory of street-level bureaucracy," in W. Hawley et al. (eds.) Theoretical Perspectives on Urban Politics. Englewood Cliff, NJ: Prentice-Hall.

LIU, B. (1976) Qualify of Life Indicators in U.S. Metropolitan Areas. New York: Praeger.

LOGAN, J. and M. SCHNEIDER (1981) "The stratification of metropolitan suburbs, 1960-1970." Amer. Soc. Rev. 46 (April): 175-186.

LOJKINE, J. (1976) Le Marxisme, L'etat et La Question Urbaine. Paris: Centre de Sociologie Urbaine.

LONG, J. (1981) Population Deconcentration in the U.S. Bureau of the Census. Washington, DC: Government Printing Office.

LOVATT, D. and B. HAM (1984) "Class formation, wage formation and community protest in a metropolitan control center." Int. J. of Urban and Regional Research 8, 3.

LOWI, T. (1967) "Machine politics—old and new." The Public Interest (Fall): 83-92.

LUKES, S. (1974) Power: A Radical View. London: Macmillan.

LUKES, S. (1977) Essays in Social Theory. New York: Columbia Univ. Press.

LYND, R. and H. LYND (1937) Middletown in Transition. New York: Harcourt.

LYON, L. and C. BONJEAN (1981) "Community power and policy outputs: the routines of local politics." Urban Affairs Q. 17, 1: 3-21.

MacIVER, R. (1969) The Modern State. New York: Oxford Univ. Press.

MAINS, J. and L. STINE (1959) "Suburban residence and political behavior." Public Opinion Q. 58-59: 483-489.

MANDEL, E. (1975) Late Capitalism. London: Velos.

MANDELBAUM, S. (1965) Boss Tweed's New York. New York: Wiley.

MARCHAND, D. (1980) The Politics of Privacy, Computers, and Criminal Justice Records. Arlington, VA: Information Resources Press.

MARKUSEN, A. (1978) "Class and urban social expenditures," pp. 90-111 in W. Tabb and L. Sawers (eds.) Marxism and the Metropolis. New York: Oxford Univ. Press.

MARLOWE, J. (1985) "Private versus public provision of refuse removal service." Urban Affairs Q. 20, 3: 355-363.

MATZER, J., Jr. (1985) "Local control of fiscal stress," pp. 63-80 in M. Gottdiener (ed.) Cities in Stress: A New Look at the Urban Crisis. Beverly Hills, CA: Sage.

MARX, K. (1967) Capital. New York: New World.

MARX, K. (1973) Grundrisse. New York: Vintage.

MAZMANIAN, D. and P. SABATIER [eds.] (1980) "Symposium on successful policy implementation." Policy Studies J. 8.

McDONALD, T. and S. WARD (1984) The Politics of Urban Fiscal Policy. Beverly Hills, CA: Sage.

MEGRET, A. (1981) "Achieving equity in an era of fiscal constraint," in R. Burchell and D. Listokin (eds.) Cities Under Stress. New Brunswick, NJ: Rutgers.

MELMAN, S. (1983) Profits Without Production. New York: Knopf.

MIKESELL, J. (1979) "The season of tax revolt," pp. 107-131 in J. Blair and D. Nachmais (eds.) Fiscal Retrenchment and Urban Policy. Beverly Hills, CA: Sage.

MILIBAND, R. (1969) The State in Capitalist Society. New York: Basic.

MINGIONE, E. (1981) Social Conflict and the City. New York: St. Martin's.

MISHAN, E. (1967) The Costs of Economic Growth. New York: Vintage.

MLANDENKA, K. and K. HILL (1977) "The distribution of benefits in an urban environment." Urban Affairs Q. 13 (September): 73-44.

MLANDENKA, K. and K. HILL (1978) "The distribution of urban police services." J. of Politics 40 (February): 112-133.

MOLLENKOPF, J. (1983) The Contested City. Princeton, NJ: Princeton Univ. Press.

MOLOTCH, A. (1976) "The city as a growth machine." Amer. J. of Sociology 82, 309-332.

MONKKONEN, E. (1985) "The sense of crisis: a historian's point of view," pp. 20-38 in M. Gottdiener (ed.) Cities in Stress: A New Look at the Urban Crisis. Beverly Hills, CA: Sage.

MORIARITY, B. et al. (1980) Industrial Location and Community Development. Chapel Hill: Univ. of North Carolina.

MULLER, P. (1981) Contemporary Suburban America. Englewood Cliffs, NJ: Prentice-Hall.

MURRAY, C. (1984) Losing Ground. New York; Basic.

MURPHY, T. and J. REHFUS (1976) Urban Politics in the Suburban Era. Homewood, IL: Dorsey.

MUSHKAT, J. (1971) Tammany: The Evolution of a Political Machine 1789-1865. Syracuse, NY: Syracuse Univ. Press.

NARDULLI, P. and J. STONECASH (1981) Politics, Professionalism and Urban Services: The Police. Cambridge, MA: Oelgeschlager, Gunn & Hain.

NEIMAN, M. (1975) Metropology. Beverly Hills, CA: Sage.

NEIMAN, M. (1982) "An exploration into class clustering and local-government inequality," in R. Rich (ed.) Analyzing Urban-Service Distributions. Lexington, MA: D. C. Heath.

NEIMAN, M. and M. GOTTDIENER (1982) "The relevance of the qualifying stage of initiative politics: the case of petition signing." Social Sci. Q. 63, 3: 582-588.

NEIMAN, M. and M. GOTTDIENER (1985) "Qualifying Initiatives." Social Sci. J. 22, 1: 99-109.

NEIMAN, M. and C. LOVELL (1980) "Federal and state requirements: impacts on local governments." The Urban Interest, 2: 45-52.

NEWFIELD, J. and DEBRUL, P. (1981) The Permanent Government. New York: Vintage.

NEWTON, K. (1976) "Feeble government and private power: urban politics and policies in the United States," pp. 37-58 in R. Lineberry and L. Masotti (eds.) The New Urban Politics. Cambridge, MA: Ballinger.

NEWTON, K. (1978) "Conflict avoidance and conflict suppression," pp. 76-93 in K. Cox (ed.) Urbanization and Conflict in Market Societies. Chicago: Maaroufa.

NISBET, R. (1968) Community and Power. New York: Oxford Univ. Press.

NORDLINGER, E. (1981) On the Autonomy of the Democratic State. Cambridge, MA: Harvard Univ. Press.

NORMAN P. (1975) "Managerialism: a review of recent work," in M. Harloe (ed.) Proceedings of the Conference on Urban Change and Conflict, 1975. London: Center for Environmental Studies.

NOVACK, M. (1982) "Mediating institutions: the communitarian individual in America." The Public Interest 68: 3-20.

NOWAK, L. (1983) Property and Power. Dordrecht: D. Reidel.

OAKES, J. (1985) Keeping Track: How Schools Structure Inequality. New Haven, CT: Yale Univ. Press.

OATES, W. (1969) Fiscal Federalism. New York: Harcourt Brace Jovanovich.

O'CONNOR, J. (1973) The Fiscal Crisis of the State. New York: St. Martin's.

O'CONNOR, J. (1981) "The fiscal crisis of the state revisited." Kapitalistate 9: 41-61.

OFFE, C. (1984) Contradictions of the Welfare State. London: Hutchinson.

OFFE, C. and V. RONGE (1975) "Theses on the theory of the state." New German Critique 6: 137-147.

OLSON, M. (1965) The Logic of Collective Action. Cambridge, MA: Harvard Univ. Press.

ORBELL, J. and T. UNO (1972) "A theory of neighborhood problem solving: political action vs. residential mobility." Amer. Pol. Sci. Rev. 66: 471-489.

OSTROM, E. (1983) "The social stratification—government inequality thesis explored." Urban Affairs Q. 19, 1: 91-112.

OSTROM, V., C. TIEBOUT, and R. WARREN (1961) "The organization of government in metropolitan areas." Amer. Pol. Sci. Rev. 55 (December): 831-842.

PADGETT, J. (1980) "Bounded rationality in budgetary research." Amer. Pol. Sci. Rev. 74: 354-372.

PAHL, R. E. (1975) "Urban managerialism reconsidered," in R. E. Pahl, Whose City? Harmondsworth, UK: Penguin.

PAHL, R. E. (1977a) "Stratification and the relation between the states and urban and regional development." Int. J. of Urban and Regional Research 1, 1: 6-17.

PAHL, R. E. (1977b) "Managers, technical experts and the state," in M. Harloe, Captive Cities. New York: John Wiley.

PAHL, R. (1978) "Castells and collective consumption." Sociology 12, 2: 309-315.

PAHL, R. E. (1979) "Socio-political factors in resource allocation," in D. Herbert and D. Smith (eds.) Social Problems and the City. Oxford: Oxford Univ. Press.

PARSONS, T. (1957) "The distribution of power in American society." World Politics 10 (October): 123-143.

PATEMAN, C. (1970) Participation and Democratic Theory. New York: Cambridge Univ. Press.

PETERSON, P. (1981) City Limits. Chicago: Univ. of Chicago Press.

PICKVANCE, C. G. (1982) The State and Collective Consumption. Milton Keynes: Open Univ. Press.

PICKVANCE, C. G. (1984a) "The structuralist critique in urban studies," pp. 31-50 in M. Smith (ed.) Cities in Transformation. Beverly Hills, CA: Sage.

PICKVANCE, C. G. (1984b) "Review of 'The City and the Grass Roots.'" Int. J. of Urban and Regional Research 8, 4: 588-591.

PICKVANCE, C. G. (1984c) "Spatial policy as territorial politics: the role of the spatial coalitions in the articulation of 'spatial' interests and in the demand for spatial policy," in G. Rees (ed.) Political Action and Social Identity: Class, Locality and Culture. London: Macmillan.

PIVEN, F. and R. CLOWARD (1971) Regulating the Poor. New York: Pantheon.

PIVEN, F. and R. CLOWARD (1979) Poor Peoples Movements: Why They Succeed, How They Fail. New York: Random House.

POLSBY, N. (1980) Community Power and Political Theory. New Haven, CT: Yale Univ. Press.

POULANTZAS, N. (1973) Political Power and Social Classes. London: New Left.

POULANTZAS, N. (1975) Classes in Contemporary Capitalism. London: New Left.

PRESSMAN, J. and A. WILDAVSKY (1973) Implementation. Berkeley: Univ. of California Press.

RAWLS, J. (1971) A Theory of Justice. Cambridge, MA: Harvard Univ. Press.

REICH, M. and R. EDWARDS (1978) "Political parties and class conflict—the U.S." Socialist Rev. 8, 3: 37-57.

REX, J. and R. MOORE (1967) Race, Community and Conflict. London: Oxford.

ROSENBAUM, W. (1975) Political Culture. New York: Praeger.

RUBIN, I. and H. RUBIN (1985) "Structural theories and urban fiscal stress," pp. 177-198 in M. Gottdiener (ed.) Cities in Stress: A New Look at the Urban Crisis. Beverly Hills, CA: Sage.

RUSSELL, R. (1984) "Using ownership to control: making workers owners in the contemporary United States." Politics and Society 13, 3: 253-294.

SACHS, S. and R. HARRIS (1974) "The determinants of state and local governmental expenditures and intergovernmental flow of funds." National Tax J. 17 (March): 78-85.

SALISBURY, R. (1979) "Why no corporatism in America?," in P. Schnitter and G. Lembruch (eds.) Trends Toward Corporatist Intermediation. Beverly Hills, CA: Sage.

SAUNDERS, P. (1978) "Domestic property and social class." Int. J. of Urban and Regional Research 11: 233-251.

SAUNDERS, P. (1981) Social Theory and the Urban Question. London: Hutchinson.

SAUNDERS, P. (1983) "On the shoulders of which giant? The case of Weberian political analysis," in P. Williams (ed.) Social Process and the City. Sydney: Allen and Unwin.

SAVAS, E. (1983) Privatizing the Public Sector. Chatham, NJ: Chatham House.

SAYRE, W. and H. Kaufman (1960) Governing New York City. New York: Russell Sage Foundation.

SBRAGIA, A. (1983) The Municipal Money Chase. Boulder, CO: Westview.

SCHNEIDER, M. (1975) "The quality of life in large American cities: objective and subjective social indicators." Social Indicators Research 1: 495-509.

SCOTT, J. (1972) Comparative Political Corruption. Englewood Cliffs, NJ: Prentice-Hall.

SENNETT, R. (1968) Classic Essays in the Culture of Cities. New York: Appleton-Century-Crofts.

SEXTON, P. (1961) Education and Income. New York: Viking.

SHALEV, M. (1983) "The social democratic model and beyond: two generations of comparative research on the Welfare State." Comparative Social Research 6.

SHALEV, M. and W. KORPI (1980) "Working class mobilization and American exceptionalism." Econ. and Industrial Democracy 1, 1: 31-61.

SHARKANSKY, I. (1970) The Routines of Politics. New York: Van Nostrand.

SHEARER, D. (1984) "Citizen participation in local government: the case of Santa Monica, California." Int. J. of Urban and Regional Research 8, 4: 573-586.

SHEFTER, M. (1977) "New York's fiscal crisis: the politics of inflation and retrenchment." The Public Interest 48 (Summer): 98-127.

SHEPHARD, W. (1975) "Metropolitan political decentralization: a test of the life styles values model." Urban Affairs Q. 10, 3: 297-313.

SKOCPOL, T. (1980) "Poltical response to capitalist crisis: neo-Marxist theories of the state and the case of the New Deal." Poltitics and Society 10, 2: 155-201.

SMITH, D. (1973) The Geography of Social Well-Being in the United States. New York: McGraw-Hill.

SMITH, M. (1980) "Critical theory and urban political theory." Comparative Urban Research 7, 3: 5-23.

SMITH, M. and D. JUDD (1984) "American cities: the production of ideology," pp. 173-196 in M. Smith (ed.) Cities in Transformation. Beverly Hills, CA: Sage.

STEIN, M. (1960) Eclipse of Community. Glencoe: Free Press.

STONE, C. (1976) Economic Growth and Neighborhood Discontent. Chapel Hill: Univ. of North Carolina Press.

STONE, C. (1980) "Systemic power in community decision making: a restatement of stratification theory." Amer. Pol. Sci. Rev. 74, 3: 978-990.

STONE, C. (1982) "Social stratification, nondecision-making, and the study of community power." Amer. Pol. Q. 10, 3: 275-302.

STONE, C., R. WHELAN, and W. MURIN (1979) Urban Policy and Politics. Englewood Cliffs, NJ: Prentice-Hall.

SUSSER, I. (1982) Norman Street. New York: Oxford Univ. Press.

SULLIVAN, W. (1985) "Individualism and civic commitment." Presented at Tocqueville Symposium, Claremont Colleges, January 26, 1985.

SUTTLES, G. (1973) The Social Construction of Communities. Chicago: Univ. of Chicago Press.

SUTTLES, G. and A. HUNTER (1973) "The defended neighborhood," in G. Suttles, The Social Construction of Community. Chicago: Univ. of Chicago Press.

SWANK, D. (1983) "Between incrementalism and revolution: protest groups and the growth of the welfare state."Amer. Behavioral Scientist 26 (January-February): 291-310.

SWANSTROM, T. (1985) The Crisis of Growth Politics: Cleveland, Kucinich and the Challenge of Urban Populism. Philadelphia: Temple Univ. Press.

TARRANCE, V. (1978) "Suffrage and voter turnout in the United States: the vanishing voter," pp. 77-85 in J. Fishel (ed.) Parties and Elections in an Anti-Party Age. Bloomington: Indiana University Press.

TAUEBER, K. and A. TAUEBER (1965) Negroes in Cities. Chicago: Aldine.

THERET, B. (1982) "Collective means of consumption, capital accumulation and the urban question." Int. J. of Urban and Regional Research 6, 3: 345-371.

THOMAS, J. (1982) "Citizen-initiated contacts with government agencies: a test of three theories." Amer. J. of Pol. Sci. 26, 3: 505-522.

THOMPKINS, G. (1975) "A causal model of state welfare expenditures." J. of Politics 37 (May): 392-416.

TIEBOUT, C. (1956) "A pure theory of local expenditures." J. of Pol. Economy 64 (October): 416-424.

VERBA, S. et al. (1978) Participation and Political Equality. New York: Cambridge

Univ. Press.

VERBA, S. and N. NIE (1972) Participation in America. New York: Harper & Row.

WARNER, W. (1949) Democracy in Jonesville. New York: Harper.

WARREN, R. (1964) "A municipal services market model of metropolitan organization." J. of Amer. Institute of Planners, 30 (August): 193-204.

WASYLENKO, M. (1981) "The location of firms: the roles of taxes and fiscal incentives," pp. 155-190 in R. Bahl (ed.) Urban Government Finance. Beverly Hills, Ca: Sage.

WEBER, M. (1962) In D. Martindale (ed.) The City. New York: Collier.

WEICHER, J. (1971) "The allocation of police protection by income class." Urban Studies 8 (October): 207-220.

WELLMAN, B. and B. LEIGHTON (1979) "Networks, neighborhoods and communities." Urban Affairs Q. 15 (March): 363-390.

WHITT, J. A. (1982) Urban Elites and Mass Transportation. Princeton, NJ: Princeton Univ. Press.

WICKMAN, W. (1970) The Political Theory of Local Government. Columbia: Univ. of South Carolina Press.

WILENSKY, H. (1975) The Welfare State and Equality. Berkeley: Univ. of California Press.

WILLIAMS, O. (1968) "Lifestyle values and political decentralization," in T. Clark (ed.) Community Structure and Decision Making. San Francisco, CA: Chandler.

WILLIAMS, O. (1971) Metropolitan Political Analysis. New York: Free Press.

WILLIAMS, O. and K. EKLUND (1978) "Segregation in a fragmented context: 1950-1970," in K. Rich (ed.) Urbanization and Conflict in Market Societies. Chicago: Maaroufa.

WINDSOR, D. (1979) Fiscal Zoning in Suburban Communities. Lexington, MA: D. C. Heath.

WINDSOR, D. and F. JAMES (1975) "Breaking the invisible wall: fiscal reform and municipal land use regulation," in R. L. Lineberry and L. Masotti (eds.) Urban Problems and Public Policy. Lexington, MA: D. C. Heath.

WIRT, F. (1974) Power in the City. Berkeley: Univ. of California Press.

WIRT, F. (1983) "The dependent city: external influences upon local autonomy." Presented at APSA meetings, Chicago, September 1-4.

WOOD, R. (1959) Suburbia: Its People and Politics. Boston: Houghton Mifflin.

WOOD, R. (1961) 1400 Governments. Cambridge, MA: Harvard Univ. Press.

WRIGHT, E. (1978) Class, Crisis and The State. London: New Left.

WRIGHT, J. (1976) The Dissent of the Governed: Alienation of Democracy in America. New York: Academic Press.

YATES, D. (1976) "Urban government as a policy-making system," in R. L. Lineberry and L. Masotti (eds.) The New Urban Politics. Cambridge, MA: Ballinger.

YATES, D. (1977) The Ungovernable City. Cambridge, MIT Press.

ZIMMERMAN, J. (1975) "The patchwork approach: adaptive responses to increasing urbanization," in A. Hawley et al. (eds). Metropolitan America in Contemporary Perspective. New York: Halsted.

ABOUT THE AUTHOR

M. GOTTDIENER is Associate Professor in the Department of Sociology at the University of California, Riverside. His principal interests are contemporary social theory, semiotics, and urban analysis. Gottdiener is the author of *The Social Production of Urban Space* and coauthor of *The City and the Sign: Introduction to Urban Semiotics.* His forthcoming book, *The Decline of Urban Politics: Political Theory and the Crisis of the Local State,* will be published by Sage in 1987.

NOTES

NOTES